ANNALS of DYSLEXIA

VOLUME 50   2000

Annals of Dyslexia is listed in *Current Contents/Social and Behavioral Sciences* (CC/ S&BS), the Social Sciences Citations Index ©(SSCI™), and *Chicoral Abstracts to Reading and Learning Disabilities*. Microfilm and photocopies are available from University Micro-films International.

The journal is annotated and indexed by the ERIC Clearinghouse on Handicapped and Gifted Children for publication in the monthly print index; *Current Index to Journals in Education* (CIJE); and the quarterly index, *Exceptional Child Education Resources* (ECER).

The International Dyslexia Association®
Chester Building/Suite 382
8600 LaSalle Road
Baltimore, MD 21286-2044

Printed in the United States of America

Notice

Members of The International Dyslexia Association® receive *Annals of Dyslexia* without charge. Additional copies of this issue are available from The International Dyslexia Association® at $15.00 each for members and $18.00 each for nonmembers plus 20% for postage and handling. Send orders prepaid to the address above.

Cover design: Joseph M. Dieter, Jr.
Compositor: Type Shoppe II Productions, Ltd.
Printer: Port City Press

ISSN 0736-9387

ANNALS OF DYSLEXIA

Volume 50   2000

Contents

FOREWORD

Annals of Dyslexia is an interdisciplinary, peer-reviewed journal published annually by The International Dyslexia Association. Our focus is on the understanding, prevention, and remediation of written language difficulties (reading, writing, spelling, handwriting) and related areas, giving primary consideration to original research papers and including significant reviews and well-documented reports of effective practices. We encourage and often solicit submissions from both members of IDA and other researchers, educators, and clinicians concerned with language disabilities.

Under the leadership of our previous editor, Anne Fowler, and those who preceded her, *Annals* has steadily increased its stature as a respected journal in the field. Throughout the years, *Annals* editors have invited leading researchers to prepare "significant" reviews for our readers of important research developments in the field. This year in Part I, *A Review of Research on the Biological Basis of Dyslexia*, Tom Zeffiro and Guinevere Eden summarize and critique evidence concerning the neurological bases of developmental dyslexia.

Though the articles submitted and solicited for *Annals of Dyslexia* each year represent an eclectic mix, they tend to cluster into themes. *Intervention Issues* continue to be one focus of this journal. On this topic, in Part II, Edward Kame'enui and his colleagues describe an integrated data-based intervention model for teaching reading in schools. Donald Compton, an IDA research grant recipient, reports on prereading variables that predict individual differences in response to regular classroom instruction and intensive, small group instruction.

Part III, *Language Development and Reading Disabilities*, contains two "complementary" research studies that examine the intriguing question of the relationship between oral language and later reading achievement.

The focus of Parts IV and V is on dyslexia and writing systems in other languages. The three articles in Part IV, *Reading and Foreign Language Learning*, address a collection of viewpoints on learning foreign languages. In Part V, *Reading Disabilities in Other Languages*, the emphasis of the two articles is on reading disabilities in other languages, in particular, Japanese and Chinese.

As Acting Editor of this issue, I would like to express my special appreciation to Associate Editor Hollis Scarborough and Editorial Advisory Board member Susan Brady for their help in soliciting authors, and for assisting me through this year of transition. Thankfully, Hollis will remain Associate Editor another year during the international search for a new editor. I am also grateful to the Editorial Advisory Board members who agreed to continue to serve during my tenure as Acting Editor, and I welcome several new members to the Board: P. G. Aaron, Nathlie Badian, Guinevere Eden, Annette Jenner, T. R. Miles, and Richard Sparks. I also appreciate the input this year from other reviewers: Emerson Dickman, Barbara Guyer, Connie Ho, George Hynd, Aleatha Kimbrough, Elaine Miles, Diane Sawyer, and Yun Yamada. The publications committee and its chair, Betty Levinson, have given me direction and support, as have IDA staff from the Baltimore office: Tom Viall, Executive Director; Cindy Ciresi, Director of Conferences and Publications; and Sharon Ringgold, Marketing Coordinator. Thanks go to Type Shoppe II for their editorial assistance and for their work facilitating the production of the journal.

Last, I want to thank the contributors to this volume and extend a special note of appreciation to Anne Fowler on behalf of the IDA staff, the Editorial Board, and our readers.

—Editor

To submit a manuscript to the *Annals of Dyslexia*, you must do so by January 10 to receive consideration for publication in the following year. Individuals interested in preparing a manuscript will find the *Guidelines for Contributors* in the back of this volume. Individuals may also obtain information about submission procedures by contacting The International Dyslexia Association, Chester Building/Suite 382, 8600 LaSalle Road, Baltimore, Maryland 21286-2044. Individual copies of papers in the current or prior issues (including those from the *Bulletin of the Orton Society*) are available at the same address. The cost of an individual paper is $4.00, including postage and handling.

THE 1999 SAMUEL T. ORTON AWARD PRESENTED TO HOWARD GARDNER

by Leonore Ganschow

Dr. Howard Gardner, MacArthur Foundation Fellow, psychologist, learning theorist, author of 18 books and several hundred articles on psychology and the science of the mind, has devoted his life to work in neuropsychology, developmental psychology, and educational reform. He is the John H. and Elisabeth A. Hobbs Professor of Cognition and Education in the Harvard Graduate School of Education.

Dr. Gardner is perhaps best known for his book, *Frames of the Mind: The Theory of Multiple Intelligences* (1983), for which he earned the American Psychological Association's National Psychology Award for Excellence in the Media, and which now has been translated into 12 languages. One might question initially why IDA selected Dr. Gardner to receive the 1999 Samuel T. Orton award at the 50th Anniversary Celebration of The International Dyslexia Association in Chicago. What is his unique contribution to our field? What does he have to say to those who study the causes and treatment of dyslexia and to individuals with dyslexia?

When I first came across *Frames of Mind* in the mid 1980s, I found his concept of seven distinct cognitive realms in the human brain fascinating and revolutionary. I remember saying to my university classes that we may be in the midst of another "paradigm shift" (Kuhn 1962) in our ways of thinking about intelligence. Now, close to 20 years later, all of us are witnesses to Dr. Gardner's forward thinking as his ideas have influenced progressive educators across the disciplines and throughout the world.

Dr. Gardner appears to have recognized connections between dyslexia and multiple intelligences at least 15 years or so before he wrote *Frames of Mind* and the many related books that followed. In 1987, readers of *Annals* (see Gardner 1987) learned that Dr. Gardner had discovered the works of Samuel T. Orton in the early 1970s when he was researching *The Shattered Mind*. Before that, he had been a student of Geschwind from whom he learned of the work of Dr. Orton and IDA, then known as The Orton Dyslexia Society. In his

1987 article, Dr. Gardner clarified for readers the connection between dyslexia and different ways of knowing and learning:

> We must confront the possibility that there may be certain subjects or concepts which will prove very difficult for students with certain kinds of deficits. . . . Part of the burden of the theory of multiple intelligences is to spell out alternative ways of communicating a concept but also to indicate when such a concept may be very difficult to convey using alternative means (p. 34).

In 1993, in the *Christian Science Monitor* (March 29, 1993, p. 11), Gardner discussed the uniqueness of each child: "They learn in very different kinds of ways, and to treat them all as if they're the same and call everybody a dummy who doesn't resemble a certain prototype is wrong." At his 1999 address in Chicago, and for his paper in this issue, Dr. Gardner again describes his early connections with our field. He presents a positive picture of where we've come but cautions us not to "declare victory . . . now that the battle is over. . . ." Rather, he presents five areas of concern to educators working on the diagnosis and treatment of dyslexia, and urges us to reexamine our "core mission" in the work we are doing.

Those of us affiliated with IDA thank Dr. Howard Gardner for his insights into the learning processes of children and adults, and for encouraging us to practice "eternal vigilance" in our profession.

The Citation:
The International Dyslexia Association
The Samuel T. Orton Award
Presented To
Howard E. Gardner, Ph.D.

In recognition of his theory of multiple intelligences
and its impact on understanding dyslexia
as a learning difference
November 6, 1999

References

Gardner, H. 1987. The theory of multiple intelligences. *Annals of Dyslexia* 37:19–35.

Gardner, H. 1983. *Frames of Mind: The Theory of Multiple Intelligences.* New York: Basic Books.

Kuhn, T. S. 1962. *The Structure of Scientific Revolutions.* Chicago, IL: University of Chicago Press.

"NOW THAT THE BATTLE'S OVER. . . "

Informal Remarks by *Howard Gardner* on the occasion of his receipt of the Samuel T. Orton Award by The International Dyslexia Association in Chicago, Illinois, *November 6, 1999.*

When I learned that I had been selected to receive the Orton Award, I had a series of thoughts. To start off, I immediately remembered an earlier recipient, the late Norman Geschwind, my mentor in all things neurological. It is a tremendous honor to receive an award that had gone previously to Geschwind and to other distinguished figures in the study of language and other learning disorders. Geschwind was also the person who first introduced me to the work of Samuel T. Orton, and to the study of congenital and acquired difficulties in reading. At the time, I was a doctoral student in developmental psychology at Harvard. As a result of this introduction, I elected to make a detour in my studies, so that I could learn more about the brain and, in particular, about the various cognitive disorders that are associated with congenital or acquired brain damage. As with certain other detours, this one lasted longer than I had anticipated. Indeed, I worked for twenty years at the Aphasia Research Center, associated with Boston University, and the Boston Veterans Administration Medical Center, and had a modest career as a research psychologist in neuropsychology. In my own mind, there is no question that I learned much more from my work in the field in which Samuel Orton pioneered than I ever contributed to the field. And so, this honor, while I do not feel worthy of it, means a great deal to me.

I first learned about alexia, dyslexia, and related disorders in 1969. That was a very different time. In my chosen field of psychology, consensus reigned that there was no need to study the brain—the "black box" it was dismissively called—and any work in education was considered to be hopelessly applied. Perhaps there was such a thing as "learning problems," but that was probably just a "fudge phrase" for laziness or low general intelligence. The earlier work of James Hinshelwood, Joseph Jules Dejerine, Samuel Orton, and others was either unknown or forgotten.

Nor was it different in most American elementary schools. My children went to an excellent progressive school in the Boston area. One of my children, we were told, was making excellent progress in school, and so it appeared to us, except for one thing. My wife and I were convinced that our child was not reading properly. The school steadfastly denied any problem, except, perhaps with pushy parents. Finally, when the child was in fourth grade, we went to see Jeanne Chall, the doyenne of reading experts in the country. "Your child is clearly dyslexic," Jeanne declared, thus clarifying a matter that had mystified us for some years. Happily, we were able to get an expert tutor; and happily, our child was able to learn to read in the next few years. I have never forgotten the well-intentioned but clearly harmful denial put forth by the school.

In the years between 1969 and the present, much has happened in the brain and cognitive sciences. (We even have fields like cognitive neuroscience, which did not exist in 1970.) It is now generally recognized that the brain is not an all-purpose machine, and that notions like "general intelligence" do not help us very much. Both in the study of brain and in the study of mind, the tide has shifted toward a more modular view: a realization that human beings are possessed of quite specific faculties that have evolved over thousands of years to allow us to survive and prosper in certain kinds of environment. My own work on "multiple intelligences" reflects this *Zeitgeist*.

Similarly, inspired in large measure by the work of Norman Geschwind and close associates like Albert Galaburda, we now know that dyslexia has a clear genetic and neural basis. Individuals can be quite intelligent in other areas of cognition; they can even appear to be linguistically talented, say, in telling jokes or learning languages orally. And yet those same individuals may have a selective disorder in making sense of written text. Perhaps if these same individuals lived in China or Japan, they might not exhibit as profound a defect in deciphering a different kind of script, but they would have difficulty in any alphabetically based language. Fortunately, except for a very small number, most individuals with reading problems can learn to read. The earlier the diagnosis, the more skilled the teaching, the more supportive the environment, the more likely that the child will be able to navigate around this cognitive obstacle and be able to become a productive and literate member of society.

Perhaps by now you have guessed the meaning of my title. In many ways, the battle waged by Samuel Orton, Norman Geschwind, and many others has been won. All over the world, the existence of specific learning problems is recognized; science is helping us to understand the nature and extent of these difficulties; and expert pedagogical interventions—both human and technological—are enabling individuals with such difficulties to master the scholastic materials that they need to master and to go on to lead full lives.

While there is an understandable temptation to "declare victory and go home," I believe that maneuver would be ill-advised. Let me mention five considerations that give me pause:

1. The proliferation of disorders. This seems a particularly American theme. Once the notion of "selected difficulty" comes to be acknowledged, there is a tendency to look for and to create labels for every conceivable difficulty. As someone who spends a lot of time in American public schools, I am continuously introduced to new kinds of problems—"right-brain syndrome," "linear sequential problems," "executive control problem," and every conceivable kind of attentional and motor disorder. Now I am not going to state that these disorders don't exist—perhaps they do. But I can assert that there is little consensus about what each disorder actually is and how it could be reliably diagnosed. The expertise that has developed with respect to dyslexia does not extend to other candidate disorders, no matter how persuasive their names might be.

2. The tendency to overdiagnose. In addition to finding a new disorder under every troubled child, there is often a correlative tendency to find instances of a disorder all over the place. Among physicians, this is often called the "medical student problem": as soon as students are introduced to a new symptom, they feel that they have it. The fact that a six-year-old child once reads "keep" as "peek" or once writes "was" for "saw" is no basis for diagnosing dyslexia or, indeed, anything else. In particular, we should not construe the fact that a child exhibits a certain problem as evidence that the child has a selective difficulty in that area. A child may have difficulty in calculating because of frank dyscalculia. But such a problem could as well be due to motivational problems or to life in a disadvantaged environment where she has not had the opportunity to construct a number line or to develop intuitions about quantity. When I hear that a class has 30 to 40 percent of children with documented learning difficulties, I suspect the absence of skilled diagnosis.

3. Insensitivity to cultural or historical factors. Even in cases in which some kind of a biologically-based difficulty is probable, one should be cautious about making a diagnosis. As suggested before, diverse cultures handle the same tasks in different ways. Just as there are different writing systems, there are also different systems of calculation, mapmaking, musical notation, and the like. A child who would have severe difficulties in one culture (or in one historical era) might not show analogous difficulties in a different culture.

Also, the presence of a difficulty need not signal a problem so long as adequate prosthetics exist. Prosthetics can range from glasses for the near-sighted to computer programs that can decode text or manipulate forms or translate from one language or symbol system to another. Possibly even dyslexia can be ameliorated if certain phonological clusters are presented auditorily in more elongated form.

The general point here is that the brain does not express itself in a vacuum. There is always a culturally developed system or domain that must be interpreted or mastered. Depending on the form that happens to have evolved in a particular culture, the same individual will exhibit more or less difficulty in performance. And depending on the power of the human or technological prosthetic, a difficulty can remain severe or be greatly ameliorated.

4. *The search, abetted by the media, for miracle cures.* No one would be happier than I (the father of two children with reading problems) if a syndrome like dyslexia could be eliminated with the same certainty as smallpox or anthrax. However, the popular literature of recent decades is littered with premature claims that dyslexia—or autism or depression—can be cured by a single intervention, a single treatment, a single drug. Perhaps reading disorders have an intimate relation with colors or shapes or elongated sounds or patterns of crawling, but perhaps they do not. While the misleading media personality suffers no penalties for having "hyped" the cure prematurely, the student and her family often do suffer. Most disorders, be they physical or cognitive, are complex, and most do not lend themselves to an instant cure. Caution should be the order of the day, particularly where another person' s welfare is concerned.

5. *The slippery biological pole.* Let me begin by asserting that I am enthralled with the new lines of research in brain science and in genetics. Both our understanding and our ability to treat will be enormously enhanced in the coming decades.

Yet, I worry that our fascination with the "hard sciences" may lead us to measures that are ill considered. Suppose, say, that we discover that a certain brain region (call it X) is important for reading, and that brain region happens to be smaller in a certain child or even a certain population. That fact could be used to help those with smaller Region X; however, it could also be used to stigmatize such individuals. Mean differences are, after all, only statistical; no doubt many individuals with small Xs read perfectly well, and others with a normal or even outsized X might have exhibited other kinds of learning or reading problems.

With the "coming of age" of genetics, the danger magnifies. Beyond doubt we will discover genes that are important for reading alphabetic scripts; and there is already evidence that a small set of genes may be related to reading problems. As with the brain evidence, such information can be helpful for early intervention; but it could easily be used for stigmatizing purposes. Indeed, it might become relevant for marriage prospects, holding a job, securing insurance, or even eugenic purposes. And no doubt, especially in our interventionist society, individuals with a genetic predisposition for reading problems will look into various kinds of genetic engineering or therapy. It is possible that such interventions will work and have no negative side effects, but it is perhaps more likely that they will have unanticipated effects. And we might even want to consider which valued human abilities—e.g., spatial or pattern recognition skills—might be placed at risk were we to target our interventions specifically at reading disorders.

*   *   *

I hope that my comments did not unsettle you, but I also hope that they served as a reminder that in life, as in science, a battle is hardly ever totally won. Indeed, to borrow a phrase from Thomas Jefferson, "eternal vigilance" must be the price of increasing knowledge about human nature. Reading is one of the most precious but also one of the most complex of human functions. It is far from being understood in its entirety. It is not cognate with other difficulties. It is not likely to be easily related to particular neural networks or genes. And whatever its biological basis, it must still be mastered within a specific culture with its own literacy system, its own institutions, its own norms and values. I suspect that over the years, the International Dyslexia Association will have to concern itself with this plethora of lenses on the human reader. When I think of the phenomenon of reading (and it is a phenomenon!), I am reminded of Albert Einstein's famous injunction: "An explanation should be as simple as possible. . . but not simpler. "

Which brings me to a closing word about my present work. Having worked for two decades in neuropsychology and developmental psychology, and a decade in educational reform, I have recently turned to issues of professional ethics. My colleagues and I are particularly concerned with the question of what happens to a sense of professional excellence, a sense of a calling, at a time when things are changing very quickly, when the market forces are very powerful, and when our senses of time and space are being radically altered by forces like the Internet.

At such times, each of us as professionals must return to fundamentals. We must ask, "What is the core mission of the work that we are doing?" In the case of most of the members of The International Dyslexia Association, I believe that you would see your core mission as "reaching each child, so that the child can use his or her strengths to master the tasks of school, and particularly those involved with written texts." If you are a teacher or therapist, you would presumably emphasize the proper methods of instruction and assessment; if you are a medical researcher, you would probably stress the design of studies that can yield firm results and the devising of diagnoses and treatments that are reliable and useful.

No matter how shielded a particular profession may be, just about all of us feel subject to some of the forces that I have mentioned. Teachers are expected to be accountable, to raise test scores, to compete against voucher or charter rivals. Physicians are expected to restrict their time with each patient, to avoid expensive treatments, to fill out vast numbers of forms. Scientific researchers compete for limited funds; they feel the temptation to work on those problems which are sexy and to cast their lots with corporations which promise higher salary "if you will only work on the following problems" or "recommend the following study kit."

I cannot, and would not, presume to advise you on what you should do under these circumstances. I am not even sure what I should do! But I will share with you that, at times when I am uncertain about my own calling, I think back to those giants of the past, investigators like Samuel Orton and Norman Geschwind, who had their priorities right. They wanted to help the victims of neurological disorders and they knew that, in order to do so, they had to understand the nature of that disorder as completely as possible. We honor them by continuing the missions that they so courageously initiated.

Dr. Howard Gardner
Larsen Hall, Rm. 201
Harvard Graduate School of Education
Cambridge, MA 02138
hgasst@pz.harvard.edu or FAX: (617) 496-4855

PART I
A Review of Research on the Biological Basis of Dyslexia

Our featured review this year on new developments in the field is a summary of research on the neural mechanisms underlying dyslexia by Tom Zeffiro and International Dyslexia Association research grant recipient Guinevere Eden. Over the last two decades, there has been an impressive development of noninvasive techniques for studying the structure and function of the brain. This paper summarizes new developments in research on the neural mechanisms underlying dyslexia.

The authors argue that studies employing this new technology indicate that the pathophysiology and localization of dyslexia extend beyond language dysfunction. Several lines of evidence suggest possible structural anomalies in the visual system and perisylvian cortical regions, including a magnocellular deficit. They describe new noninvasive techniques that have assisted researchers in examining brain mechanisms that underly phonological processing and the neural mechanisms that might be involved in rapid automatized naming and phonological coding in working memory. The authors summarize current knowledge about the cortical areas thought to be involved in phonological processing, reading silently, and reading aloud. Finally, they discuss which findings appear to have the strongest empirical support, as well as limitations of the results to date.

Readers will appreciate the importance of this research in advancing our understanding of the possible biological bases and heritability of dyslexia. Finding neural "correlates" of the primary causes and their associated behavioral characteristics of dyslexia will provide external validation of dyslexia and inform our efforts toward a more accurate definition of dyslexia.

The Neural Basis of Developmental Dyslexia

Thomas Zeffiro

Guinevere Eden

Georgetown University Medical Center
Washington, DC

Until recently, many thought developmental dyslexia was a behavioral disorder that primarily affected reading. In fact, it is a partly heritable condition, the clinical manifestations of which are extremely complex including deficits in reading, working memory, sensorimotor coordination, and early sensory processing. Even though extensive research has characterized these behavioral abnormalities carefully, the biological mechanisms of the clinical manifestations still are poorly understood. Recent research into both the nature of the structural and functional abnormalities in developmental dyslexia and the functional neuroanatomy of reading have rapidly advanced our understanding of the localization of the processes responsible for the signs and symptoms of dyslexia. This paper reviews recent evidence supporting a biological basis for developmental dyslexia.

This article was made possible by grant NICI ID IID36461 from The Charles A. Dana Foundation and The International Dyslexia Association.

Annals of Dyslexia, Vol. 50, 2000
Copyright ©2000 by The International Dyslexia Association®
ISSN 0736-9387

INTRODUCTION

As our lives become more dependent on information obtained from printed and electronic sources, rapid mastery of reading skills necessarily assumes an increasingly prominent position in early education. An important prerequisite for subsequent achievement, failure to acquire reading competency adversely affects acquisition of other fundamental cognitive skills. In contrast to spoken language, the more recently developed human skill of reading involves abilities that have to be explicitly, and sometimes painstakingly, taught. Although reading impairment is common, with an incidence of 5 to 10 percent among school-age children, our understanding of its causes is not consistent with the prevalence of the problem.

One cause of reading problems is developmental dyslexia. Although there is a long tradition of behavioral research that has characterized carefully abnormalities such as deficits in reading, motor control, and early sensory processing, the specific neural mechanisms that may explain the myriad behavioral manifestations of dyslexia are still poorly understood. Because reading is a uniquely human endeavor, we do not have access to the sorts of experimental animal models that have so richly informed investigations of other skills involving complex sensorimotor integration. Instead, behavioral studies of patients suffering focal brain damage, with a consequent loss of reading skills, reveal some useful information concerning the large-scale anatomical organization of reading systems in adults. Nevertheless, evidence from these sources does not provide much information about the processes responsible for reading acquisition. With structural and functional brain imaging, investigators now may explore the neural mechanisms underlying reading in children and how these representations change as reading skills are acquired during early schooling. Using these efficient and noninvasive tools, it is possible to study children from their first halting attempts at letter recognition until reading has become an automatic and effortless process. Similarly, these same experimental methods allow examination of the neural mechanisms underlying failure to achieve an adequate degree of reading fluency and automaticity. Although the investigations reviewed here have as their principal goal a more through understanding of brain mechanisms responsible for normal and impaired reading, the information obtained from these experimental studies may provide a foundation for the development of better techniques for early identification and treatment of children who are at high risk of experiencing later reading failure.

As regards the biological origins of developmental dyslexia, even though its behavioral manifestations are discussed extensively, the neurobiological foundations of dyslexia are still poorly understood. Recent advances in structural and functional neuroimaging techniques now provide means to identify the regional specialization and spatial congruence of the cortical areas engaged in reading and related cognitive processes. While these new techniques make possible novel investigations of the pathophysiology of the reading disorder called developmental dyslexia, their direct application is limited by problems establishing an unambiguous behavioral characterization of reading disorders.

BEHAVIORAL MANIFESTATIONS IN ADDITION TO LANGUAGE

Perhaps one reason for the slow progress toward a fuller understanding of the neural mechanisms responsible for developmental reading disorders is their behavioral complexity. It has long been known that the clinical manifestations of developmental dyslexia are many and varied. In addition to global impairments in reading fluency and comprehension, dyslexics exhibit specific difficulties decoding and recognizing single words. They commonly have abnormalities processing the phonological features of written and spoken language. A large body of research supports the contention that successful reading is dependent on development of an awareness of the phonemic structure of language, so-called phonological awareness. For over three decades, the evidence has been strong that the ability to isolate and manipulate the constituent sounds of words is related to reading proficiency (Bruce 1964), and that individuals with developmental dyslexia exhibit deficits in numerous measures of phonological awareness (Bradley and Bryant 1978; Catts 1993; Goswami 1990; Snowling 1981).

Although many researchers consider the core deficit in dyslexia to involve dysfunction of language mechanisms (Bradley and Bryant 1983; Felton and Wood 1992; Liberman and Mattingly 1985; Snowling 1981), others have emphasized the possible role of failure of early sensory processing mechanisms (Eden et al. 1996b; Lovegrove 1993b; Tallal, Miller, and Fitch 1993; Wright et al. 1997). The precise nature of behavioral abnormalities attributable to dysfunction of sensory systems has been more difficult to describe unambiguously. Using a variety of experimental approaches, researchers have demonstrated that dyslexics show impairments on a number of tasks heavily dependent on early sensory mechanisms (Lovegrove 1993a; Lovegrove, Heddle, and Slaghuis 1980) including visuomotor (Eden et al. 1994), visuospatial (Eden et al. 1996a), and visual motion processing (Eden et al. 1996b). These results suggest that the pathophysiology and localization of dyslexia is more complex than originally thought, extending beyond the classically defined language areas. Possibly related to this abnormality in sensory processing is growing evidence that dyslexics have a disorder involving sensorimotor coordination (Fawcett and Nicolson 1992; Nicolson and Fawcett 1990) evidenced by deficits in performance of speeded, bimanual movement tasks (Moore et al. 1995; Rousselle and Wolff 1991; Wolff, Cohen, and Drake 1984). This increasingly detailed behavioral characterization of the varied clinical manifestations of developmental dyslexia makes any simple account of the pathophysiology of the disorder difficult to envision.

EVIDENCE FOR INVOLVEMENT OF SPECIFIC BIOLOGIC SYSTEMS

BRAIN STRUCTURE ABNORMALITIES

One approach to determining the neural systems affected in any behavioral disorder is to search for coincident microscopic or macroscopic neuroanatomical abnormalities with the hope that the known functional anatomy of the structurally abnormal areas might correspond to the behavioral abnormalities known to characterize the disorder in question. In dyslexia, structural abnormalities have been detected in visual system structures, the thalamus, the corpus callosum, and perisylvian cortical regions.

The evidence for perisylvian cortical abnormalities largely has taken the form of reports of structural anomalies of different types in the temporal and parietal banks of the sylvian fissure. Reported macrostructural abnormalities also include the insula (Hynd et al. 1990), a finding consistent with microstructural abnormalities reported in the same area (Klingberg et al. 2000). The planum temporale is an expanse of neocortex on the temporal bank of the sylvian fissure. Its anterior border is defined by Heschl's gyrus and the left planum temporale is larger than the homologous region in the right hemisphere in 70 to 80 percent of individuals (Geschwind and Levitzkiy 1968). This leftward asymmetry is present from the time of birth (Chi, Dooling, and Gilles 1977; Witelson and Pallie 1973). Although there have been a number of reports documenting reductions or reversals of this leftward asymmetry in individuals with developmental dyslexia (Galaburda et al. 1985b; Humphreys, Kaufmann, and Galaburda 1990; Hynd et al. 1990; Larsen et al. 1990), some recent studies failed to find evidence for this specific abnormality (Best and Demb 1999; Leonard et al. 1993; Rumsey et al. 1997a). Arguments presented to explain the differing experimental results include a possible variable occurrence of planum abnormalities in different dyslexia subtypes (Best and Demb 1999; Rumsey et al. 1997a) in relation to hand dominance (Moffat, Hampson, and Lee 1998), or resulting from technical image analysis and anatomical nomenclature differences (Leonard et al. 1993; Morgan and Hynd 1998). In summary, it seems safe to conclude that developmental dyslexia is accompanied by subtle macroscopic structural anomalies in perisylvian cortical morphology, even if the precise nature of those abnormalities and their relation to particular dyslexic subtypes remains an open question. Future studies employing more uniform criteria for subject behavioral characterization and brain structural quantification may produce a more consistent account of the circumstances in which dyslexia is associated with macrostructural perisylvian cortical abnormalities.

Of importance for theories positing disordered interhemispheric communication as a basis for the behavioral manifestations of dyslexia are reports of callosal structural anomalies. Variations in cross-sectional areas of the corpus callosum have been reported, with dyslexics exhibiting a larger splenium (Duara et al. 1991) or a smaller genu than controls (Hynd et al. 1995).

Evidence for neuronal abnormalities detectable at the microscopic level demonstrates involvement of perisylvian cortical structures as well as cortical and subcortical structures in the visual system. Galaburda and colleagues described microscopic abnormalities including foci of myelinated glial scarring and molecular layer ectopias in the perisylvian neocortex of both male and female dyslexics (Galaburda et al. 1985b; Humphreys, Kaufmann, and Galaburda 1990). These histopathological findings have been interpreted as evidence supporting intrauterine damage resulting from an autoimmune process. Evidence for selective involvement of magnocellular pathways of the visual system also has accumulated, beginning with the demonstration that neuronal cell bodies in the magnocellular layers of the lateral geniculate nucleus are small in dyslexia (Livingstone et al. 1991). The location and distribution of these microscopic abnormalities may explain some of the visual behavioral abnormalities seen in dyslexia (see below). More recently, it was demonstrated that the normal neuronal size asymmetry present in primary visual cortex is absent in developmental dyslexia (Jenner, Rosen, and Galaburda 1999). In these studies, it was observed that control brains had larger neurons in the left hemisphere, whereas dyslexic brains had no such size asymmetry. The functional correlate of this morphological abnormality is not yet clear.

Concerning connections among cortical areas responsible for reading, abnormalities in left hemisphere perisylvian white matter tracts were observed in individuals with below-average reading abilities, although these subjects did not have a documented childhood history of developmental dyslexia. Diffusion tensor imaging, a novel, noninvasive, structural neuroimaging technique, was utilized to examine the relationship between word and nonword reading skills, and the microstructural integrity of cerebral white matter (Klingberg et al. 2000). This measure of structural integrity, the white matter diffusion anisotropy, correlated positively with the subject's reading ability in a spatial distribution confined to left posterior perisylvian regions. These results are consistent with the notion that damage to the fiber tracts connecting cortical structures responsible for visual and phonological processing may result in the behavioral abnormalities seen in individuals with developmental reading disorders.

PHONOLOGICAL PROCESSING SYSTEMS

Another approach to localizing the neural processes impaired in dyslexia originates with an analysis of its defining behavioral abnormalities. The most widely accepted current explanation for dyslexic reading difficulties makes reference to coexisting abnormal phonological processing. The term "phonological awareness" has been used as an umbrella term for the skill of manipulation and segmentation of the constituent sounds of words. Phonological awareness was first described by Bruce (1964) who asked children to repeat words after a particular sound had been taken away. Liberman and colleagues (Liberman et al. 1974) devised a similar task, in which mono-

and polysyllabic words were read to children, who, in turn, tapped out the number of phonemes and syllables of particular words. Since then, a large body of evidence has shown that certain phonological abilities can predict reading acquisition (Bradley and Bryant 1983; Goswami 1990; Snowling 1991; Stanovich 1988). Therefore, examination of the neural basis of phonological processing, specifically phonemic awareness, might identify candidate regions affected by dyslexia. Phonological skills are of particular interest in studying reading disabilities as children with reading problems struggle with such tasks.

Studies to date have demonstrated that reading and phonological processing involve coordinated activity in numerous perisylvian areas, predominantly in the left hemisphere. Using functional brain imaging, it is possible to monitor in detail the various processes involved in word processing. For example, during a visual discrimination task involving word form information, areas in visual cortex are engaged strongly. However, as subjects make an explicit judgment about the sound structure or the semantic meanings of a word, the areas involved shift to the temporal, parietal, and frontal lobes. Tasks requiring explicit phonological processing involve areas in the occipito-temporal junction, the intraparietal sulcus, and inferior frontal areas (Eden et al. 1999).

It is possible to measure phonological awareness, the ability to identify the sound structure in words, by asking individuals to translate words into Pig Latin (Olson et al. 1994). This task requires identifying the first sound of a word (the first sound is not necessarily the first letter), moving it to the end of the word, and finally adding an additional sound. Throughout this process, the word substructure has to be maintained online for manipulation, just as sounds have to be kept in memory during the process of sounding out a new word. Children with dyslexia who attempt this task typically make more mistakes and take significantly longer than children with good reading skills. Functional brain imaging studies, performed in adults and children with dyslexia, have shown that when poor readers are asked to perform a task that requires phonological awareness, less activity is identified in certain temporal, occipital, and parietal areas than in good readers. There has been a continuous effort to study systematically individuals with normal cognitive development to understand the functional organization of the brain for language and the effects of development, instruction, and gender (Bookheimer et al. 1995; Sergent et al. 1992;

Shaywitz et al. 1996; Shaywitz 1996). Positron Emission Tomography (PET) and functional MRI (fMRI) studies have provided new information about the cortical areas involved in object and word naming (Bookheimer et al. 1995) and phonological processing (Demonet et al. 1992; Paulesu et al. 1996; Petersen et al. 1988; Rumsey et al. 1997b; Sergent et al. 1992; Zatorre et al. 1992). Although there has been some discrepancy among functional neuroimaging and lesion studies concerning the neuroanatomical localization of phonological coding, it is possible that the observed differences are due to task differences among the different studies. Evidence in support of this interpretation is that these processes may be strongly influenced by the type of test used such as lexical decisions (word-nonword judgment) versus naming (pronouncing aloud) or word presentation rates (Price et al. 1992; Price et al. 1994; Share, Silva, and Adler 1987). Despite abundant evidence supporting the relationship between phonological awareness and reading ability, the mechanisms underlying the "sounding out" of words and the location of a phonological processing module in the brain are just beginning to emerge from a controversial body of literature (Bookheimer et al. 1995; Demonet, Wise, and Frackowiak 1993; Frackowiak 1994; Paulesu, Frith, and Frackowiak 1993; Pugh et al. 1996). Figure 1 summarizes these results.

Another experimental approach has been to determine whether or not there are separate neural processing systems underlying different aspects of reading. Some words cannot be decoded unambiguously by means of grapheme-to-phoneme mapping and, therefore, must be processed by other means, such as whole word reading. Comparison of tasks that engage this "direct" orthographic route (e.g., reading the word "yacht") with the "indirect" phonologic route (reading a novel regular- or low-frequency word) has been one approach to delineate language processes in individuals. Some neuroimaging studies have demonstrated functional specialization for orthography and phonology. One proposal has been that the locus of orthographic processing is in extrastriate visual regions, whereas phonological processing engages lateral orbital, dorsolateral prefrontal, and inferior frontal cortex (Pugh et al. 1996). Other studies, however, have shown that these aspects of reading share a large common network (Rumsey et al. 1997b). As a further complication, the regions engaged during reading tasks are not necessarily specific to reading. For example, object naming, assumed to engage the "direct route," appears to involve a subset of the areas engaged during word reading (Bookheimer et al.

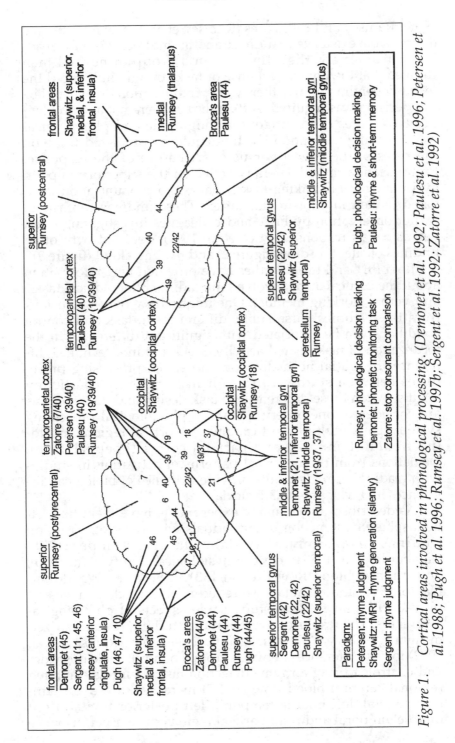

Figure 1.   Cortical areas involved in phonological processing. (Demonet et al. 1992; Paulesu et al. 1996; Petersen et al. 1988; Rumsey et al. 1997b; Sergent et al. 1992; Zatorre et al. 1992)

1995). Rumsey and colleagues (Rumsey et al. 1997c) investigated the possible existence of a direct and an indirect route for reading. Surprisingly, their findings in a group of normal men showed that the type of response or task strongly influenced the result depending on whether word pronunciation or a silent lexical decision was required. Although they were not able to identify two routes differentiating orthographic and phonological word reading, activation location could be predicted more on the basis of the covert versus overt nature of the response. Pronunciation tasks bilaterally activated the superior temporal gyri but decision-making tasks (that is, no pronunciation) activated the left inferior frontal cortex. These findings confirm an earlier observation by Price and colleagues investigating overt versus covert responses (Price et al. 1994), depicted with other findings of silent reading (figure 2) and reading aloud (figure 3).

Both PET and fMRI studies have provided new information about the cortical areas involved in reading, phonological tasks, and verbal working memory. One might draw two conclusions from these studies. First, subtle differences in task and control conditions can be associated with significant differences in the localization of task-related activity. Second, minor technical differences in spatial normalization and signal processing procedures between studies can result in apparently conflicting results. When these differences in task design and data analysis are considered, one observes that the phonological processing system spans multiple cortical and subcortical regions including frontal, temporal, and parietal cortex (Poeppel 1996). Deviations from these normal patterns of activation in studies with reading disabled adults provide evidence of biological differences in developmental dyslexia.

As described above, many experiments have identified left hemisphere dysfunction in individuals with dyslexia based on findings of anatomical (Galaburda and Kemper 1978; Galaburda et al. 1985a), electrophysiological (Duffy et al. 1980), and cerebral blood flow (Xenon-133) (Flowers, Wood, and Naylor 1991) abnormalities. More recently, researchers have employed PET and fMRI to study some aspects of phonological awareness. The results of some of these studies are summarized in figure 4. Using PET, Rumsey and colleagues (Rumsey et al. 1992) found differences between groups of adult male dyslexics and controls during a rhyme detection task. Controls exhibited regional cerebral blood flow (rCBF) increases in the left temporoparietal, left middle temporal, left posterior frontal, right middle temporal and right parietal regions during performance

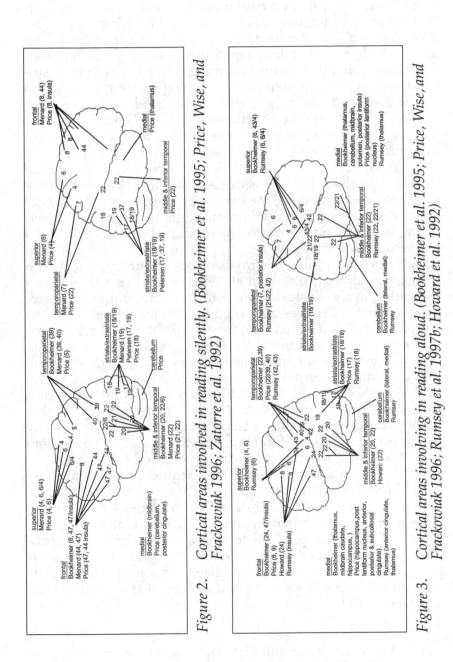

Figure 2. Cortical areas involved in reading silently. (Bookheimer et al. 1995; Price, Wise, and Frackowiak 1996; Zatorre et al. 1992)

Figure 3. Cortical areas involving in reading aloud. (Bookheimer et al. 1995; Price, Wise, and Frackowiak 1996; Rumsey et al. 1997b; Howard et al. 1992)

of the task. Dyslexics, however, showed significantly less increase than controls in two temporoparietal areas of the left hemisphere. Differences also were measured between these groups in the left inferior frontal and right anterior frontal regions. Paulesu and colleagues (Paulesu et al. 1996) reported functional activation during rhyming (subvocal rehearsal system) and short-term memory (phonological store) tasks in a small group of controls and compensated dyslexics. The dyslexic group exhibited increased rCBF in Broca's area (BA 44) during rhyming and increases in Wernicke's area/supramarginal gyrus during the short-term memory task. However, the controls activated both these areas as well as the insula during both tasks. The absence of activation in the insula in the dyslexics, an area linking the two other sites, led the authors to suggest that dyslexia is a "disconnection" syndrome. This use of the term expanded Geschwind's original description of disconnection syndromes as resulting from acquired, rather than developmental, insults. The rhyming results are consistent with Rumsey's studies (Rumsey et al. 1992) with respect to deficient activation in the dyslexic group in the temporoparietal area. Rumsey and colleagues also report deficient activation in the dyslexics in Broca's area (Rumsey et al. 1992), a finding that contradicts those reported by Paulesu et al. (Paulesu et al. 1996). A more recent study by Rumsey et al. (Rumsey et al. 1997c) confirmed earlier findings of altered patterns of activation in dyslexics in the bilateral posterior temporal cortex and inferior parietal cortex. Recently, it was demonstrated that dyslexics show phonological task-related relative hyperactivity in the left inferior frontal gyrus (Shaywitz et al. 1998) consistent with the motor theory of speech perception (Liberman and Mattingly 1985). The same study documents deficient task-related activity in the posterior superior temporal gyrus, angular gyrus, and extrastriate cortex. The enhanced activity in the inferior frontal gyrus may represent a compensatory response to failure of phonological processing mechanisms in more posterior cortical areas. Variation in results among these studies may reflect differing approaches to subject selection and subtle differences in the cognitive components of the phonological awareness test utilized.

RAPID NAMING

In addition to these phonological tasks, two other measures can predict reading ability: rapid automatized naming (RAN) (Denckla and Rudel 1976), which has been thought of as

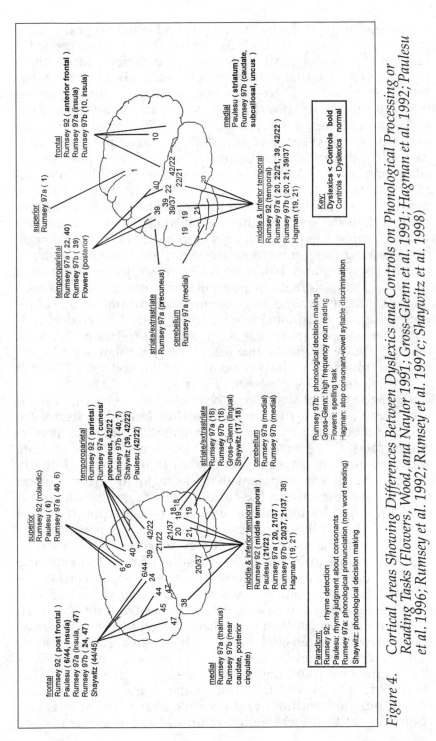

Figure 4. Cortical Areas Showing Differences Between Dyslexics and Controls on Phonological Processing or Reading Tasks (Flowers, Wood, and Naylor 1991; Gross-Glenn et al. 1991; Hagman et al. 1992; Paulesu et al. 1996; Rumsey et al. 1992; Rumsey et al. 1997c; Shaywitz et al. 1998)

a measure of phonological recoding; and phonological coding in working memory (Jorm 1983). Although both these tasks differ from the phonological manipulations described above, there is much evidence that deficits in both skills are commonly observed in dyslexia. There have been numerous investigations into the precise relationship between performance on these tasks and reading at different age levels (Badian 1997; Bowers and Wolf 1993; Wagner et al. 1993). For example, in kindergarten, children who later become reading disabled are slower at naming letters, numbers, colors, and objects (Wolf, Bally, and Morris 1986; Wolf and Goodglass 1986). Children with poor rapid automatized naming and phonological deficits are poorer readers than those with either deficit alone (Bowers and Wolf 1993). Compensated dyslexics perform better on rapid automatized naming tasks than those dyslexics who remain impaired (Felton, Naylor, and Wood 1990). Even so, these "improved readers" retain deficits in phonological manipulation tasks. Phonological awareness (e.g., segmentation), phonological recoding (e.g., rapid automatized naming), and phonological coding in working memory (e.g., digit span) correlate highly with reading ability (Denckla and Rudel 1976; Kaplan, Goodglass, and Weintraub 1983; Lindamood and Lindamood 1971; Olson et al. 1989; Rosner 1975; Wechsler 1974).

Using tasks that share some characteristics with rapid naming, there is suggestive evidence that neural systems are strongly modulated by stimulus presentation and task performance rates. One focus of interest has been the effects of rate and exposure duration on task-related brain activity. In early experiments, it was apparent that the regional cerebral blood flow (rCBF) response in the primary visual cortex was influenced strongly by the rate of stimulus presentation (Fox and Raichle 1984). In these studies, an 8Hz stimulus produced the maximal activation. As more complex processes have been examined with neuroimaging, the question of rate and exposure duration has become more complicated and controversial. We address this issue here for two reasons. First, we found that some visual deficits in dyslexia were associated with abnormal processing in a subsystem specialized for rapid visual information processing (Eden et al. 1996b). It has been argued that analogous problems may exist in the auditory system and have a direct effect on phonological processing in dyslexics (Tallal 1980; Wright et al. 1997). Although the causal connection between impaired auditory and phonological processing is still controversial (Studdert-Kennedy and Mody 1995), it is clear that the ability to read requires high rates of information processing, and that dyslexics have impairments of rapid visual naming speed (Denckla and Rudel 1976; Wolf and Goodglass 1986). Second, findings indicate that stimulus rate alone can modulate the amplitude task-related brain activity. Specifically, the effect of exposure duration has been studied systematically with PET during oral reading (Price et al. 1994) and listening to words (Price et al. 1992). This latter experiment revealed a linear relationship between the rate of heard words and rCBF bilaterally in the superior temporal gyrus, primary auditory cortex and right posterior superior temporal gyrus. The left posterior superior temporal gyrus failed to show this linear rate dependence. In a comparison of reading aloud versus lexical decision (Price et al. 1994), Price and colleagues found bilateral posterior temporal and inferior parietal areas, or Brodmann's area 39, (as well as the cingulate gyrus and left hippocampus) to be significantly more active during reading aloud. However, this was the case only when words were presented for brief durations (150 ms). These differences disappeared when stimuli were presented at longer durations (1000 ms). Together, these findings suggest that stimulus duration and presentation rate may jointly modulate activity in superior temporal and inferior parietal areas. Because impairments of fluency and processing rate are prominent in dyslexia, the neural mechanisms engaged during rapid object, letter, and color naming require further study.

In a preliminary study, we employed fMRI techniques to examine the functional neuroanatomy of the RAN task using sequential visual presentation at varying stimulus presentation rates. After controlling for purely sensorimotor aspects of the task, activity in the right lateral cerebellum was parametrically related to RAN rate, consistent with its involvement in the retrieval component of the task (Eden et al. 2000a). Further work is required to gain a deeper understanding of the neural systems engaged when subjects rapidly name letters, numbers, objects, or colors.

EARLY SENSORY PROCESSING SYSTEMS

In the last two decades, a large body of research has been carried out documenting visual processing abnormalities in dyslexia. The initial work focused on the early processing of temporal sequences of visual stimuli; for example, presenting two separate stimuli in close succession and determining when the two stimuli are perceived since one may be used as a measure of visual persistence. One such study demonstrated that reading disabled children had significantly longer separation thresholds than controls (Stanley, Smith, and Howell 1983). These results were confirmed (Lovegrove and Brown 1978) using a technique by which subjects make a judgment about their perception of a grating (e.g., orientation of horizontal black and white bars). In these experiments, the operator varies the stimulus' appearance (by changing the spatial frequency) and then measures the effect on the subject's response. Lovegrove and colleagues found that the results varied with the nature of the grating (Lovegrove, Heddle, and Slaghuis 1980). In adults, the duration of visible persistence increases as spatial frequency increases (as the gratings become less coarse). Lovegrove and colleagues found this increase to be less in reading disabled children compared to normal children (Lovegrove, Heddle, and Slaghuis 1980). Therefore, at low spatial frequencies, reading disabled children exhibit longer visible persistence. Further, reading disabled children exhibit reduced luminance contrast sensitivity at mesopic luminance levels (Cornelissen et al. 1995), and the biggest effects are observed at low grating contrast (Martin and Lovegrove 1984). Lovegrove et al. explain these differences in the framework of sustained and transient channels of the visual pathway (Lovegrove 1993a), sometimes referred to as the parvocellular and magnocellular system, respectively. These channels can be distinguished by their spatial frequency preference, their temporal properties, and their contrast sensitivity. Since both contrast sensitivity and visible persistence varied in reading disabled children, Lovegrove concluded that these children have disturbances in the transient system which mediates global form, movement, and temporal resolution. Experiments in which flicker thresholds were used to measure the efficiency of the transient system also have differentiated normal and reading disabled children successfully (Felmingham and Jakobson 1995; Martin and Lovegrove 1988). Against the mounting evidence demonstrating psychophysical abnormalities consistent with magnocellular system dysfunction in dyslexia is the fact that attempts to link reading deficits and visual system impairments causally have never been widely persuasive. Recent progress along these lines is the proposal that one way in which this visual abnormality could influence the reading process would be by preventing the processing of crucial information required for reading such as the accuracy of letter position encoding (Cornelissen et al. 1998). Nevertheless, it is possible that there is no "causal" link between visual system abnormalities and reading disorders in developmental dyslexia. Rather, both behavioral manifestations may result from damage to common neural processing systems (Eden and Zeffiro 1998).

Other evidence for visual system abnormalities comes from experiments in which children were tested on their ability to process temporal and spatial visual stimuli in order to investigate the role these processes play in reading (Eden et al. 1995). Normal (n = 39) and dyslexic (n = 26) children were compared on a visual computer game that consisted of a Temporal Dot and an analogous Spatial Dot counting task. Dyslexic children performed significantly worse than the control group on the Temporal Dot task but were only mildly impaired when the same kind of visual information was presented spatially. For the Temporal Dot task, it appeared that the stimulus presentation rate caused the dyslexics to perform worse than controls. On the other hand, the Spatial Dot task permitted the children to control their own temporal sampling rate while performing a visuospatially challenging task. Even though the differences between dyslexics and controls on this spatial task did not reach significance, a visuospatial impairment was measured on other visuospatial tasks such as Benton's classic Judgment of Lines task (Eden et al. 1996a). Taken together, these findings provide evidence for a rate-related visual processing deficit that lends further support to the theory of abnormal magnocellular processing in dyslexia. While the deficit appears to be most obvious during rapid processing, it may well involve processes where functions are localized in cortical parietal areas and also receive strong projections from the magnocellular system. To evaluate the importance of visual processing rate, we estimated its contribution to reading in the same group of 65 children. Computing a regression model with age, verbal IQ, phonological awareness (Pig Latin), and visual temporal processing ability (the Temporal Dot task), we were able to predict 73 percent of the variance in reading ability. The fact that dyslexics perform worse on tasks requiring speeded, sequential processing may provide a partial explanation for their reading difficulties.

Unlike language, studies of human visual processing have had the benefit of a more detailed understanding of the anatomy and physiology of the visual system gained from experiments with nonhuman primates. Anatomical data from nonhuman primate (Livingstone and Hubel 1988; Maunsell and Newsome 1987; Ungerleider and Mishkin 1982; Van Essen and Maunsell 1983) and human postmortem studies suggest that the magnocellular system has strong projections to the V5/MT complex. Further, PET and fMRI studies have been able to identify task-related activity in the human V5/MT complex during motion perception (Corbetta et al. 1990; Watson et al. 1993). To investigate the magnocellular deficit in dyslexia, we studied activity in area V5/MT during visual motion processing in normal and dyslexic men using fMRI (Eden et al. 1996c). Controls were carefully matched to dyslexics on IQ, age, and other behavioral measures. We used a stimulus velocity judgment task to behaviorally quantify any visual motion deficit in the dyslexic subjects using measurements made outside the MRI scanner. The results demonstrated a significant performance difference between controls and dyslexics (p<.03) on this task. During fMRI, blood oxygenation level dependent (BOLD) contrast signals were measured while the subjects viewed one of three stimuli. First, a fixation point on an isoluminant background was used as the neutral baseline condition. Differences in the BOLD signal were compared between this stimulus and a coherently moving, low-contrast, random-dot stimulus that was the magnocellular stimulus (M-stimulus). In order to assure that any differences between the control and dyslexic subjects were not due to a general deficit in visual processing, a stationary, high-contrast patterned stimulus was used. The pattern stimulus consisted of small squares that were spatially correlated, thereby forming a texture (Julesz, Gilbert, and Victor 1978; Victor and Zemon 1985). The motion stimulus was created from the same basic components (achromatic dark squares on a light background) and was, therefore, similar to the pattern stimulus in terms of its basic visual features (e.g., global spatial frequency). For each subject, V5/MT was identified in a search volume by its preferential sensitivity to motion in those spatial coordinates of the Talairach atlas (Talairach and Tournoux 1988) previously identified by Watson and colleagues (Watson et al. 1993).

The results revealed that the presentation of moving stimuli in dyslexics failed to produce the same task-related functional activation in area V5/MT observed in controls. This deficit was confined to the motion processing system since presentation of stationary patterns resulted in equivalent activations in both groups in other extrastriate areas. In the single-subject analysis, we found that all controls showed significant signal changes related to motion perception in the search volume defined as V5/MT. Only one of the six dyslexics showed task-related changes in this area and it was seen on the left side only. This activation lay in the most anterior extent of the search volume. The group analysis confirmed the single subject analysis. The control group exhibited bilateral motion sensitivity in the area specialized for motion processing. No activation was detected in any of the dyslexics in this search volume. Responses in other motion sensitive visual cortical areas were seen in both groups in the anterior portion of temporal cortex, identified as the superior temporal gyrus (BA 42/22). These temporal motion sensitive areas have been reported to show particular sensitivity to coherent motion (Cheng et al. 1995).

Confirmation of the sensitivity and selectivity of this finding in a larger experimental group is the next step in furthering our understanding of this physiological difference. Recently, Demb and colleagues demonstrated a direct correlation between the amount of signal change in the V5/MT complex and reading levels (Demb, Boynton, and Heeger 1997). An individual mildly affected with dyslexia is predicted to show weaker signals in this extrastriate area. Very low or absent signals are expected in the case of severe dyslexia. Although the V5/MT complex may not be the primary site of altered function in dyslexia, disruption of V5/MT activity may offer an explanation for the visual and oculomotor abnormalities seen in some dyslexics (Eden et al. 1994). In future studies, investigators could study these phenomena in the context of dysfunction of other neural information processing systems such as those involved in phonological awareness. It also may be useful in the early identification of children at risk for developing reading disorders later in life. First steps in this direction include recent evidence in children that, after controlling for intelligence and overall reading ability, visual motion sensitivity explained independent variance in orthographic skill (Talcott et al. 2000) and that reading level is correlated with visual motion processing in the V5/MT complex (Eden et al. 2000b).

It should be noted that, unlike patients with destructive lesions involving areas in the V5/MT complex (Zihl, von Cramon, and Mai 1983) and surrounding structures, the dyslexics' motion detection deficit is subtle. It is not seen in a normal ophthalmologic or orthoptic investigation, but only during careful psychophysical testing in the laboratory. One likely reason for the subtle nature of the behavioral impairment is that a considerable degree of compensation for this deficit may have occurred. A useful analogy is the visual motion deficit seen in nonhuman primates after recovery from focal MT lesions. Ibotenic acid injection into MT causes severe and acute motion detection deficits, but motion sensitivity recovers over days to weeks. The animals eventually show only minimal motion detection impairment, despite complete destruction of neurons in area MT (Newsome and Pare 1988).

Finally, the role of the anterior temporal motion processing areas is not understood and the analogous areas in the macaque are not known. Their location in the superior temporal gyrus places them in an area of the brain usually associated with language processing. Neuroimaging studies have shown that deaf subjects exhibit both functional reorganization for language (much less activation is seen in the left temporal lobe compared to hearing subjects during reading) and functional reorganization of cortical areas devoted to visual motion processing in temporal cortex. This reorganization is paralleled by an advantage over hearing subjects during the performance of psychophysical tasks requiring magnocellular system functions (Neville 1997). These findings suggest that functional reorganization may be occurring between visual motion and language processing areas. The mechanism by which this reorganization might occur is not understood but it raises the possibility of an association between cortical areas devoted to visual motion processing and those devoted to language processing. This relationship may be important in explaining the co-occurrence of visual motion and language processing deficits in dyslexia.

SUMMARY

As noted above, the clinical manifestations of dyslexia are numerous and complex. Although some may reflect the behavioral consequences of damage to neural systems directly, others may result from compensatory mechanisms activated in response to the original lesion. Of particular concern in this context is the interpretation of findings from functional brain imaging experiments in which differences in task-related hemodynamic change are observed. Although neuroimaging techniques have dramatically improved our ability to localize specific cognitive processes to particular brain regions, their application in the analysis of neural dysfunction in disease states is complicated. While reduced activity in a particular region could result from focal neuronal dysfunction, it could as easily result from compensatory neural mechanisms associated with spatial reorganization of task-related activity. Similarly, increases in task-related activity may result from either increased local neuronal excitatory or inhibitory influences, making it difficult to employ solely information from functional neuroimaging experiments to test models of information processing. Future studies combining information gained from studies of task-related hemodynamic change with independent measures of anatomical connectivity using diffusion tensor imaging and neural process timing using electrophysiological techniques will allow a more detailed picture of the spatiotemporal patterns of the brain activity underlying reading in health and disease.

At present, the combined evidence demonstrating macroscopic morphologic, microscopic neuronal, and microstructural white matter abnormalities in dyslexia is consistent with a localization of the principal pathophysiological process to perisylvian structures predominantly in the left hemisphere. In children and adults, functional imaging shows that numerous perisylvian cortical areas are involved in reading (see figure 5). A review of the results of a number of neuroimaging studies of reading and early sensory processing also are consistent with this localization (Eden and Zeffiro 1998), with the occipitotemporal sulcus, the posterior superior temporal gyrus, and the inferior parietal cortex of the left hemisphere emerging as likely sites of dysfunction in dyslexia. As regards causal connection between reading and brain function differences, future work combining structural and functional brain imaging with careful behavioral subject characterization may provide a clearer picture of the relation between observed biological and behavioral variations in individuals with developmental dyslexia.

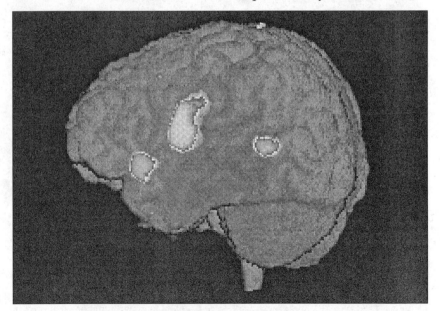

Figure 5.   An example of the spatial distribution of task-related changes
             in hemodynamic activity in a twelve-year old child reading
             aloud. The colored areas represent statistically significant
             hemodynamic changes in relation to single-word reading.

Address correspondence to: Thomas Zeffiro, M.D. Ph.D., Department of Neurology, Research, Building EP04, Georgetown University Medical Center, 3900 Reservoir Road, NW, Washington, DC 20007. Telephone: 202 687 6776. Fax: 202 687 6914. Email zeffiro@giccs.georgetown.edu.

References

Badian, N. 1997. Dyslexia and the double deficit hypothesis. *Annals of Dyslexia* 47:69–87.

Best, M., and Demb, J. B. 1999. Normal planum temporale asymmetry in dyslexics with a magnocellular pathway deficit. *Neuroreport* 10:607–12.

Bookheimer, S., Zeffiro, T. A., Blaxton, T., Gaillard, W., and Theodore, W. 1995. Regional cerebral blood flow during object naming and word reading. *Human Brain Mapping* 3:93–106.

Bowers, P., and Wolf, M. 1993. Theoretical links among naming speed, precise timing mechanisms, and orthographic skill in dyslexia. *Reading and Writing* 5:69–86.

Bradley, L., and Bryant, P. 1978. Difficulties in auditory organisation as a possible cause of reading backwardness. *Nature* 271:746–47.

Bradley, L., and Bryant, P. E. 1983. Categorizing sounds and learning to read—a causal connection. *Nature* 301:419–21.

Bruce, D. J. 1964. The analysis of word sounds. *British Journal of Educational Psychology* 34:158–70.

Catts, H. W. 1993. The relationship between speech-language impairments and reading disabilities. *Journal of Speech and Hearing Research* 36:948–58.

Cheng, K., Fujita, H., Kanno, I., Miura, S., and Tanaka, K. 1995. Human cortical regions activated by a wide-field visual motion: An H2 15O study. *Journal of Neurophysiology* 74:413–27.

Chi, J. G., Dooling, E. C., and Gilles, F. H. 1977. Left-right asymmetries of the temporal speech areas of the human fetus. *Archives of Neurology* 34:346–48.

Corbetta, M., Miezin, F. M., Dobmeyer, S., Shulman, G. L., and Petersen, S. E. 1990. Attentional modulation of neural processing of shape, color, and velocity in humans. *Science* 248:1556–59.

Cornelissen, P., Richardson, A., Mason, A., Fowler, M. S., and Stein, J. 1995. Contrast sensitivity and coherent motion detection measured at photopic luminance levels in dyslexic controls. *Vision Research* 35:1483–94.

Cornelissen, P. L., Hansen, P. C., Gilchrist, I., Cormack, F., Essex, J., and Frankish, C. 1998. Coherent motion detection and letter position encoding. *Vision Research* 38:2181–91.

Demb, J. B., Boynton, G. M., and Heeger, D. J. 1997. Brain activity in visual cortex predicts individual differences in reading performance. *Proceedings of the National Academy of Sciences of the United States of America* 94:13363–66.

Demonet, J. F., Chollet, F., Ramsay, S., Cardebat, D., Nespoulous, J. L., Wise, R., Rascol, A., and Frackowiak, R. 1992. The anatomy of phonological and semantic processing in normal subjects. *Brain* 115:1753–68.

Demonet, J. F., Wise, R., and Frackowiak, R. S. J. 1993. Language functions explored in normal subjects by positron emission tomography: A critical review. *Human Brain Mapping* 1:39–47.

Denckla, M. B., and Rudel, R. G. 1976. Rapid "automatized" naming (RAN): Dyslexia differentiated from other learning disabilities. *Neuropsychologia* 14:471–79.

Duara, R., Kushch, A., Gross-Glenn, K., Barker, W. W., Jallad, B., Pascal, S., Loewenstein, D. A., Sheldon, J., Rabin, M., Levin, B., et al. 1991. Neuroanatomic differences between dyslexic and normal readers on magnetic resonance imaging scans. *Archives of Neurology* 48:410–16.

Duffy, F. H., Denckla, M. B., Bartels, P. H., and Sandini, G. 1980. Dyslexia: Regional differences in brain electrical activity by topographic mapping. *Annals of Neurology* 7:412–20.

Eden, G., Jones, K., Zeffiro, T., and Joseph, J. 2000a. A functional resonance imaging study of naming and articulation rate. Paper read at Cognitive Neuroscience Society Annual Meeting Program.

Eden, G., Joseph, J., Jones, K., Berger, J., and Zeffiro, T. 1999. Functional neuroanatomy of phonological processing: Visual versus auditory stimuli. *Neuroimage* 9:S1065.

Eden, G. F., Brown, C. P., Jones, K., Given, B., and Zeffiro, T. A. 2000b. Phonological and Visual Motion Processing in Reading Impaired Children. *Neuroimage* 11:S183.

Eden, G. F., Stein, J. F., Wood, H. M., and Wood, F. B. 1994. Differences in eye movements and reading problems in dyslexic and normal children. *Vision Research* 34:1345–58.

Eden, G. F., Stein, J. F., Wood, M. H., and Wood, F. B. 1995. Temporal and spatial processing in reading disabled and normal children. *Cortex* 31:451–68.

Eden, G. F., Stein, J. F., Wood, M. H., and Wood, F. B. 1996a. Differences in visuospatial judgment in reading disabled and normal children. *Perceptual and Motor Skills* 82:155–77.

Eden, G. F., vanMeter, J. W., Rumsey, J., Maisog, J. M., Woods, R. P., and Zeffiro, T. A. 1996b. Abnormal processing of visual motion in dyslexia revealed by functional brain imaging. *Nature* 382:66–69.

Eden, G. F., VanMeter, J. W., Rumsey, J. M., Maisog, J. M., Woods, R. P., and Zeffiro, T. A. 1996c. Abnormal processing of visual motion in dyslexia revealed by functional brain imaging. *Nature* 382:66–69.

Eden, G. F., and Zeffiro, T. A. 1998. Neural systems affected in developmental dyslexia revealed by functional neuroimaging. *Neuron* 21:279–82.

Fawcett, A. J., and Nicolson, R. I. 1992. Automatisation deficits in balance for dyslexic children. *Perceptual and Motor Skills* 75:507–29.

Felmingham, K. L., and Jakobson, L. S. 1995. Visual and visuomotor performance in dyslexic children. *Experimental Brain Research* 106:467–74.

Felton, R. H., Naylor, C. E., and Wood, F. B. 1990. Neuropsychological profile of adult dyslexics. *Brain and Language* 39:485–97.

Felton, R. H., and Wood, F. B. 1992. Cognitive deficits in reading disability and attention deficit disorder. *Journal of Learning Disabilities* 25:318–26.

Flowers, D. L., Wood, F. B., and Naylor, C. E. 1991. Regional cerebral blood flow correlates of language processes in reading disability. *Archives of Neurology* 48:637–43.

Fox, P. T., and Raichle, M. E. 1984. Stimulus rate dependence of regional cerebral blood flow in human striate cortex, demonstrated by positron emission tomography. *Journal of Neurophysiology* 51:1109–20.

Frackowiak, R. S. J. 1994. Functional mapping of verbal memory and language. *Trends in Neuroscience* 17:109–14.

Galaburda, A. M., and Kemper, T. L. 1978. Cytoarchitectonic abnormalities in developmental dyslexia: A case study. *Annals of Neurology* 6:94–100.

Galaburda, A. M., Sherman, G., Rosen, G. D., Aboitiz, F., and Geschwind, N. 1985a. Developmental dyslexia: Four consecutive cases with cortical anomalies. *Annals of Neurology* 18:222–33.

Galaburda, A. M., Sherman, G. F., Rosen, G. D., Aboitiz, F., and Geschwind, N. 1985b. Developmental dyslexia: Four consecutive patients with cortical anomalies. *Annals of Neurology* 18:222–33.

Geschwind, N., and Levitzky, W. 1968. Human brain: Left-right asymmetries in temporal speech region. *Science* 161:186–87.

Goswami, U. 1990. A special link between rhyming skills and the use of orthographic analogies by beginning readers. *Journal of Child Psychology and Psychiatry* 31:301–11.

Gross-Glenn, K., Duara, R., Barker, W. W., Loewenstein, D., Chang, J. Y., Yoshii, F., Apicella, A. M., Pascal, S., Boothe, T., Sevush, S., *et al.* 1991. Positron emission tomographic studies during serial word-reading by normal and dyslexic adults. *J Clin Exp Neuropsychol* 13:531–44.

Hagman, J. O., Wood, F., Buchsbaum, M. S., Tallal, P., Flowers, L., and Katz, W. 1992. Cerebral brain metabolism in adult dyslexic subjects assessed with PET during performance of an auditory task. *Archives of Neurology* 49:734–39.

Howard, D., Patterson, K., Wise, R., Brown, W. D., Friston, K., Weiller, C., and Frackowiak, R. 1992. The cortical localization of the lexicons. Positron emission tomography evidence. *Brain* 115:1769–82.

Humphreys, P., Kaufmann, W. E., and Galaburda, A. M. 1990. Developmental dyslexia in women: Neuropathological findings in three patients. *Annals of Neurology* 28:727–38.

Hynd, G. W., Hall, J., Novey, E. S., Eliopulos, D., Black, K., Gonzalez, J. J., Edmonds, J. E., Riccio, C., and Cohen, M. 1995. Dyslexia and corpus callosum morphology. *Archives of Neurology* 52:32–38.

Hynd, G. W., Semrud-Clikeman, M., Lorys, A. R., Novey, E. S., and Eliopulos, D. 1990. Brain morphology in developmental dyslexia and attention deficit disorder/hyperactivity. *Archives of Neurology* 47:919–26.

Jenner, A. R., Rosen, G. D., and Galaburda, A. M. 1999. Neuronal asymmetries in primary visual cortex of dyslexic and nondyslexic brains. *Annals of Neurology* 46:189–96.

Jorm, A. F. 1983. Specific reading retardation and working memory: A review. *British Journal of Psychology* 74:311–42.

Julesz, B., Gilbert, E. N., and Victor, J. D. 1978. Visual discrimination of textures with identical third-order statistics. *Biological Cybernetics* 31:137–40.

Kaplan, E., Goodglass, H., and Weintraub, S. 1983. *The Boston Naming Test.* Philadelphia: Lea & Febiger.

Klingberg, T., Hedehus, M., Temple, E., Salz, T., Gabrieli, J. D., Moseley, M. E., and Poldrack, R. A. 2000. Microstructure of temporo-parietal white matter as a basis for reading ability: Evidence from diffusion tensor magnetic resonance imaging. *Neuron* 25:493–500.

Larsen, J. P., Hoien, T., Lundberg, I., and Odegaard, H. 1990. MRI evaluation of the size and symmetry of the planum temporale in adolescents with developmental dyslexia. *Brain and Language* 39:289–301.

Leonard, C. M., Voeller, K. K., Lombardino, L. J., Morris, M. K., Hynd, G. W., Alexander, A. W., Andersen, H. G., Garofalakis, M., Honeyman, J. C., Mao, J., Agee, O. F., and Staab, E. V. 1993. Anomalous cerebral structure in dyslexia revealed with MRI. *Archives of Neurology* 50:461–69.

Liberman, A. M., and Mattingly, I. G. 1985. The motor theory of speech perception revised. *Cognition* 21:1–36.

Liberman, I. Y., Shankweiler, D., Fischer, F. W., and Carter, B. 1974. Explicit syllable and phoneme segmantation in the young child. *Journal of Experimental Child Psychology* 18:201–12.

Lindamood, C., and Lindamood, P. 1971. *Lindamood Auditory Conceptualization (LAC) Test.* Austin, TX: PRO-ED.

Livingstone, M., and Hubel, D. 1988. Segregation of form, colour, movement and depth: Anatomy, physiology, and perception. *Science* 240:740–49.

Livingstone, M. S., Rosen, G. D., Drislane, F. W., and Galaburda, A. M. 1991. Physiological and anatomical evidence for a magnocellular deficit in developmental dyslexia. *Proceedings of the National Academy of Sciences of the United States of America* 88:7943–47.

Lovegrove, W. 1993a. Weakness in the transient visual system: A causal factor in dyslexia? *Annals of the New York Academy of Sciences* 682:57–69.

Lovegrove, W. 1993b. Weakness in transient visual system: A causal factor in dyslexia? In *Temporal Information Processing in the Nervous System: Special Reference to Dyslexia and Dysphasia*, eds. P. Tallal, A. M. Galaburda, R. R. Llinas, and C. von Euler. New York: New York Academy of Sciences.

Lovegrove, W., and Brown, C. 1978. Development of information processing in normal and disabled readers. *Perceptual and Motor Skills* 46:1047–54.

Lovegrove, W. J., Heddle, M., and Slaghuis, W. 1980. Reading disability: Spatial frequency specific deficits in visual information store. *Neuropsychologia* 18:111–15.

Martin, F., and Lovegrove, W. 1984. The effect of field size and luminance on contrast sensitivity differences between specifically reading disabled and normal children. *Neuropsychologia* 22:73–77.

Martin, F., and Lovegrove, W. 1988. Uniform and field flicker in control and specifically-disabled readers. *Perception* 17:203–14.

Maunsell, J. H. R., and Newsome, W. T. 1987. Visual processing in monkey extrastriate cortex. *Annual Review of Neuroscience* 10:363–401.

Moffat, S. D., Hampson, E., and Lee, D. H. 1998. Morphology of the planum temporale and corpus callosum in left handers with evidence of left and right hemisphere speech representation. *Brain* 121:2369–79.

Moore, L. H., Brown, W. S., Markee, T. E., Theberge, D. C., and Zvi, J. C. 1995. Bimanual coordination in dyslexic adults. *Neuropsychologia* 33:781–93.

Morgan, A. E., and Hynd, G. W. 1998. Dyslexia, neurolinguistic ability, and anatomical variation of the planum temporale. *Neuropsychology Rev* 8:79–93.

Neville, H. 1997. Specificity and plasticity in human brain development: ERP and fMRI studies. In *Proceedings of the Rodin Remediation Academy*, eds.

Newsome, W. T., and Pare, E. B. 1988. A selective impairment of motion perception following lesions of the middle temporal visual area (MT). *Journal of Neuroscience* 8:2201–11.

Nicolson, R. I., and Fawcett, A. J. 1990. Automaticity: A new framework for dyslexia research? *Cognition* 35:159–82.

Olson, R., Forsberg, H., Wise, B., and Rack, J. Eds. 1994. Measurement of word recognition, orthographic, and phonological skills. In *Frames of Reference for Assessment of Learning Disabilities*, ed. G. Lyon. Baltimore: Paul H. Brookes Publishing.

Olson, R., Wise, B., Conners, F., Rack, J., and Fulker, D. 1989. Specific deficits in component reading and language skills: Genetic and environmental influences. *Journal of Learning Disabilities* 22:339–48.

Paulesu, E., Frith, C. D., and Frackowiak, R. S. J. 1993. The neural correlates of the verbal component of working memory. *Nature* 362:342–44.

Paulesu, E., Frith, U., Snowling, M., Gallagher, A., Morton, J., Frackowiak, R. S., and Frith, C. D. 1996. Is developmental dyslexia a disconnection syndrome? Evidence from PET scanning. *Brain* 119:143–57.

Petersen, S. E., Fox, P. T., Posner, M. I., Mintun, M., and Raichle, M. E. 1988. Positron emission tomographic studies of the cortical anatomy of single-word processing. *Nature* 331:585–89.

Poeppel, D. 1996. A critical review of PET studies of phonological processing. *Brain and Language* 55:317–51.

Price, C., Wise, R., Ramsay, S., Friston, K., Howard, D., Patterson, K., and Frackowiak, R. 1992. Regional response differences within the human auditory cortex when listening to words. *Neuroscience Letters* 146:179–82.

Price, C. J., Wise, R. J., and Frackowiak, R. S. 1996. Demonstrating the implicit processing of visually presented words and pseudowords. *Cerebral Cortex* 6:62–70.

Price, C. J., Wise, R. J., Watson, J. D., Patterson, K., Howard, D., and Frackowiak, R. S. 1994. Brain activity during reading. The effects of exposure duration and task. *Brain* 117:1255–69.

Pugh, K. R., Shaywitz, B. A., Shaywitz, S. E., Constable, R. T., Skudlarski, P., Fulbright, R. K., Bronen, R. A., Shankweiler, D. P., Katz, L., Fletcher, J. M., and Gore, J. C. 1996. Cerebral organization of component processes in reading. *Brain* 119:1221–38.

Rosner, J. 1975. *Helping Children Overcome Learning Difficulties.* New York: Walker Educational Publishers.

Rousselle, C., and Wolff, P. H. 1991. The dynamics of bimanual coordination in developmental dyslexia. *Neuropsychologia* 29:907–24.

Rumsey, J. M., Andreason, P., Zametkin, A. J., Aquino, T., King, A. C., Hamburger, S. D., Pikus, A., Rapoport, J. L., and Cohen, R. M. 1992. Failure to activate the left temporoparietal cortex in dyslexia. *Archives of Neurology* 49:527–34.

Rumsey, J. M., Donohue, B. C., Brady, D. R., Nace, K., Giedd, J. N., and Andreason, P. 1997a. A magnetic resonance imaging study of planum temporale asymmetry in men with developmental dyslexia. *Archives of Neurology* 54:1481–89.

Rumsey, J. M., and Eden, G. F. 1997. Functional neuroimaging of developmental dyslexia: Regional cerebral blood flow in dyslexic men. In *Specific Reading Disability: A View of the Spectrum*, eds. B. Shapiro, P. J. Accardo, and A. J. Capute. Timonium, MD: York Press, Inc.

Rumsey, J. M., Horwitz, B., Donohue, B. C., Nace, K., Maisog, J. M., and Andreason, P. 1997b. Phonological and orthographic components of word recognition. A PET-rCBF study. *Brain* 120:739–59.

Rumsey, J. M., Nace, K., Donohue, B., Wise, D., Maisog, J. M., and Andreason, P. 1997c. A positron emission tomographic study of impaired word recognition and phonological processing in dyslexic men. *Archives of Neurology* 54:562–73.

Sergent, J., Zuck, E., Levesque, M., and MacDonald, B. 1992. Positron emission tomography study of letter and object processing: Empirical findings and methodological considerations. *Cerebral Cortex* 2:68–80.

Share, D. L., Silva, P. A., and Adler, C. J. 1987. Factors associated with reading-plus-spelling retardation and specific spelling retardation. *Developmental Medicine and Child Neurology* 29:72–84.

Shaywitz, B. A., Shaywitz, S. E., Pugh, K. R., Skudlarski, P., Fulbright, R. K., Constable, R. T., Bronen, R. A., Fletcher, J. M., Liberman, A. M., Shankweiler, D. P., Katz, L., Lacadie, C., Marchione, K. E., and Gore, J. C. 1996. Functional magnetic resonance imaging as a tool to understand reading and reading disability. In *Developmental Neuroimaging: Mapping the Development of Brain and Behavior*, eds. R. W. Thatcher, G. R. Lyon, J. Rumsey, and N. Krasnegor. San Diego: Academic Press, Inc.

Shaywitz, S. E. 1996. Dyslexia. *Sci Am* 275:98–104.

Shaywitz, S. E., Shaywitz, B. A., Pugh, K. R., Fulbright, R. K., Constable, R. T., Mencl, W. B., Shankweiler, D. P., Liberman, A. M., Skudlarski, P., Fletcher, J. M., Katz, L., Marchione, K. E., Lacadie, C., Gatenby, C., and Gore, J. C. 1998. Functional disruption in the organization of the brain for reading in dyslexia. *Proceedings of the National Academy of Sciences of the United States of America* 95:2636–41.

Snowling, M. J. 1981. Phonemic deficits in developmental dyslexia. *Psychological Research* 43:219–34.

Snowling, M. J. 1991. Developmental reading disorders. *Journal of Child Psychiatry* 32:49–77.

Stanley, G., Smith, G. A., and Howell, G. A. 1983. Eye movements and sequential tracking in dyslexic and control children. *British Journal of Psychology* 74:181–87.

Stanovich, K. E. 1988. Explaining the differences between the dyslexic and the garden-variety poor reader: The phonological-core variable-difference model. *Journal of Learning Disabilities* 21:590–604.

Studdert-Kennedy, M., and Mody, M. 1995. Auditory temporal perception deficits in reading-impaired: A critical review of the evidence. *Psychonomic Bulletin Review* 2:508–14.

Talairach, J., and Tournoux, P. 1988. *Co-planar Stereotaxic Atlas of the Human Brain*. Trans. by M. Rayport. New York: Thieme Medical Publishers, Inc.

Talcott, J. B., Witton, C., McLean, M. F., Hansen, P. C., Rees, A., Green, G. G., and Stein, J. F. 2000. Dynamic sensory sensitivity and children's word decoding skills. *Proceedings of the National Academy of Sciences USA* 97:2952–57.

Tallal, P. 1980. Auditory temporal perception, phonics, and reading disabilities in children. *Brain and Language* 9:182-98

Tallal, P., Miller, S., and Fitch, R. H. 1993. Neurobiological basis of speech: A case for the preminence of temporal processing. In *Temporal Information Processing in the Nervous System: Special Reference to Dyslexia and Dysphasia*, eds. P. Tallal, A. M. Galaburda, R. R. Llinas, and C. von Euler. New York: New York Academy of Sciences.

Ungerleider, L. G., and Mishkin, M. 1982. Two cortical visual systems. In *Analysis of Visual Behavior*, eds. D. J. Ingle, M. A. Goodale, and R. J. W. Mansfield. Cambridge, MA: MIT Press.

Van Essen, D., and Maunsell, J. H. R. 1983. Hierarchical organization and functional streams in the visual cortex. *Trends in Neurosciences* 9:370–75.

Victor, J. D., and Zemon, V. 1985. The human visual evoked potential: Analysis of components due to elementary and complex aspects of forms. *Vision Research* 25:1829–42.

Wagner, R. K., Torgesen, J. K., Laughon, P., Simmons, K., and Rashotte, C. A. 1993. Development of young readers' phonological processing abilities. *Journal of Educational Psychology* 85:83–103.

Watson, J. D. G., Myers, R., Frackowiak, R. S. J., Hajnal, J. V., Woods, R. P., Mazziotta, J. C., Shipp, S., and Zeki, S. 1993. Area V5 of the human brain: Evidence from a combined study using positron emission tomography and magnetic resonance imaging. *Cerebral Cortex* 3:79–94.

Wechsler, D. 1974. *Manual for the Wechsler Intelligence Scale for Children*. New York: Psychological Corporation.

Witelson, S. F., and Pallie, W. 1973. Left hemisphere specialization for language in the newborn. Neuroanatomical evidence of asymmetry. *Brain* 96:641–46.

Wolf, M., Bally, H., and Morris, R. 1986. Automaticity, retrieval processes, and reading: A longitudinal study in average and impaired readers. *Child Development* 57:988–1000.

Wolf, M., and Goodglass, H. 1986. Dyslexia, dysnomia, and lexical retrieval: A longitudinal investigation. *Brain and Language* 28:154–68.

Wolff, P. H., Cohen, C., and Drake, C. 1984. Impaired motor timing control in specific reading retardation. *Neuropsychologia* 22:587–600.

Wright, B. A., Lombardino, L. J., King, W. M., Puranik, C. S., Leonard, C. M., and Merzenich, M. M. 1997. Deficits in auditory temporal and spectral resolution in language-impaired children. *Nature* 387:176–78.

Zatorre, R., Evans, A., Meyer, E., and Gjedde, A. 1992. Lateralization of phonetic and pitch discrimination in speech processing. *Science* 256:846–49.

Zihl, J., von Cramon, D., and Mai, N. 1983. Selective disturbance of movement vision after bilateral brain damage. *Brain* 106:313–40.

PART II
Intervention Issues

In keeping with one of the goals of *Annals of Dyslexia*—to provide well-documented reports of effective practice—we feature two very different perspectives on intervention.

The first article provides an exemplary model of effective reading instruction; the second presents a research study on individual differences in reading.

Kame'enui, Simmons, and Coyne describe a school-wide reading model that has shown success in a small suburban school district in Oregon. The first author had presented some of this material at the IDA Preconference Symposium, "Reading: The Urban Challenge," in Chicago in November, 1999. In this article, the authors explain how their approach can apply to school districts of any size. Importantly, their model reflects some of the best current research and thinking on beginning reading in terms of its integration of research in assessment, instructional design principles, methods of early reading instruction, and interventions. The authors present a five-stage approach that includes analyzing context and assessing global performance, analyzing individual performance and planning instructional groups, designing a range of instructional interventions, setting and monitoring goals, evaluating effectiveness of interventions, and adjusting interventions accordingly. They make a special point of saying that school districts should take advantage of the general nature of the school-wide Reading Improvement Model by adapting it to the unique context(s) of their school system. In their words, "The singular act of teaching reading . . . cannot be separated from the contexts in which it takes place."

The second paper is based on research resulting from an IDA grant. Donald Compton makes an important contribution to a growing body of research that examines the efficacy of direct, systematic instruction on word reading skills and individual differences in responsiveness to reading instruction. Compton describes individual differences prior to intervention during the first semester, and the results of systematic small-group intervention over the second semester with a select group of at-risk first graders over a relatively short period of time (12 weeks). Despite intervention, the at-risk learners in his study did not reach the same proficiency levels as the typically performing students, although they did not fall further behind. Compton's findings indicate that the assessment measures he used, such as curriculum-based management (CBM) and hierarchical linear modeling (HLM), appear to work well for measuring reading growth. He was able to identify important subject characteristics that predicted individual differences in responsiveness to word reading instruction.

Both articles should provide useful information for educators on how to develop appropriate programs for beginning reading instruction. The first article provides a global, "school-wide" view that will assist educators in setting up empirically based reading programs in their school systems. The second article adds evidence to a growing body of literature on child characteristics that predict responsiveness to early reading intervention, and on ways to assess and monitor reading growth.

Schools as Host Environments: Toward a Schoolwide Reading Improvement Model

Edward J. Kame'enui

Deborah C. Simmons

Michael D. Coyne

University of Oregon
Eugene, Oregon

Despite vast differences among school districts across the country, all students must learn how to read in a complex "host-environment" called a school. A challenge in beginning reading, therefore, is to transcend these differences and focus, instead, on the essential task of teaching reading in schools. Teaching reading involves attending to what we know about beginning reading and the alphabetic writing system, the difficulties of reading, and the challenges associated with dyslexia. Teaching reading in a school requires that interventions be tailored to the unique needs of an individual school and implemented and sustained at the school building level. In this article, we outline the Schoolwide Reading Improvement Model (SRIM). This model is characterized by the strategic integration of research-based practices in assessment, instructional design, and beginning reading instruction. Additionally, the SRIM acknowledges the specific needs of individual schools and is customized to provide the best fit with each unique "host-environment." First we provide a description of each major stage of the SRIM and then an example of its application in a school district in western Oregon.

Annals of Dyslexia, Vol. 50, 2000
Copyright ©2000 by The International Dyslexia Association®
ISSN 0736-9387

Schools are inherently complex environments that are made even more complex by significant social, political, economic, pedagogical, legal, cultural, demographic, and historical forces. Although some of these forces are whimsical and others are coercive, they unwittingly shape the very nature and function of schools. As a result, the over 85,000 public elementary and secondary schools in the United States vary in any number of ways. To give just one example, schools come in all sizes, and size matters. Urban schools tend to be larger than rural schools. Moreover, urban school districts usually consist of a vast number of schools. Not surprisingly, bigger, urban schools are likely to be more complex fiscally and administratively than smaller, rural schools. By way of illustration, the Los Angeles Unified School District (LAUSD), the second largest school district in the country, has 420 elementary schools, 72 middle schools, and 49 senior high schools, and an enrollment of 697,143 students who speak more than 80 different languages and dialects, a certified staff of more than 41,000, and a total district budget of $6.5 billion. In fact, the budget for the LAUSD is bigger than the state budgets, for example, of Alaska, Colorado, Delaware, Hawaii, New Hampshire, and Wyoming. In contrast to the LAUSD, the Bethel School District (BSD) in Eugene, Oregon, has six elementary schools, two middle schools, and one high school, with a total enrollment of 5,246, a certified staff of 272, and an entire district budget of $30 million. The numerical differences between these disparate districts are staggering and provocative. Specifically, the Los Angeles School District has 70 times more schools, 133 times more students, 150 times more certified staff, and a budget that is 220 times greater than the Bethel School District. Size matters, and sometimes, in a very big way.

Students in both Los Angeles and Bethel, however, share a fundamental similarity despite the differences in the size of their schools and districts. They all have to learn to read. Furthermore, they all have to learn to read in a complex environment of people, pedagogy, policies, and programs called a school. One challenge in beginning reading, therefore, is to get beyond the often overwhelming differences among school districts and focus, instead, on the essential task of teaching reading in schools. Teaching reading involves attending to what we know about beginning reading and the alphabetic writing system, the difficulties of reading, and the challenges associated with dyslexia. Teaching reading in a school requires that interventions be tailored to the unique needs of an individual school and implemented and sustained at the school building level. These are the essential components necessary to improve the reading outcomes of students, irrespective of the school or district they attend.

Domain-specific knowledge should inform our efforts to teach reading and prevent reading failure. Fortunately, we know more about reading disability than about all the other learning disabilities put together. This assertion, recently expressed by Stanovich (1999), underscores the substantial knowledge base that exists in our field. This knowledge base comes from the sizable body of converging research evidence accumulated over the past thirty years and reflects a significant advancement in our understanding of both the nature of dyslexia and the ways in which we as educators and parents can work to ensure that children become successful readers (National Research Council 1998; Adams 1990). We know that reading failure is a serious and pervasive concern in our society (U.S. Department of Education 1999). We know that a clear and unforgiving "line in the sand" exists at the end of grade 3 after which students who are poor readers almost never catch up to their peers who are good readers (Felton and Pepper 1995; Juel 1988). We know that we must identify students at risk of reading failure early, that systematic and strategic intervention should begin no later than kindergarten, and that monitoring of student progress should be formative and ongoing (Kame'enui, Simmons, and Coyne 1999). We know that interventions targeted toward students at risk of reading failure should focus on at least the three "big ideas" of beginning reading: phonological awareness, alphabetic understanding, and automaticity with the code (Simmons and Kame'enui 1998; Kame'enui and Carnine 1998).

The singular act of teaching reading, however, cannot be separated from the contexts in which it takes place. Too often, effective reading programs are insufficient because educators consider only one "context" (i.e., the learner context) of the learning, teaching, and schooling process (Carroll 1963, 1989; Mosenthal 1984). In addition, such interventions fail to reflect and accommodate the vagaries of changing student performance in the shifting milieu of classrooms and schools (Hedges and Waddington 1993). As Mosenthal (1984) noted more than a decade ago, there is not "one ideal and absolute geometry," but multiple geometries or contexts that influence the teaching and learning space (p. 206). Teaching reading takes place in a complex "host environment" (Zins and Ponti 1990; Sugai and

Horner 1999) and the host environment that holds constant across all of public education is the school. Therefore, it is necessary to take into account the distinctive combination of multiple contexts that exist within an individual school and customize interventions to provide the best fit with each unique school environment.

What we now know about reading disability and the intricacies of schools compels us to intervene in more complex, comprehensive, and coordinated ways. It is not enough to teach reading by relying on vague and general guidelines that attempt to span all disciplines. Teaching reading is, indeed, rocket science (Moats 1999); therefore, we must focus our efforts on the specifics of dyslexia and beginning reading in an alphabetic writing system (Stanovich 1999). Neither is it enough to assume that individual teachers, working independently, can implement and sustain the host of research-based practices that we know are necessary to prevent reading failure. Rather, our scope should extend beyond individual teachers to mirror and capture the genuine complexities in "real world" schools (Kame'enui and Simmons 1998). We are at a point in our field where we have the knowledge to effect schoolwide, coordinated efforts to ensure that every student learns to read, from the rural areas of Eugene, Oregon, to the sprawling urban neighborhoods of Los Angeles. What we know requires that we do no less.

Below, we outline the Schoolwide Reading Improvement Model (SRIM). This model attempts to integrate what we know about the specifics of dyslexia and beginning reading with what we know of the realities of implementing and sustaining effective practices in complex host environments called schools. In the sections that follow, we provide a description of each major stage of the SRIM and then an example of its application in a school district in western Oregon.

A SCHOOLWIDE READING IMPROVEMENT MODEL (SRIM)

The SRIM consists of five stages (see figure 1) and combines four primary components:
1. dynamic assessment of big ideas or target performance indicators
2. research-based practices and procedures in beginning reading

3. validated principles of effective curriculum and instruction

4. customized interventions in integrated contexts as the basis for reading improvement models that fit the host environment.

A key feature of this model is the essential linkage of assessment and instruction. Though integrating assessment and intervention is not a novel concept and is indeed a signature of effective special education (Deno 1992; Fuchs and Fuchs 1994), what is innovative and effective about this process is the timely, strategic fit of the measures (what to assess), the targets of reading improvement (what to teach), and interventions that have a high probability of improving reading (how to teach). This confluence of performance indicators and instructional intervention positions a school to identify children early who are at serious risk of reading failure, intervene strategically, and modify instruction responsively in accord with learner performance.

The model and its decision-making processes draw extensively on the work in reading assessment of Shinn (1997) and Kaminski and Good (1996) and combine their procedures for identifying, grouping, problem solving, and performance monitoring with Kame'enui and Simmons' (1998) components of contextual interventions to reflect an integrated and comprehensive intervention model anchored to the distinguishing characteristics of individual schools.

STAGE I: ANALYZE CONTEXTS AND ASSESS STUDENT PERFORMANCE USING DYNAMIC INDICATORS OF BIG IDEAS

Description. The goals of Stage I are twofold and operate concurrently. The first goal is to determine what is currently in place in the school with respect to instructional priorities, time allocation to reading instruction, instructional materials and programs, organizational strategies, and overall student performance. Schools conduct an internal audit guided by a "Planning and Evaluation Tool for Effective Schoolwide Reading Programs" (Kame'enui and Simmons 1999) that examines school goals, instructional priorities, teacher philosophy, and current practices. Results of the inventory illuminate the unique interactions of the multiple contexts existing within a school and provide a framework for anchoring decisions made during subsequent stages of the SRIM to the particular realities of the host environment or school.

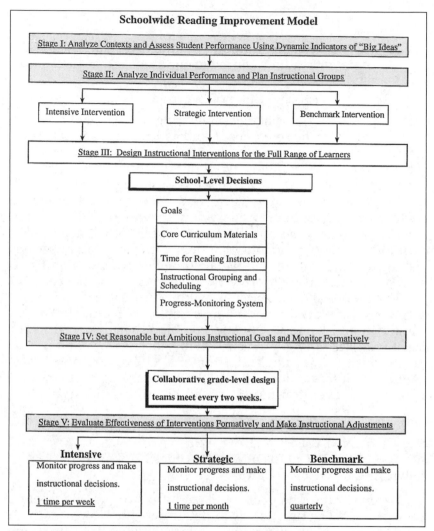

Figure 1.   Schoolwide reading improvement model.

The second goal of Stage I is to identify children who are at risk of reading disabilities or delay. Kaminski and Good (1996) describe this process as "problem identification." At the beginning of the school year, all children, kindergarten through Grade 3, are screened with measures that correspond to the big ideas in beginning reading: phonological awareness, alphabetic understanding, and automaticity with the code. The premise behind big idea indicators is that while these screening measures do not tell us everything about reading achievement, they serve as valid and reliable predictors of skills highly associated with later reading achievement. Deno (1992) describes such measures as indicators or "vital signs of growth in basic skills comparable to the vital signs of health used by physicians" (Deno 1992, p. 6). Performance indicators provide fast and efficient indication of the reading *well being* of students with respect to reading skills essential to successful performance in the general education curriculum (Kaminski and Good 1998).

Screening measures differ according to grade and learner performance. For example, in kindergarten and first grade, *Dynamic Indicators of Basic Early Literacy Skills* (DIBELS) (Kaminski and Good 1998), which include onset recognition, phonemic segmentation, letter naming, and nonsense word reading, are used to identify and monitor children whose performance differs significantly from their same-age peers. Once students are able to read words in connected text (approximately mid-first grade through third grade), measures of oral reading fluency from curriculum-based passages are used as indicators of reading achievement (Shinn 1997). Students' performance on these indicators is then compared to performance expectations, or "where we would expect children to perform," to identify children at risk of reading disability or delay. Performance expectations may be derived from two sources: local normative data or performance associated with early reading success (Kaminski and Good 1996).

This stage integrates several contexts including setting (school), task (specific reading measures), and learner (performance on critical indicators). This integrative model allows schools to examine learner performance not only at the individual level, but also at the school level, to determine the magnitude of the problem. From this big-picture analysis, the scope and intensity of the intervention can be assessed. Furthermore, schools are better able to respond to children's needs proactively through early screening and identification. Stage I involves initiating and maintaining a centralized system for managing student-performance data at the school level to enable timely and informed decisions. This dynamic database and record-keeping system is a common feature of effective schools and is an essential feature of SRIM.

Application. A small, suburban school district in western Oregon with an enrollment of approximately 5,000 students has recently embarked on the process of implementing the SRIM in six elementary schools. The school district had been experiencing a significant and recurring increase in the percentage of students identified with special needs (e.g., approximately 20 percent identified for special education). After examining the results of the six schoolwide inventories (Kame'enui and Simmons 1999), the district concertedly identified beginning reading as a top instructional priority and made a commitment to improve the reading outcomes of all students in kindergarten through Grade 3. In addition, the district pledged to provide the administrative support necessary to build the capacity to implement and sustain a comprehensive districtwide reading intervention. The first-year focus was on implementing the model in kindergarten. In subsequent years, the implementation will expand to encompass the other primary grades (Grades 1 to 3).

During sessions in the fall, administrators and kindergarten teachers, as well as Title I teachers, special education teachers, and instructional assistants that work with kindergarten students, evaluated their current assessment and instructional practices and became familiar with the goals and components of the SRIM. The participants also received training in administering and interpreting the DIBELS measures that assess the three big ideas of phonological awareness, alphabetic understanding, and automaticity with the code. Two types of measures have been particularly effective for early identification: (1) a test of letter names or sounds, and (2) a measure of phonemic awareness (Torgesen 1998). Measures of letter knowledge are strong predictors of reading difficulties, and measures of phonemic awareness enhance the accuracy of the prediction. In the fall of kindergarten, a letter naming fluency measure was used to assess students' familiarity with the letters of the alphabet, and a phonemic awareness measure was used to assess students' ability to recognize the first sounds in words. In winter and spring, a measure of letter-sound knowledge (i.e., nonsense word fluency) and a more sophisticated measure of phonemic awareness (i.e., phonemic segmentation fluency) was used to assess a student's progressive skill with the individual sound units in words.

In November 1998, all kindergarten students received assessments on the following performance indicators:

> *Letter Naming Fluency:* ability to name letters accurately and rapidly.
> *Onset Recognition Fluency:* ability to recognize the first sounds in words.

In February and May 1999, all students received assessments on the previous measures and the following indicators:

> *Phonemic Segmentation Fluency:* ability to produce phonemes in words (auditory).

Nonsense Word Fluency: ability to produce letter-sound correspondences and use them to read words.

The school district established a computer-based data management system that allowed teachers to input student data and then analyzed and graphed results. The district reported results of the November, February, and May assessments for the entire district, each of six schools, and for all 20 of the individual kindergarten sessions (morning and afternoon). Figure 2 presents an example of the districtwide results of Phonemic Segmentation Fluency. These results indicated the magnitude of the problem in kindergarten. The benchmark goal for the Phonemic Segmentation Fluency measure is a score of 35 to 45 phoneme segments per minute by spring of kindergarten (Kaminski and Good 1998). According to these data, only 20 percent of students in the district demonstrated established segmentation skills on the February assessment. More worrisome, 32 percent of the students (N = 127) scored below 10 segments and were at serious risk to meet the spring benchmark (Kaminski and Good 1998). By examining these results, along with those of the other measures, the district was able to confirm that there was a significant reading problem in kindergarten. Moreover, this performance data served as an anchor for guiding decisions related to the development of the components of the SRIM outlined in Stages II-V.

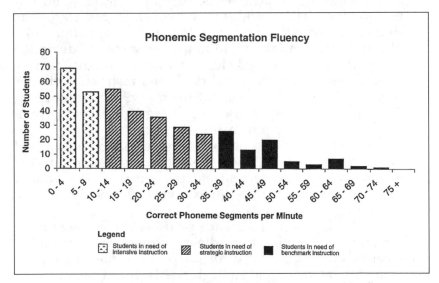

Figure 2.   Districtwide results of phonemic segmentation fluency measure, February, 1999.

STAGE II: ANALYZE INDIVIDUAL PERFORMANCE AND PLAN INSTRUCTIONAL GROUPS

Description.   Using normative information from performance indicators of big ideas, an analysis of individual student results determines the child's current level of performance and other children who have similar performance profiles. Using a process developed by Shinn (1997), children's results on big-idea indicators and other information from teachers are used to perform "instructional triage"; that is, children who are at greatest risk are identified from those with less risk. To make this process operational, we use the following criteria:

Intensive students are those who are seriously at risk based on extremely low performance on one or more performance indicators. The greater the number of measures and the lower the performance, the greater the risk. In general, these children are performing more than two standard deviations below the mean on local norms or expected levels of performance. Similar to children with serious medical conditions, children in need of intensive care in reading are in acute need of the most effective interventions available and require frequent monitoring to ensure that their reading performance does not remain seriously low. Educators must intervene with a sense of urgency.

Strategic students need systematic, strategic intervention and monitoring because of increased risk factors and low performance. Their condition, however, is less acute than students in the intensive group. In general, the performance of these children falls more than one standard deviation below the mean. Nonetheless, strategic students require more carefully designed and delivered instruction than is typical of most classrooms. Shinn (1997) recommends monthly monitoring on critical reading indicators to evaluate these students' performance.

Benchmark students' performance seems to be on target on critical literacy skills, and these students are not at risk of reading delay, based on current performance. We monitor benchmark students three times a year—in the fall, winter, and spring.

Once children's performance profiles are analyzed, we group children according to reading performance in small homogeneous groups designed for purposeful intervention for children with intensive and strategic needs. As a rule, the number of students in intensive groups should be smaller than either the strategic or benchmark groups and comprise no more than five students. A word of caution is warranted regarding grouping. The purpose of grouping is to enable children to receive instruction (e.g., increased opportunities to respond) that is appropriate for the needs of the learner. Groups should remain dynamic. Strategic and frequent monitoring of performance provides a mechanism for adjusting groups in response to instruction and assessment.

Application. The districtwide results from the western Oregon school district's February assessment indicated the scope of the problem in kindergarten and emphasized the need for developing comprehensive reading interventions at each school. School teams then examined the results of individual student performance and determined instructional groupings. By comparing students' results on the different kindergarten measures to performance expectations (i.e., benchmarks) that were known to reliably predict future reading success, teachers were able to identify students as benchmark, strategic, or intensive (Kaminski and Good 1998). For example, individual student performance on the *Phonemic Segmentation Fluency* measure (see figure 2) indicated that in February, 20 percent of kindergarten students should be considered benchmark students, 48 percent strategic students, and 32 percent intensive students. Identifying instructional groups based on student performance set the stage for school teams to plan interventions that would address the needs of all students.

STAGE III: DESIGN INSTRUCTIONAL INTERVENTIONS FOR THE FULL RANGE OF LEARNERS

Description. In Stages I–II, the context is set for what is arguably the most critical and complex component of the SRIM process: intervention. Stage III focuses on the multiple contexts that must be considered when designing interventions and the importance of instructional fit with the host environment. Too often, interventions fail because *Intervention A* has been implemented in *School B* with *Teachers C and D* without really understanding the fit among factors A, B, C, and D. A key difference of the SRIM from other models is the focus of intervention that moves beyond the learner to the school, classroom, teacher, curriculum, materials, and tasks (Kame'enui and Simmons 1998). Site-based coordinators (e.g., a teacher or administrator serving as a building coordinator for SRIM) facilitate the analysis of contexts and the development of intervention elements with collaborative grade-level intervention teams. In this process, grade-level teams work from a framework of research-based practices (e.g., specific curriculum, supplemental practices) and alterable variables (e.g., instructional time, groupings, concentration of low performers, delivery of instruction) to customize intervention models.

In this model, there are standard intervention dimensions across all grades and classrooms within the school, and there are dimensions that are discretionary. At a minimum, we recommend considering a "core" set of features to address at a schoolwide level. These core features include:

- setting reading goals based on research-based targets;
- adopting and implementing core curriculum programs of documented efficacy;
- scheduling fixed and protected times for teacher-directed daily reading instruction;
- differentiating instruction based on learners' current level of reading performance;
- instituting a centralized system of student achievement data collection;
- coordinating the delivery of instruction across school personnel (e.g., general education, special education, Title I); and
- establishing and supporting grade-level teams who study, analyze, and respond to students who fail to make adequate progress (Simmons et al. in press).

At every stage of the intervention definition process, collaborative intervention teams construct or customize the intervention from a menu of validated options. For example, in selecting a core reading program, teams review programs of documented efficacy (American Federation of Teachers 1999) such as *SRA Open Court Reading* (SRA 2000), *Success for All* (Slavin et al. 1996), and *Reading Mastery* (Engelmann and Bruner 1998) to determine the fit of those research-based programs with the philosophy, needs, and resources of the school. It is this customization or "fit" within the school that further distinguishes the SRIM from more traditional translations of research into practice.

Application.   In Stage III, kindergarten teachers and administrators from the school district in western Oregon worked together to customize instructional interventions that targeted the full range of learners and acknowledged the unique host environment of each school. First, school teams reviewed several phonological awareness/reading programs that would serve as the core curriculum for all students and supplemental programs that would augment instruction for strategic and intensive students. All kindergarten teachers received training and guidance on the review and selection of core and supplemental reading programs. Kindergarten programs reviewed included *Open Court, Reading Mastery, Phonemic Awareness in Young Children* (Adams et al. 1997), *Ladders to Literacy* (Notari-Syverson et al. 1998), and *Phonological Awareness Training for Reading* (Torgesen and Bryant 1994). School teams selected core and supplemental programs on the basis of strong research support and the contextual fit with the needs of each school.

Next, the schools determined the minimum amount of time that would be set aside for teacher-directed reading instruction during the half-day kindergarten sessions. School teams decided that between 30 to 45 minutes of direct reading instruction each day was essential to meet the needs of all kindergarten students within the district. Furthermore, some schools concluded that intensive students would require an additional period (i.e., "double dose") of reading instruction daily. Teachers and administrators also discussed options for the grouping of students and the scheduling of reading instruction. Depending on the instructional preferences of teachers and the availability of additional staff support at each school, teams considered grouping possibilities (e.g., within class, across class, and across grade) and discussed options for the delivery of instruction to intensive and strategic students utilizing classroom, Title I, and special education teachers, and instructional assistants. In general, intensive intervention groups were no larger than five students. The inclusion of administrators on each school team permitted conversations about ways in which schoolwide scheduling could help facilitate these various grouping and service delivery alternatives. Finally, individual teachers made decisions about additional curricular materials and instructional practices that they would use to enhance the reading instruction in their classrooms.

STAGE IV: SET REASONABLE BUT AMBITIOUS INSTRUCTIONAL GOALS AND MONITOR FORMATIVELY

Description. The next stage of the Schoolwide Reading Improvement Model involves using individual student performance to set four-week and long-term instructional goals. In early literacy, we have a reliable knowledge base to determine expected performance for early literacy success (Fuchs and Fuchs 1994; Kaminski and Good 1996; Hasbrouck and Tindal 1992; Markell and Deno 1997). For example, in second grade, children gain approximately 1.46 words correct per minute per week in oral reading fluency (Fuchs, et al. 1993) and students in the 50th percentile exit second grade reading approximately 90 correct words per minute (Hasbrouck and Tindal 1992). Children who are successful early readers orally segment words into phonemes at a rate of approximately 35 to 45 phonemes per minute by spring of kindergarten (Kaminski and Good 1998). These levels of expected performance are critical as we develop goals for children whose early reading trajectories are less than adequate, and they serve an important function in the SRIM process.

It is sometimes necessary to establish goals for multiple measures and monitor progress formatively. Shinn (1997) recommends weekly monitoring for intensive students, and monthly monitoring for strategic students. All students are measured quarterly on critical performance indicators to determine their progress toward long-term goals. Teachers also can calculate four week and even weekly instructional goals for intensive students by using current student achievement on dynamic measures, expected performance (i.e., benchmark goals), and time remaining until the next measurement point to ascertain the rate of learning necessary to reach the benchmarks. Teachers can use this same process for each target measure of reading.

Application. The western Oregon school district used research-based performance objectives to establish benchmark goals for the phonological awareness measures administered in kindergarten. The goals for kindergarten students were to score between 25 to 35 onsets per minute on the *Onset Recognition Fluency* measure by winter and between 35 to 45 segments per minute on the *Phonemic Segmentation Fluency* measure by spring. Because phonological segmentation is such a strong predictor of reading success in first grade, the goal was for all students to have established phonological segmentation skills by the end of kindergarten. Additionally, the *Nonsense Word Fluency* measure that assesses alphabetic understanding also was administered throughout kindergarten. By using these results, teachers could set short term instructional goals to ensure that students would meet the first grade benchmark of between 40 to 50 letter-sound correspondences per minute on this measure by the following winter.

School teams decided to assess benchmark students in the fall, winter, and spring and monitor strategic students monthly. Some schools planned to monitor intensive students every week while other schools decided to assess these students every other week. By establishing clear goals of expected performance and instituting an assessment schedule based on degree of student risk, schools created a feedback loop that allowed for formative evaluation of instruction.

STAGE V: EVALUATE EFFECTIVENESS OF INTERVENTIONS FORMATIVELY AND MAKE INSTRUCTIONAL ADJUSTMENTS

Description. In this final stage of the SRIM, we illustrate the critical linkage between assessment and instruction. Using students' performance on big ideas as indicators collected weekly for intensive students and monthly for strategic students, teachers evaluate progress toward goals to determine whether the rate of progress is adequate to achieve performance benchmarks and, therefore, eliminate risk of long-term reading difficulty. In essence, we address the questions: Is the students' current rate of progress sufficient to close the gap, *and* is the rate sufficient so the student will *learn enough* (Carnine 1997) to be on a positive trajectory toward reading success? Grade level teams meet frequently (e.g., every two weeks) to monitor the effectiveness of interventions and make instructional adjustments. Teams work collaboratively to alter instructional variables based on student data. At meetings, teachers make decisions about the allocation of instructional time, ways to regroup students, the use of supplemental materials, assessment schedules, short-term objectives, and instructional focus. In this way, teams are able to customize interventions for intensive and strategic students in a way that is dynamic and integrally linked to student performance.

Application. School teams from the western Oregon school district made a commitment to meet frequently to monitor the effectiveness of their kindergarten interventions and to make instructional adjustments. The scheduling and frequency of meetings varied by school and were guided by time and staffing considerations. All teams met every week or every other week. Teams worked collaboratively to alter instructional variables based on student data. At meetings, decisions were made about the allocation of instructional time, ways to regroup students, the use of supplemental materials, assessment schedules, short-term objectives, and instructional focus. In this way, teams were able to customize interventions for intensive and strategic students in a way that was dynamic and integrally linked to student performance.

Results of the districtwide SRIM implementation in kindergarten indicate that students' phonemic awareness skills increased substantially from February to May (see figure 3). In

May, only 7 percent of kindergarten students had phonemic awareness skills of the level that would require intensive intervention, as opposed to 32 percent in February. In the absence of a control group, we cannot draw conclusions about relative growth; however, we can conclude that in an absolute sense, students made notable growth in phonemic segmentation, which is a reliable predictor of word reading in Grade 1.

CONCLUSION

The SRIM is an integrated, data-based intervention model for teaching reading in schools. This model is based on the methodological integration of (a) general and special education research in assessment (e.g., Good, Simmons, and Smith 1998), (b) effective instructional design principles (Kame'enui and Carnine 1998), (c) validated methods of early reading instruction (Simmons and Kame'enui 1998), and (d) interventions that fit the school as the host environment (Sugai and Horner 1999). The Schoolwide Reading Improvement Model can intercept and prevent early reading risk from becoming long-term, intractable difficulties.

If we take seriously the widespread call to educate all children, and not view it as just another slogan in which "the rhetoric" of educating all is in effect the reality of educating

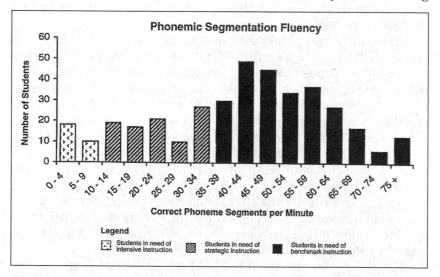

Figure 3. Districtwide results of phonemic segmentation fluency measure, May, 1999.

some or even most (Kame'enui 1998), then we face enormous challenges. Perhaps the most important challenge is that of designating beginning reading as the top instructional priority for elementary schools in kindergarten through Grade 3, making a schoolwide commitment to focus relentlessly and strategically on this priority, and implementing a data-based intervention model that provides a formative and continuous feedback loop about student reading performance. Finally, if we embrace an intervention model that acknowledges and honors the differences among individual schools, wherever they may be located, we can truly say, yes, size matters, but teaching reading matters more.

ACKNOWLEDGMENTS

The contents of this document were developed in part for the Office of Special Education Programs, U.S. Department of Education under Grant Number H324M980127. This material does not necessarily represent the policy of the U.S. Department of Education, nor is the material necessarily endorsed by the Federal Government.

We gratefully acknowledge and warmly thank the dedicated, hard-working, and enthusiastic Bethel District elementary administrators, teachers, and educational assistants who so expertly implemented the Schoolwide Reading Model. We extend a special thanks to the reading coordinators for their leadership and perseverance.

Address correspondence to: Edward J. Kame'enui, Institute for the Development of Educational Achievement, Education Annex, 1211 University of Oregon, Eugene, OR 97403-1211

References

Adams, M. J. 1990. *Beginning To Read: Thinking and Learning About Print.* Cambridge, MA: The MIT Press.

Adams, M. J., Foorman, B. R., Lundberg, I., and Beeler, T. D. 1997. *Phonemic Awareness in Young Children: A Classroom Curriculum.* Baltimore, MD: Paul H. Brookes Publishing Co.

American Federation of Teachers. 1999. *Building on the Best, Learning From What Works: Seven Promising Reading and English Language Arts Programs.* Washington, DC.

Carnine, D. 1997. Instructional design in mathematics for students with learning disabilities. *Journal of Learning Disabilities* 30:130–31.

Carroll, J. B. 1963. A model of school learning. *Teachers College Record* 64:723–33.

Carroll, J. B. 1989. The Carroll model: A 25-year retrospective and prospective view. *Educational Researcher* 18:26–31.

Deno, S. L. 1992. The nature and development of curriculum-based measurement. *Preventing School Failure* 36:5–10.

Engelmann, S., and Bruner, E. 1998. *Reading Mastery I: Distar Reading*. Chicago, IL: Science Research Associates, Inc.

Felton, R. H., and Pepper, P. P. 1995. Early identification and intervention of phonological deficits in kindergarten and early elementary children at risk for reading disability. *School Psychology Review* 24:405–14.

Fuchs, D., and Fuchs, L. 1994. Classwide curriculum-based measurement: Helping general educators meet the challenge of student diversity. *Exceptional Children* 60:518–37.

Fuchs, L. S., Fuchs, D., Hamlett, C. L., Walz, L., and Germann, G. 1993. Formative evaluation of academic progress: How much growth can we expect? *School Psychology Review* 22:27–48.

Good, R., III, Simmons, D. C., and Smith, S. 1998. Effective academic interventions in the United States: Evaluating and enhancing the acquisition of early reading skills. *School Psychology Review* 27:740–53.

Hasbrouck, J. E., and Tindal, G. 1992. Curriculum-based oral reading fluency norms for students in grades 2 through 5. *Teaching Exceptional Children* 24:41–44.

Hedges, L. V., and Waddington, T. 1993. From evidence to knowledge to policy: Research synthesis for policy formation. *Review of Educational Research* 63:345–52.

Juel, C. 1988. Learning to read and write: A longitudinal study of 54 children from first through fourth grades. *Journal of Educational Psychology* 80:437–47.

Kame'enui, E. J. 1998. The rhetoric of all, the reality of some, and the unmistakable smell of mortality. In *Literacy for All: Issues in Teaching and Learning*, eds. J. Osborn and F. Lehr. New York: Guilford.

Kame'enui, E. J., and Carnine, D. W. 1998. *Effective Teaching Strategies That Accommodate Diverse Learners*. Columbus, OH: Merrill, Prentice Hall.

Kame'enui, E. J., and Simmons, D. C. 1998. Beyond effective practice to schools as host environments: Building and sustaining a school-wide intervention model in reading. *Oregon School Study Council Bulletin* 41:3–24.

Kame'enui, E. J., and Simmons, D. C. 1999. *Planning and Evaluation Tool for Effective Schoolwide Reading Programs*. Unpublished document.

Kame'enui, E. J., Simmons, D. C., and Coyne, M. D. 1999. *Kindergarten Reading Instruction and the Tyranny Of Time: Toward a Schoolwide Reading Improvement Model*. Manuscript submitted for publication.

Kaminski, R. A., and Good, R. H., III. 1996. Toward a technology for assessing basic early literacy skills. *School Psychology Review* 25:215–27.

Kaminski, R. A., and Good, R. H., III. 1998. Assessing early literacy skills in a problem-solving model: Dynamic indicators of basic early literacy skills. In *Advanced Applications of Curriculum-Based Measurement*, ed. M. R. Shinn. New York: Guilford.

Markell, M. A., and Deno, S. L. 1997. Effects of increasing oral reading: Generalization across reading tasks. *The Journal of Special Education* 31:233–50.

Moats, L. C. 1999. *Teaching Reading Is Rocket Science: What Expert Teachers of Reading Should Know and Be Able To Do*. Washington, D.C: American Federation of Teachers.

Mosenthal, P. 1984. The problem of partial specification in translating reading research into practice. *The Elementary School Journal* 85:199–227.

National Research Council 1998. *Preventing Reading Difficulties in Young Children*. Washington, DC: National Academy Press.

Notari-Syverson, A., O'Connor, R. E., and Vadasy, P. F. 1998. *Ladders to Literacy: A Kindergarten Activity Book*. Baltimore: Paul H. Brookes Publishing Co.

SRA Open Court Reading 2000. Columbus, OH: SRA McGraw-Hill.

Shinn, M. 1997. *Instructional Decision Making Using Curriculum-Based Measurement*. Unpublished workshop materials.

Simmons, D. C., and Kame'enui, E. J. 1998. *What Reading Research Tells Us About Children With Diverse Learning Needs: Bases and Basics*. Mahwah, NJ: Lawrence Erlbaum Associates, Inc.

Simmons, D., King, K., Kuykendall, K., Cornachione, C., and Kame'enui, E. J. 2000. Implementation of a school-wide reading improvement model: No one ever told us it would be this hard. *Learning Disabilities Research and Practice 15* (2):92–100.

Slavin, R. E., Madden, N. A., Dolan, L. J., and Wasik, B. A. 1996. *Every Child, Every School: Success for All*. Thousand Oaks, CA: Corwin.

Stanovich, K. E. 1999. The sociopsychometrics of learning disabilities. *Journal of Learning Disabilities 32*:350–61.

Sugai, G., and Horner, R. H. 1999. Discipline and behavioral support: Practices, pitfalls, and promises. *Effective School Practices 17*:10–22.

Torgesen, J. K. 1998. Catch them before they fall: Identification and assessment to prevent reading failure in young children. *American Educator 22* :32–39.

Torgesen, J. K., and Bryant, B. T. 1994. *Phonological Awareness Training for Reading*. Austin, TX: PRO-ED.

U. S. Department of Education. 1999. *Start Early, Finish Strong: How To Help Every Child Become a Reader*. Washington, DC: U.S. Department of Education, America Reads Challenge.

Zins, J. E., and Ponti, C. R. 1990. Best practices in school-based consultation. In *Best Practices in School Psychology - II*, eds. A. Thomas and J. Grimes. Washington, DC: National Association of School Psychologists.

Modeling the Response of Normally Achieving and At-Risk First Grade Children to Word Reading Instruction

Donald L. Compton

University of Colorado
Boulder, Colorado

The purpose of this study was to identify important subject character-istics that predicted individual differences in responsiveness to word reading instruction in normally achieving and at-risk first grade chil-dren. This was accomplished by modeling individual word and non-word reading growth, and the correlates of change in these skills, in first grade students during two different phases of the school year. In the first phase of the study (October–January), word and nonword reading skill was modeled in normally achieving and at-risk children. Results of growth modeling indicated significant group differences in word and nonword reading growth parameters. A combination of phonemic awareness skill, advanced graphophoneme knowledge, and initial word/nonword reading skill predicted word and nonword read-ing growth in the control group, whereas, a combination of rapid nam-ing speed, letter sound knowledge, and phonemic awareness skill predicted word and nonword reading growth in the at-risk group. In the second phase of the study (January–April), a subgroup of the at-risk subjects who exhibited limited growth in word reading skills dur-ing the first phase of the study was enrolled in 12 weeks of small group reading intervention designed to improve reading skills. Results of growth modeling indicated significant increases in word and nonword

Annals of Dyslexia, Vol. 50, 2000
ISSN 0736-9387

*reading growth rates in this group during the intervention phase.
Only rapid naming speed uniquely predicted word and nonword reading growth in the group of subjects receiving intervention.*

As early as first grade, individual differences in word reading skills are significant predictors of later reading performance
(e.g., Foorman et al. 1997a; Juel 1988; Wagner et al. 1997).
Considering the importance of word reading development in
first grade, and the fact that an estimated 20 percent of all children in the United States will experience significant difficulties
learning to read (Shaywitz et al. 1990), it is not surprising that
there has been increasing interest in programs aimed at improving the basic reading skills of first grade children at risk of developing reading problems. Results from various intervention
studies support the general conclusion that intensive early intervention programs can significantly improve the reading
skills of at-risk and reading disabled (RD) children (e.g., Abbott
et al. 1997; Berninger et al. 1999; Blachman et al. 1999; Felton
1993; Felton and Pepper 1995; Foorman et al. 1997b; Foorman et
al. 1998; Hatcher, Hulme, and Ellis 1994; Invernizzi et al. 1997;
Iversen and Tunmer 1993; Marston et al. 1995; Lovett et al. 1994;
McCarthy, Newby, and Recht 1995; Olson et al. 1997; Pikulski
1994; Santa and Høien 1999; Shanahan and Barr 1995; Torgesen,
Wagner, and Rashotte 1997; Torgesen et al. 1999; Vellutino et al.
1996). Nevertheless, results from these intervention studies,
with the possible exception of the Toregsen et al. (1999) study,
have generally failed to demonstrate robust and long lasting
treatment effects based on specific components of various intervention programs. (For a review see Snow, Burns, and Griffin
1998.) Instead, there is growing evidence to suggest that successful intervention programs provide at-risk children with
structured opportunities to acquire a wide array of skills aimed
at improving various aspects of phonological processing, understanding of the alphabetic principle, basic decoding and
spelling skills, orthographic knowledge, reading fluency, and
reading connected text. In addition, effective intervention programs are generally designed to take place in one-on-one or
small group situations where instruction can be designed to
match the developmental level of the child and be paced at an
appropriate rate.

While systematic early intervention has generally been
shown to improve the basic reading skills of at-risk and RD
children, it is also true that there is considerable individual variation in the responsiveness of at-risk and RD children to treat-

ment (e.g., Foorman et al. 1997a, 1997b; Hatcher and Hulme 1999; Torgesen et al. 1999; Vellutino et al. 1996). For instance, Torgesen et al. (1999) have reported that over 20 percent of a sample of kindergarten children, identified as having phonological processing difficulties who received 88 hours of one-to-one instruction (beginning the second semester of kindergarten and extending through second grade), remained significantly impaired in both word and nonword reading skill. In the Torgesen study (1999), individual differences in word and nonword reading growth were predicted by a combination of phonological processing variables, a home background measure, and classroom behavior rating. Vellutino et al. (1996) also reported significant individual variation in the response of first grade poor readers to systematic reading intervention. Similar to the Torgesen study, Vellutino and colleagues found that the children who were the least responsive to remediation generally had very weak phonological processing skills. These results suggest that there are important child characteristics that predict responsiveness to early reading intervention.

The purpose of this study was to further identify subject characteristics that predicted individual differences in responsiveness to early reading intervention. This was accomplished by modeling individual word and nonword reading growth in at-risk first grade students during two different phases of the school year. In the first phase of the study (October–January), individual growth of word and nonword reading skill was modeled in 75 first grade children, and differences in growth characteristics between children considered at relatively high (at-risk subjects) versus relatively low (control subjects) risk of developing reading problems were examined. In the second phase of the study (January–April), a subgroup of the at-risk subjects who exhibited limited growth in word reading skills during the first phase of the study was enrolled in 12 weeks of small group reading intervention designed to improve reading skills. Individual growth in word and nonword reading skill was modeled in this subgroup of at-risk subjects during intervention and compared to a subgroup of at-risk subjects who exhibited relatively normal growth rates in word reading skill development. Finally, various cognitive processing skills and measures of emergent print knowledge were evaluated as predictors of responsiveness to intervention in the at-risk readers.

While sharing various key components with the Foorman et al. (1997b), Torgesen et al. (1999), and Vellutino et al. (1996) studies, the present study differs in several important ways.

First, unlike the Foorman et al. and Torgesen et al. studies that attempted to evaluate differential effects across various treatments, this study was designed to identify important subject characteristics (i.e., cognitive processes and emergent print knowledge) that predicted individual differences in responsiveness to a single balanced intervention program. Second, unlike the Torgesen et al. and Vellutino et al. studies which used standardized measures to assess reading growth, this study employed curriculum-based measurement techniques to model word reading growth and investigate the factors that predict rate of growth in at-risk readers. This made it possible to directly assess children's response to the curriculum over much shorter periods of time (one month intervals) than could be done with traditional standardized measures. Third, the design of this study allowed for comparisons to be made between word and nonword reading growth rates in a subgroup of the at-risk sample during two different phases of reading instruction. In the first phase of the study (October–January), reading instruction was provided to at-risk students solely by their regular classroom teachers. In the second phase of the study (January–April), at-risk students received the same amount of reading instruction as their normally achieving peers; however, it included both regular classroom instruction and small group intervention. Finally, in this study, intervention was provided to at-risk students in small groups (three to four students) by preservice teachers enrolled in a special education methods class, as opposed to studies that used specially trained teachers (e.g., Foorman et al. 1997a, 1997b; Torgesen et al. 1999; Vellutino et al. 1996).

METHOD

SUBJECTS

The sample for this study consisted of first grade children in four classrooms in the same elementary school (representing the entire first grade class). The school was located in a predominantly lower- to middle-class, semi-rural area of the southern United States. Participants in the study were native speakers of English and the sample included the full range of cognitive and reading abilities present in the four classrooms. During the course of the study, the subjects did not receive special education services. The initial sample consisted of 96 children, 47 of whom were female. At the start of the school year, subjects ranged in age from 5.9 to 7.6 years (M = 6.56; SD = .41). Individual growth curve modeling of word reading and nonword development, using hierarchical linear modeling (HLM) techniques, took place during two different phases of the study (October–January and January–April).[1] Subject selection criteria for each modeling phase are presented below.

Phase I: October to January. The first phase of the study was to model the growth of word and nonword reading skills from October–January in groups of children considered at relatively high versus relatively low risk of developing basic word reading problems. In order to accomplish this, the original sample of children was subdivided after the initial testing session (October), at which time children were designated as either at risk of developing word reading difficulties or normal controls. Children were considered at risk if they were unable to recognize any of the words on the first experimental word reading list (which included simple high frequency CVC words such as *man* and *big*) administered during the first week of October. The inability of at-risk children to read simple high frequency CVC words was used as an indicator that these children did not enter first grade with minimal word reading skills. The at-risk group of children consisted of 41 children from the original sample of 96 children. The control group was defined as children who were able to read at least one word, but no more than five words, on the first experimental word reading list. The upper limit on word reading skill was an attempt to remove those children whose word reading skills were sufficient to allow independent reading. This procedure maximized the likelihood that word reading skill development in both groups was primarily the result of the reading curriculum that the children were receiving within the classroom, and to limit the possibility of ceiling effects in word and nonword reading performance over time in the control sample. Of the original sample of 96 children, 34 were selected as control subjects. Thus, individual word and nonword reading growth in this sample of at-risk and control subjects during the first phase of the study served as a proxy for subject responsiveness to reading instruction provided in the classroom.

---

[1] January served as the anchoring month for modeling during the two phases of the study. The first phase, in which the at-risk children received reading instruction only in the regular classroom, ended in early January. The second phase of the study, in which the at-risk children received reading instruction in the regular classroom and in small intervention groups, began late in January.

Phase II: January to April. The at-risk group was further divided in January, based on growth rates in word reading skills (during the time period of October to January), into those exhibiting normal growth in word reading skills and those still considered at risk of developing word reading difficulties. The group of children still considered at-risk students were then enrolled in 12 weeks of systematic small group reading intervention designed to improve reading skills. Individual word and nonword reading skill growth was modeled (using HLM techniques) during the period of January–April in the two groups of at-risk children, and the correlates of change in each group were evaluated. To be considered still at risk of developing reading difficulties in January, children in the original at-risk sample had to meet three different inclusion criteria. The first was that each at-risk child had to be identified by his classroom teacher as having "significant difficulties" learning to read words. The second was that the child scored below the 25th percentile on the WRAT-3 Reading (Wilkinson 1993) subtest administered late in January. Finally, the child's rate of growth (October–January) had to be at least .75 *SD* below the overall mean growth rate of the entire sample.[2] Of the 41 children considered at-risk of developing word reading difficulties in October, 21 children met the criteria for still being considered as at risk in January. During this phase of this study, these 21 at-risk subjects received approximately 27 hours of specialized small group instruction. The other 20 at-risk subjects served as control during this phase of the study (hereby referred to as normally achieving at-risk children).[3]

MEASURES

Word Reading. Seven word lists were developed to assess word reading growth during the two phases of the study. A different list was administered during each of the seven assessment waves. Lists were constructed by using a modified form of curriculum-based measurement in which children were assessed using the curriculum they were expected to learn (e.g., Deno 1985; Shinn 1989). Each list consisted of 15 single syllable words

---

[2] Researchers advocate the use of growth rate data as a means of identifying children at-risk of developing future academic problems prior to the presence of measurable deficits in academic functioning (e.g., Fletcher and Foorman 1994).

[3] The normally achieving at-risk children can be thought of as a group of "false positives" in that they were falsely identified as at risk of reading failure at the beginning of the first phase of the study.

and represented a random mix of decodable words that followed the word reading/spelling skills taught within the curriculum. This method was used in order to construct parallel word lists that would allow for the measurement of individual growth of word reading skills due to direct instruction in the curriculum. (For details see Compton 2000.) Words could be read through sight recognition or application of learned spelling-sound relationships. The majority of the words on each list could not be re-coded correctly by applying simple one-to-one correspondence rules between letters and sounds; more advanced knowledge of grapheme-phoneme relations were required. (An example of a word reading list is provided in Appendix A.) Scores ranged from 0 to 15 on the word reading task. None of the words found on the seven experimental word lists were target words for instruction in the intervention phase of this study.

Nonword Reading.   Seven parallel nonword lists were developed to assess nonword reading growth. A different list was administered during each of the seven assessment waves. Lists were constructed by stripping off the initial consonant(s) from the first 10 words on the word reading lists and replacing them with a consonant(s) which produced a decodable nonword (an example of a nonword reading list is provided in Appendix A). Scores ranged from 0 to 10 on the nonword reading task.

Phonemic Awareness.   Each child received two measures of phonemic awareness. The first measure of phonemic awareness was a segmentation task in which the child listened to a word and then was instructed to "tell me each sound you hear in the word in the order that you hear it." There were two practice items for which feedback was given, followed by six test items with each consisting of a single-syllable, three-phoneme word. Different sets of words were used during each of the assessments. The second phonemic awareness task was a phoneme blending task. In the blending task, the child listened to words presented phoneme by phoneme and was instructed to "tell me the word you get when you put these sounds together." There were also two practice items for which feedback was given, and then six items consisting of three-phoneme, single-syllable words. Again, different sets of words were used during each of the assessment waves. Combined results from the segmentation and blending tasks yielded a single phonemic awareness score for each assessment wave. Scores ranged from 0 to 12 on the phonemic awareness task.

Rapid Naming Speed.   Five rows containing six numbers (one to five) in random order were used to assess rapid naming speed. Children were instructed to name the numbers as fast as possible without making errors, beginning with the top row and continuing to the bottom. The time to complete the task was recorded using a stopwatch. Results were converted into numbers/second scores so as to make higher scores indicative of better performance.

Letter Sound Knowledge. Children were asked to produce the sound(s) associated with all 26 lowercase letters. Letters were displayed in random order on a single piece of paper using SchoolText font. The first grade curriculum includes both the long and short sounds for the five vowels, as well as the hard and soft sounds of c and g, and children then were asked to give both sounds for each of these letters. Children received credit only if they were able to provide both sounds associated with these letters either spontaneously or when prompted. Scores on this task ranged from 0 to 26.

Advanced Graphophoneme Knowledge. Children were asked to produce the sounds associated with letter combinations found commonly in the words that made up the experimental word lists. Sixteen different letter combinations were displayed in large print using SchoolText font on a single piece of paper. The letter combinations included consonant blends (e.g., *dr*), consonant digraphs (e.g., *sh*), vowel digraphs (e.g., *ai*), r-controlled vowels (e.g., *er*), and other letter combinations (e.g., *igh*). Children were instructed, "Tell me the sound these letters would make if you saw them in a word." Scores on this task ranged from 0 to 16.

PROCEDURE

The first grade children were assessed seven times, once a month between October and April. Every effort was made to ensure that the time interval between assessment waves for each child was exactly one month. During each of the assessment waves, children's word and nonword reading skill were evaluated. During the October, January, and April assessment waves measures also included cognitive processing skills (phonemic awareness and rapid naming speed) and print knowledge variables (letters-sound knowledge and graphophoneme knowledge). Each assessment wave lasted approximately five to eight minutes. For each assessment, children were tested individually at the end of a shared hall outside of their rooms during regular school hours. Testing took place during midmorning instructional time when all children were expected to be in their classrooms. Additional tests included the

WRAT-3 Reading and Spelling (Wilkinson 1993) subtests in January (Blue form) and May (Tan form). The spelling portion of the WRAT-3 was group-administered to entire classrooms. Testers were the author and four trained graduate students. The testers did not participate in any aspect of the intervention phase of this study. The monthly assessment of skill growth was separate from the reading intervention portion of the study.

CLASSROOM INSTRUCTION

Each of the four first grade classrooms provided a balanced reading and writing program. School policy requires that at least 90 minutes of literacy instruction be provided to children in first grade each day. This instructional time was divided between work in basic decoding and spelling skills and numerous activities focusing on reading connected text along with various writing activities. Reading of connected text usually took the form of reading selected children's literature with associated writing activities. Teachers were responsible for selecting their own literature and written language activities.

The decoding and spelling program varied much less across classrooms. As a group, the four first grade teachers developed a decoding and spelling sequence that each of the teachers followed during the course of the year. During the year, the teachers also developed and expanded a "word wall" representing the spelling patterns mastered. Furthermore, throughout the year, teachers added high frequency irregular words and important content words to the children's sight-word vocabularies. In general, the first grade instruction in decoding and spelling can be characterized best as explicit, systematic, and somewhat decontextualized in nature.

DESCRIPTION OF INTERVENTION

The intervention was a multifaceted program aimed at improving phonological awareness, understanding of the alphabetic principle, basic decoding and spelling skills, orthographic knowledge, reading fluency, and reading in connected text. This intervention program might be described as a hybrid, based on several well-known and established methodologies (Orton-Gillingham and the Benchmark Word Identification). It relied heavily on direct instruction that emphasized both synthetic and analytic phonics methods that engaged students in mastering basic word recognition and spelling skills, and transferring this knowledge to unfamiliar words. In addition, this program borrowed key components from Sandra McCormick's

Multiexposure-Multicontext Method (1995) in which children are given the opportunity to read and spell target words in a variety of contexts.

The principal investigator designed and prepared scripts for five separate units. Each unit included a vowel sound, five to seven new consonant sounds, three to four word families based on the unit's vowel and consonants, a set of sight words, and some context words. (The scope and sequence for the five lessons is provided in Appendix B.) Each unit built upon the previous units and followed a set order which included a variety of teaching tasks and materials (e.g., mnemonic letter-sound cards, Elkonin boxes—for phoneme segmenting and blending, word stretching exercises, sorting of rhyming words, magnetic letters—for manipulation of sounds in words, and spelling with Elkonin boxes), reading of connected text (e.g., reading sentences, rearranging scrambled sentences, and reading short stories), and games (e.g., word concentration, board games, word bingo, word fish, and word around the world). A rodeo theme was used to construct meaningful sentences and stories using the sight words, context words, and decodable words. Pre- and posttests (measuring knowledge of unit letter names, letter sounds, sight words, context words, and sentence reading) were given for each unit and a mastery level of 90 percent or above accuracy was set before the next unit began.

The intervention program took place during the Spring semester (January–April) of the first grade school year. Children received instruction three times a week (M, W, F) for approximately 45 minutes each lesson. Senior level preservice teachers from a special education methods class delivered the lessons. Two university students worked with three to four at-risk first grade students grouped homogeneously by reading ability by their classroom teachers. It is important to note that intervention took place during classroom reading instruction time, and, therefore, the at-risk subjects enrolled in the intervention program received the same amount of reading instruction as their normally achieving peers.

RESULTS

PHASE I: MODELING WORD READING GROWTH (OCTOBER TO JANUARY)

Table I presents intercorrelations among the experimental variables for the entire sample of subjects during the October and

Table I. Correlations Among Experimental Variables in October Assessment and January Assessment and the Standardized Word Reading and Spelling Measures in the Total Sample (n = 75).

Variable	October Assessment						January Assessment						WRAT-3	
	1	2	3	4	5	6	7	8	9	10	11	12	13	14
October Assessment														
1. Word Reading	—													
2. Nonword Reading	.87	—												
3. Phonemic Awareness	.56	.48	—											
4. Rapid Naming Speed	.63	.54	.52	—										
5. Letter Sounds	.55	.45	.58	.55	—									
6. Graphophonemes	.64	.53	.55	.52	.65	—								
January Assessment														
7. Word Reading	.63	.50	.72	.52	.66	.66	—							
8. Nonword Reading	.55	.48	.67	.45	.56	.44	.81	—						
9. Phonemic Awareness	.37	.30	.62	.52	.69	.50	.65	.52	—					
10. Rapid Naming Speed	.67	.56	.53	.81	.61	.62	.68	.54	.56	—				
11. Letter Sounds	.33	.26	.43	.45	.73	.46	.53	.44	.55	.51	—			
12. Graphophonemes	.43	.38	.45	.46	.64	.55	.59	.42	.53	.53	.59	—		
WRAT-3 (January)														
13. Reading	.71	.58	.61	.68	.71	.76	.76	.60	.59	.74	.55	.68	—	
14. Spelling	.38	.28	.51	.63	.58	.50	.58	.48	.58	.54	.59	.58	.65	—

Note. All correlations are significant at the $p < .01$ level (two-tailed).

January assessment waves and standardized measures of word reading and spelling administered in January. All the experimental measures correlated significantly with reading and spelling measures. In addition, the experimental measures had moderate to high stability coefficients which were calculated by correlating performance during the October assessment with performance during the January assessment on the same measures. These test-retest correlations ranged from a low of .48 for nonword reading to a high of .81 for rapid naming speed.

Table II presents descriptive statistics and mean comparisons for the control and at-risk groups on the experimental measures assessed in October. The two groups differed significantly on each of the six experimental measures, with the control group out-performing the at-risk group on all measures. Results of these comparisons indicate that the selection criteria used to identify at-risk children resulted in a group of children having lower ability compared to controls on all reading related skills assessed. Therefore, results tend to suggest that the means of identifying at-risk children during the initial testing wave in October was appropriate.

Growth rates and final status for the measures of word and nonword reading in the at-risk and control groups were modeled using HLM (Bryk, Raudenbush, and Congdon 1996). In addition, HLM was used to examine the extent to which initial status in cognitive processing abilities (i.e., phonemic awareness and rapid naming speed) and measures of print knowledge (i.e., letter sound and more advanced graphophoneme knowledge) contribute variance to word and nonword reading

Table II. Descriptive Statistics and Mean Comparisons for the Control and At-Risk Groups on the Experimental Measures (October).

Variable	Control Group (n = 34)		At-Risk Group (n = 41)		t-Value
	Mean	SD	Mean	SD	
Age	6.60	.35	6.52	.46	.92
Phonemic Awareness	8.09	4.21	2.85	3.77	5.62***
Rapid Naming Speed	1.34	.37	.97	.24	4.83***
Letter Sounds	20.57	7.17	15.41	5.05	3.37**
Graphophenemes	7.15	4.60	2.75	3.38	4.57***
Word Reading	3.13	1.81	.00	.00	10.10***
Nonword Reading	2.13	1.62	.00	.00	8.41***

** $p < .01$, *** $p < .001$

growth parameters in each of the groups. Word and nonword growth was fitted over the four assessment waves (October–January) using a person-level linear model (Bryk and Raudenbush 1992). In the person-level model, a growth curve that describes the amount of true change that takes place over time in a particular skill (in this case word and nonword reading) is modeled for each subject.

Each assessment wave was equally spaced (separated by one month) and the four observation points were coded as -3, -2, -1, 0 from the first observation (see McBride-Chang, Wagner, and Chang 1997; Torgesen et al. 1999). Table III presents results of the unconditional growth models for the word and nonword reading variables for both at-risk and control groups. In this coding scheme, the intercept coefficient for each experimental variable represents the mean value from the fitted model at the last observation in January. For instance, in the at-risk group, the estimated mean word reading score in January was 2.263 words read correctly. The slope term for each experimental variable indicates the average amount of growth in that variable over each assessment period (one month). Therefore, in the case

Table III. Linear Growth Models for Word and Nonword Reading in the At-Risk and Control Groups (October–January).

Variable	Fixed Effects			Random Effects		
	Coefficient	SE	t	Variance	χ^2	Reliability
At-Risk Group ($n = 41$)						
Word Reading						
Intercept	2.263	.369	6.328***	5.074	660.43***	.902
Slope	.789	.134	6.033***	.617	278.79***	.815
Nonword Reading						
Intercept	1.493	.276	5.707***	2.698	405.99***	.860
Slope	.546	.107	5.318***	.372	202.98***	.765
Control Group ($n = 34$)						
Word Reading						
Intercept	7.315	.661	11.091***	13.322	354.65***	.890
Slope	1.541	.198	7.402***	.885	98.68***	.659
Nonword Reading						
Intercept	5.388	.458	11.527***	4.394	80.70***	.605
Slope	1.296	.156	7.289***	.472	58.83**	.515

Note. Intercept refers to performance in January; Slope refers to the rate of change October–January.

**$p < .01$, ***$p < .001$

of word reading, at-risk children read on average .789 more words correctly each month on the word reading measures. As can be seen, the control group's rate of growth in word and nonword reading skill was approximately double that of the at-risk group. Furthermore, the control group was able to read approximately five more words and four more nonwords than the at-risk group on the January assessment. These group differences in the estimated rate of growth and final intercept in both word and nonword reading were statistically significant.

Hypothesis testing for fixed effects revealed large and highly significant t-statistics for all of the estimated intercepts and slopes values, indicating that both parameters are necessary for describing the mean growth trajectory. The test of homogeneity of growth parameters (χ^2 statistic) revealed that in all of the variables, significant variation existed within individual growth trajectories. Finally, the relatively high estimated measures of reliability for the individual growth parameters in the experimental variables demonstrated that there was a substantial signal in these data in terms of individual differences in intercept and slope. Overall, these results support the general conclusion that growth in word and nonword reading skill can be measured over relatively short time periods using curriculum-based measurement procedures and accurately modeled using HLM techniques.

In the next set of analyses, an attempt was made to identify the cognitive processing and print knowledge factors most responsible for individual growth in word and nonword reading skills in the at-risk and control groups. The correlations between individual change in word and nonword reading and initial status in cognitive processing abilities and measures of print knowledge were examined using a between-person model (Bryk and Raudenbush 1992).[4] Table IV presents results of these analyses. The first two columns evaluate the importance of each factor individually as a predictor of growth parameters (i.e., intercept and slope) in word and nonword reading. Since the control group was able to read words and nonwords during the October assessment, initial performance in word and nonword reading was also used to predict growth parameters in the control group. Initial status variables designated as significant predictors of the final intercept in word or nonword reading indicated that, on average, children with greater skills on these variables at the time of the first assessment wave in October achieved a higher

---

[4] Initial status variables used to predict word and nonword growth characteristics refer to performance at single point in time (i.e., October assessment wave).

Table IV.   Individual and Simultaneous Prediction of Growth Curve Parameters (October–January) for Word and Nonword Reading in the At-Risk and Control Groups.

Variable	Individual Predictor Regression Coefficients		Simultaneous Predictors Regression Coefficients[a]	
	Intercept	Slope	Intercept[b]	Slope[c]
At-Risk Group (n = 41)				
Word Reading				
Phonemic Awareness	.180*	.072*	—	—
Rapid Naming Speed	3.909*	1.424**	2.898*	1.034**
Letter Sounds	.196**	.069**	.149*	.071*
Graphophenemes	.273*	.095*	—	—
Nonword Reading				
Phonemic Awareness	.185*	.069*	.143*	.055*
Rapid Naming Speed	1.569	.570	—	—
Letter Sounds	.140**	.049*	.109*	.047*
Graphophenemes	.168	.047	—	—
Control Group (n = 34)				
Word Reading				
Phonemic Awareness	.601***	.114*	.339*	.126*
Rapid Naming Speed	3.758*	.067	—	—
Letter Sounds	.373***	.061*	—	—
Graphophenemes	.599***	.082*	.350*	.096*
Word Reading	.852**	.055*	.299*	.248**
Nonword Reading				
Phonemic Awareness	.442***	.076*	.297**	.106*
Rapid Naming Speed	2.555*	.387	—	—
Letter Sounds	.289***	.056*	—	—
Graphophenemes	.399***	.041	.210*	.051*
Nonword Reading	.605**	.130*	.121*	.281**

Note. Intercept refers to performance in January; Slope refers to rate of change October – January. Predictor variables for the Intercept and Slope are values from the October assessment wave.

[a] Predictor variables were entered into the model simultaneously and non-significant terms were removed from the model using a backward stepwise deletion procedure.

[b] Percent variance predicted in the estimated intercept: At-Risk Group word reading = 22.26%, At-Risk Group nonword reading = 23.83%; Control Group word reading = 60.59%, Control Group nonword reading = 55.35%.

[c] Percent variance predicted in the estimated slope: At-Risk Group word reading = 23.66%, At-Risk Group nonword reading = 23.34%; Control Group word reading = 50.76%, Control Group nonword reading = 47.31%.

* $p < .05$, ** $p < .01$, *** $p < .001$

level of estimated performance in word and/or nonword reading in January. Similarly, initial status variables specified as significant predictors of word or nonword reading slope indicated faster growth rates in these decoding skills for those children scoring higher on the predictor variables at the time of the first assessment wave in October.

The next two columns contain results from modeling the correlations between predictors and growth when all predictors are entered into the model simultaneously. Results indicated a differential set of unique predictors for word and nonword growth parameters in the at-risk and control groups. In the at-risk group, both word and nonword reading growth parameters were uniquely predicted by letter-sound knowledge. However, in this group of readers, the other unique predictor of growth parameters differed between word and nonword reading with rapid naming speed predicting word reading growth and phonemic awareness predicting nonword reading. In the control group phonemic awareness, graphophoneme knowledge, and initial reading skill uniquely predicted both word and nonword reading growth parameters.

Finally, an examination of the word reading growth curve parameters for each individual during the first phase of the study revealed that a significant number of the at-risk children exhibited fairly flat growth in word reading. This lack of word reading growth was considered to be an indicator of nonresponsiveness to the regular classroom word reading instruction. Of the 41 children initially identified as being at risk in October, 12 children had growth estimates of 0 words gained per month, while another nine children had growth estimates that were less than 0.5 words gained per month. This level of word reading growth was significantly below the mean growth rate for the entire sample of children and, as such, put this subgroup of children further at risk of developing reading difficulties. In the next phase of the study, the group of at-risk students that did not respond to regular classroom word reading instruction received small group reading intervention. Individual growth in word and nonword reading skill was modeled in this at-risk group during intervention as a means of evaluating the extent to which these children responded to intervention.

PHASE II: MODELING AT-RISK CHILDREN'S RESPONSE TO INTERVENTION (JANUARY TO APRIL)

Table V presents intercorrelations among the experimental variables for the entire sample of at-risk subjects during the January

Table V. Correlations Among Experimental Variables in January Assessment and April Assessment and the Standardized Word Reading and Spelling Measures in the At-Risk Sample ($n = 41$).

Variable	January Assessment						April Assessment				WRAT-3	
	1	2	3	4	5	6	7	8	9	10	11	12
January Assessment												
1. Word Reading	—											
2. Nonword Reading	.65	—										
3. Phonemic Awareness	.63	.38	—									
4. Rapid Naming Speed	.56	.30	.42	—								
5. Letter Sounds	.50	.27	.34	.34	—							
6. Graphophonemes	.43	.13	.28	.28	.37	—						
April Assessment												
7. Word Reading	.66	.32	.30	.48	.48	.46	—					
8. Nonword Reading	.53	.41	.26	.57	.44	.33	.82	—				
9. Rapid Naming Speed	.49	.28	.43	.72	.25	.35	.32	.30	—			
10. Graphophonemes	.38	.20	.10	.42	.55	.57	.55	.40	.29	—		
WRAT-3 (May)												
11. Reading	.68	.44	.41	.52	.44	.53	.71	.63	.33	.49	—	
12. Spelling	.36	.35	.36	.46	.24	.37	.47	.51	.35	.34	.68	—

Note. Correlations above .32 are significant at the $p < .05$ level; correlations above .43 are significant at the $p < .01$ level (two-tailed).

and April assessment waves and standardized measures of word reading and spelling administered in May. As in the first phase, all the variables had moderate to high stability coefficients. These test-retest correlations ranged from a low of .41 for nonword reading to a high of .72 for rapid naming speed. Due to significant ceiling effects, April performance in phonemic awareness and letter-sound knowledge were removed from the table. In general, the correlations between the experimental variables and reading and spelling measures were statistically significant.

Table VI presents descriptive statistics and mean comparisons for the control, normally achieving at risk, and intervention groups on the experimental and standardized measures assessed in January and the word and nonword reading growth rates (October–January). As expected, the three groups differed significantly on measures of absolute proficiency in word reading, nonword reading, and spelling. The normally achieving at-risk group and control group did not differ on several important reading related measures at the time of the January assessment. Namely, the two groups were statistically equivalent in phonemic awareness skill, letter-sound knowledge, and graphophoneme knowledge. In addition, the rate at which the two groups developed word and nonword reading skills did not differ during the first phase of the study (October–January). On the other hand, the intervention group performed significantly lower than either the control or normally achieving at-risk groups on all measures assessed in January except letter-sound knowledge. In addition, the intervention group differed significantly from the other two groups on the rate of word and nonword reading growth during the October–January phase of the study.

Similar to the first phase of the study, a linear model for word and nonword reading variables was fitted separately on data for children in the normally achieving at-risk and intervention groups. Table VII presents results of the unconditional growth models for the word and nonword reading variables for both groups. In this set of analyses, the intercept coefficient for each experimental variable represents the mean value from the fitted model at the last observation in April. The slope term for each experimental variable indicates the average amount of growth in that variable over each assessment period from January to April. As can be seen from the table, the difference in estimated intercept between the two groups was still quite large, whereas the rate of word and nonword reading growth

Table VI. Descriptive Statistics and Mean Comparisons for the Control, Normally Achieving At-Risk, and Intervention Groups on the Standardized Measures (January), Experimental Measures (January), and Growth Measures (October–January).

Variable	Control (C) (n = 34)		Normally Achieving At-Risk (N) (n = 20)		Intervention (I) (n = 21)		Comparisons
	Mean	SD	Mean	SD	Mean	SD	
Standardized Measures (January)							
WRAT – Reading (standard score)	110.35	14.38	99.95	5.47	84.92	4.37	C > N > I
WRAT – Spelling (standard score)	105.20	9.04	100.01	5.35	89.41	4.62	C > N > I
Experimental Measures (January)							
Phonemic Awareness	10.93	2.59	10.11	3.34	7.00	3.58	C = N > I
Rapid Naming Speed	1.72	0.43	1.48	0.26	1.19	0.24	C > N > I
Letter Sounds	24.58	4.61	24.36	1.64	22.35	2.56	C = N = I
Graphophenemes	10.94	4.57	9.60	3.87	5.33	4.15	C = N > I
Word Reading	7.31	3.78	4.23	2.43	0.76	0.72	C > N > I
Nonword Reading	5.38	2.80	2.95	1.90	0.57	0.41	C > N > I
Growth Measures (Oct. – Jan.)							
Word Reading	1.54	1.11	1.47	0.74	0.25	0.27	C = N > I
Nonword Reading	1.29	1.02	0.99	0.62	0.13	0.21	C = N > I

Note. Post hoc comparisons based on Tukey HDS procedure, $p < .05$

Table VII.   Linear Growth Models for Word and Nonword Reading
in the Normally Achieving At-Risk and
Intervention Groups (January–April).

Variable	Coefficient	SE	t	Variance	χ^2	Reliability
		Fixed Effects			Random Effects	
		Intervention Group (n = 21)				
Word Reading						
Intercept	6.842	.473	14.648***	3.051	61.77***	.637
Slope	2.146	.189	11.227***	.274	38.41**	.443
Nonword Reading						
Intercept	5.331	.380	14.150***	2.078	68.38***	.676
Slope	1.581	.157	10.106***	.234	41.76**	.472
		Normally Achieving At-Risk Group (n = 20)				
Word Reading						
Intercept	10.373	.577	18.759***	4.169	54.65***	.607
Slope	1.993	.189	12.170***	.168	32.42*	.359
Nonword Reading						
Intercept	7.200	.445	16.610***	2.219	45.58**	.615
Slope	1.508	.185	8.350***	.188	36.83*	.366

Note. Intercept refers to performance in April; Slope refers to the rate of change January – April.

$*p < .05, **p < .01, ***p < .001$

in the at-risk children receiving intervention was now comparable to the normally achieving at-risk group. Therefore, it appears that during the intervention period, it was possible to produce relatively normal rates of word and nonword reading growth in the intervention group. This result is consistent with the vast majority of intervention studies that have reported positive gains in reading performance in poor readers during intervention.

Again, an attempt was made to identify the cognitive processing and emergent print knowledge factors most responsible for individual growth in word and nonword reading skills in the normally achieving at-risk and intervention groups. Table VIII presents results of these analyses. Performance on cognitive processing skill, knowledge about print, and reading performance assessed in January were used to predict word and nonword growth parameters in the two groups. In the intervention group, the only unique predictor of word and nonword growth was rapid naming speed. In the normally achieving at-risk

Table VIII. Individual and Simultaneous Prediction of Growth Curve Parameters (January–April) for Word and Nonword Reading in the Intervention Group.

Variable	Individual Predictor Regression Coefficients		Simultaneous Predictors Regression Coefficients[a]	
	Intercept	Slope	Intercept[b]	Slope[c]
Intervention Group (n = 21)				
Word Reading				
Phonemic Awareness	.090	.046	—	—
Rapid Naming Speed	3.909*	1.621*	3.909*	1.621*
Letter Sounds	.030	.053	—	—
Graphophenemes	.172	.062	—	—
Word Reading	.391	.187	—	—
Nonword Reading				
Phonemic Awareness	.185*	.055*	—	—
Rapid Naming Speed	3.923*	1.680*	2.689*	1.687*
Letter Sounds	.053	.036	—	—
Graphophenemes	.274	.048	—	—
Nonword Reading	.393	.143	—	—
Normally Achieving At-Risk Group (n = 20)				
Word Reading				
Phonemic Awareness	.380**	.058*	—	—
Rapid Naming Speed	4.653*	3.529*	2.601*	3.135*
Letter Sounds	.371	.048	—	—
Graphophenemes	.415***	.079*	.245***	.064*
Word Reading	.769***	.065*	.571***	.203*
Nonword Reading				
Phonemic Awareness	.241*	.066*	.297**	.106*
Rapid Naming Speed	1.555	.387	—	—
Letter Sounds	.242	.033	—	—
Graphophenemes	.299**	.141*	.220*	.051*
Nonword Reading	.418*	.182*	.121*	.281**

Note. Intercept refers to performance in April; Slope refers to rate of change January - April. Predictor variables for the Intercept and Slope are values from the January assessment wave.

[a] Predictor variables were entered into the model simultaneously and nonsignificant terms were removed from the model using a backward stepwise deletion procedure.

[b] Percent variance predicted in the estimated intercept: Intervention Group word reading = 34.17%, Intervention Group nonword reading = 32.57%; Normally Achieving At-Risk Group word reading = 54.32%, Normally Achieving At-Risk Group nonword reading = 52.35%.

[c] Percent variance predicted in the estimated slope: Intervention Group word reading = 46.33%, Intervention Group nonword reading = 41.83%; Normally Achieving At-Risk Group word reading = 60.59%, Normally Achieving At-Risk Group nonword reading = 55.35%.

$* p < .05, ** p < .01, *** p < .001$

group, a more balanced set of unique predictors of word (i.e., rapid naming speed, graphophoneme knowledge, and initial word reading) and nonword (i.e., phonemic awareness, graphophoneme knowledge, and initial nonword reading) growth were identified.

Tables IX presents between-group comparisons on the standardized measures (May), experimental measures (April), and growth measures (January–April). Group comparisons indicate that the normally achieving at-risk and intervention group differed in absolute word, nonword, and spelling performance. However, there was not a statistical difference between the two groups on any of the cognitive processing skills or print knowledge measures. In addition, the rate of growth in word and nonword reading skill was similar between the two groups during the intervention phase. Therefore, results from these comparisons suggest that while the intervention group still

Table IX.   Descriptive Statistics and Mean Comparisons Between the Normally Achieving At-Risk and Intervention Groups on the Standardized Measures (May), Experimental Measures (April), and Growth Measures (January–April).

Variable	Normally Achieving At-Risk Group (*n* = 20)		Intervention Group (*n* = 21)		*t*-Value
	Mean	SD	Mean	SD	
Standardized Measures (May)					
WRAT – Reading (standard score)	104.75	6.55	89.43	4.82	9.11***
WRAT – Spelling (standard score)	102.65	4.83	96.38	4.77	4.18***
Experimental Measures (April)					
Phonemic Awareness	11.50	0.82	10.95	2.01	1.16
Rapid Naming Speed	1.79	0.35	1.66	0.31	1.21
Letter Sounds	25.20	1.44	25.01	1.38	0.45
Graphophenemes	13.36	2.36	13.35	3.93	0.02
Word Reading	10.37	2.81	6.84	2.23	4.46***
Nonword Reading	7.20	2.44	5.33	1.72	2.86**
Growth Measures (Jan. – April)					
Word Reading	1.99	1.37	2.15	1.17	–0.39
Nonword Reading	1.51	0.96	1.58	0.73	0.27

** $p < .01$, *** $p < .001$

lagged behind their peers in reading skill, during intervention the group did not appear to lose further ground in word and nonword reading skills to their peers.

Finally, Table X presents within-group comparisons on word and nonword growth rates during the October–January and January–April phases in the intervention and normally achieving at-risk groups. Results indicate that during the intervention phase, a significant change in both the absolute level of word and nonword reading ability (January versus April) and the rate of word and nonword reading skill growth occurred in the intervention group. This result is consistent with the idea that intervention had a positive effect on the overall rate of word and nonword reading acquisition in this group of at-risk readers. In contrast, the normally achieving at-risk group showed significant differences in the absolute level of word

Table X. Comparisons of Estimated Word and Nonword Reading Intercepts and Growth Rates Within the Normally Achieving At-Risk and Intervention Groups During the Periods October–January and January–April.

| Variable | October–January | | January–April | | |
	Mean	SD	Mean	SD	t-Value
Intervention					
Intercept Measures[a]					
Word Reading	0.86	1.03	6.84	2.23	−12.25***
Nonword Reading	0.67	1.02	5.33	1.72	−12.66***
Growth Measures[b]					
Word Reading	0.25	0.27	2.15	1.17	−6.58***
Nonword Reading	0.13	0.21	1.58	0.73	−6.89***
Normally Achieving At-Risk					
Intercept Measures[a]					
Word Reading	4.23	2.43	10.37	2.81	−9.41***
Nonword Reading	2.95	1.90	7.20	2.44	−6.84***
Growth Measures[b]					
Word Reading	1.47	0.74	1.99	1.37	−1.68
Nonword Reading	1.29	1.02	1.51	0.96	−1.59

[a] The intercept measure for the October – January period refers to estimated performance in January and the intercept measure for the January – April period refers to estimated performance in April.

[b] The growth measure for the October – January refers to the estimated linear slope during the period and the growth measure for the January – April refers to the estimated linear slope during the period.

*** $p < .001$

and nonword reading ability (January versus April), but no difference in word and nonword reading growth rates across the two phases of the study. This result implies that in the normally achieving at-risk group word and nonword reading growth was fairly constant across the year. Taken together, results of the between- and within-group comparisons suggest that increases in word and nonword reading growth within the intervention group were associated with intervention activities. However, due to the quasiexperimental design employed in this study, it is impossible to make causal inferences concerning the effectiveness of the intervention program.[5]

DISCUSSION

In general, results from this study demonstrate the utility of using a combination of curriculum-based measurement and HLM techniques to explore the factors that influence individual growth of word and nonwords reading skills in at-risk first grade children. During the initial phase of the study (October–January), there were large differences between the word and nonword reading growth parameters in the at-risk and control groups, with the control group outperforming the at-risk group on all measures. In addition, predictors of growth curve parameters for word and nonword reading differed between the at-risk and normally achieving control groups. In the control group, a combination of phonemic awareness skill, advanced graphophoneme knowledge, and initial word/nonword reading skill predicted word and nonword reading growth. In the at-risk group, rapid naming speed and letter-sound knowledge predicted word reading growth, whereas phonemic awareness and letter-sound knowledge predicted nonword reading growth. The differential loading of predictors across groups is interesting for several reasons. First, the relative importance of letter-sound knowledge in the at-risk group and graphophoneme knowledge in the control group as predictors of word and nonword reading growth indicate a possible shift in the size of the unit used to recognize words as a function of reading skill. This result is consistent with arguments forwarded by Ehri (1992, 1998; Ehri and Soffer 1999; Scarborough et al. 1998) and Perfetti (1991, 1992) that as children

---

[5] Only randomizing the assignment of at-risk subjects meeting the criteria for intervention into separate control and intervention groups allows causal inferences to be made concerning the effectiveness of the intervention program.

develop word recognition skills, graphophoneme connections move from simple letter-sound correspondences to more complex connections that include the sounds associated with multi-letter grapheme units (e.g., common consonant blends, consonant digraphs, vowel digraphs, and larger subword connections). Second, the differential importance of rapid naming speed as a predictor of word reading growth in the at-risk group compared to the control group is consistent with recent findings that rapid naming speed is particularly predictive of word reading skill in poor readers (for a review see Wolf and Bowers 1999). Therefore, results of modeling word and nonword reading growth in the at-risk and control groups during the first phase of the study are consistent with general theories of word reading development and specific theories of reading disability. Finally, results from the first phase of the study also indicate that there were a substantial number of at-risk children that failed to respond to the regular classroom word reading instruction.

Results from the second phase of the study (January–April) indicate that the growth rate of word and nonword reading skills in at-risk first grade children with fairly flat growth parameters were significantly larger during intervention. In fact, intervention was associated with comparable growth rates between the intervention group and the normally achieving at-risk group. A different set of predictors of word and nonword reading growth were identified in the normally achieving and intervention groups. In the normally achieving at-risk group predictors of word and nonword reading growth resembled the control group in the first phase of the study, whereas in the intervention group, only rapid naming speed predicted word and nonword reading growth. Again, this differential loading of predictors across groups is important for several reasons. First, the set of factors predicting word and nonword reading growth in the normally achieving at-risk group was similar to the pattern of predictors in the control group during the first phase of the study. The only difference was the relative importance of rapid naming speed and phonemic awareness skill in predicting word reading growth in the two groups. This result suggests that word and nonword reading growth in these two groups was mediated by a similar set of processes. Second is the fact that rapid naming speed was the only unique predictor of growth in both word and nonword reading in the intervention group. Wolf and Bowers (Bowers et al. 1994; Bowers, Sunseth, and Golden 1999; Wolf and Bowers 1999) have hypothesized that slow naming speed contributes to poor reading in three ways:

a. "By impeding the appropriate amalgamation of connections between phonemes and orthographic patterns at subword and word levels of representation,

b. By limiting the quality of orthographic codes in memory.

c. By increasing the amount of repeated practice needed to unitize codes before representations of adequate quality are achieved" (Wolf and Bowers 1999).

Results from the intervention phase of this study are consistent with this hypothesis. The children with faster naming speed at the onset of intervention achieved higher rates of word and nonword reading growth during intervention.

The finding that rapid naming speed was the only factor that uniquely predicted word reading growth in the intervention group is similar to results reported by Torgesen et al. (1999). However, the fact that rapid naming speed was the only unique predictor of nonword reading growth in the intervention group is somewhat at odds with results from the Torgesen et al. study. In the Torgesen et al. study, a combination of phonemic awareness, naming speed, and verbal memory skills predicted growth in nonword reading. Differences in the subject selection criteria used in the two studies probably contributed to this discrepancy in results. The Torgesen et al. study identified children with fairly severe phonological processing deficits that may have contributed to the importance of individual differences in phonological processing skills as predictors of nonword reading skill growth. In the present study, the intervention group was able to perform basic blending and segmenting tasks (albeit somewhat less accurately than the normally achieving group), and thus this group should not be thought of as possessing severe phonological processing deficits. As such, individual differences in phonemic awareness may not be as important in this sample of at-risk children.

Finally, the combined use of curriculum-based measurement and HLM techniques to monitor and model growth in word reading skills in the early phases of reading development needs further exploration. There have been important discussions within the research literature advocating the use of such procedures to distinguish between learning disabilities in children resulting from basic cognitive deficits versus experiential deficits (e.g., Berninger and Abbott 1994; Fletcher and Foorman

1994; Vellutino et al. 1996). For instance, Berninger and Abbott (1994) have argued that, ". . . one approach would be to use static assessment—that is, administration of multivariate batteries to identify or flag 'at-risk' individuals—but to defer the final diagnosis of learning disability pending the outcome of dynamic assessment using response to treatment protocols validated for remediating specific kinds of disabilities" (p. 166). The label of "learning disabled" would only be applied to a child who did not show measurable gains to validated treatment. In such a system, individual growth would be evaluated within a particular curriculum to evaluate a child's potential to benefit from specific instruction. Therefore, there appears to be a need for general techniques that would allow for individual modeling of growth within a particular curriculum over relatively short periods of time. This study represents an initial attempt to demonstrate the utility of merging curriculum-based measurement procedures and growth modeling using HLM techniques to examine factors that affect individual differences in word reading skill growth in groups of first grade children receiving different types of reading instruction.

ACKNOWLEDGMENTS

This research was supported by grants from the International Dyslexia Association (formerly the Orton Dyslexia Society) and the Department of Curriculum and Instruction, University of Arkansas, Fayetteville. I would like to thank the children and educators of T. G. Smith Elementary School in Springdale, Arkansas, for their participation in this project. I would also like to thank Jackie Flanagan, Richard Petty, Sarah Sanders, and Paul Sims for their help in the data collection phase of this project. Finally, I would like to thank the preservice special education students enrolled in SPED 4036 for their enthusiasm, commitment, and professionalism during the structured intervention phase of this study.

Address correspondence to: Dr. Donald L. Compton, Department of Special Education, Box 328, Peabody College, Vanderbilt University, Nashville, TN 37203. Telephone: (615) 322-8282. E-mail: donald.l.compton@vanderbilt.edu

APPENDIX A

Sample Word and Nonword Reading Test

Words	*Nonwords*
map	dap
late	vate
red	med
block	plock
coal	noal
high	kigh
club	gub
feet	deet
drip	crip
tune	hune
shout	
king	
hair	
form	
play	

APPENDIX B

Intervention: Scope and Sequence

Teaching Tasks and Materials	*Games*
Mnemonics for Letter Names and Sounds	Concentration
Elkonin Boxes	Board Games
Stretching Words	Bingo
Scrambled Sentences	Fish
Sorting Rhyming Words	Round the World
Word Manipulation	
Spelling-Elkonin Boxes	
Sentence Reading	
Reading Short Stories	

Unit 1

Letters:	*a, b, c, s, t, n, r, p*
Word Families:	*-at, -an, -ap, -ab*
Sight Words:	*the, and, are, I, to, is, a, has*
Content Words:	*two, black, stallion, cowboy*

Unit 2

Letters:	*a, b, c, s, t, n, r, p, e, f, m, d, h*
Word Families:	*-at, -an, -ap, -ab, -ed, -en, -ed, -et*
Sight Words:	*the, and, are, I, to, is, a, has, have, for, she, he, put*
Content Words:	*two, black, stallion, cowboy, three, red, saddle, rodeo, cowgirl*

Unit 3

Letters:	*a, b, c, s, t, n, r, p, e, f, m, d, h, o, g, l, k, v, w, j*
Word Families:	*-at, -an, -ap, -ab, -ed, -en, -ed, -et, -ot, -op, -og,*
Sight Words:	*the, and, are, I, to, is, a, has, have, for, she, he, put, you, from, on, more, or, see, two,*
Content Words:	*black, stallion, cowboy, three, red, saddle, rodeo, cowgirl, blue, six, sky, rope*

Unit 4

Letters:	*a, b, c, s, t, n, r, p, e, f, m, d, h, o, g, l, k, v, w, j, i*
Word Families:	*-at, -an, -ap, -ab, -ed, -en, -ed, -et, -ot, -op, -og, -ip, -in, -it, -id*
Sight Words:	*the, and, are, I, to, is, a, has, have, for, she, he, put, you, from, on, more, or, see*
Content Words:	*two, black, stallion, cowboy, three, blue, six red, saddle, rodeo, cowgirl, sky, rope*

Unit 5

Letters:	*a, b, c, s, t, n, r, p, e, f, m, d, h, o, g, l, k, v, w, j, I, u*
Word Families:	*-at, -an, -ap, -ab, -ed, -en, -ed, -et, -ot, -op, -og, -ip, -in, -it, -id, -ug, -ut, -un*
Sight Words:	*the, and, are, I, to, is, a, has, have, for, she, he, put, you, from, on, more, or, see*
Content Words:	*two, black, stallion, cowboy, three, blue, six, red, saddle, rodeo, cowgirl, sky, rope*

References

Abbott, S., Reed, E., Abbott, R. D., and Berninger, V. W. 1997. Year-long balanced reading/writing tutorial: A design experiment used for dynamic assessment. *Learning Disability Quarterly* 20:249–63.

Berninger, V. W., and Abbott, R. D. 1994. Redefining learning disabilities: Moving beyond aptitude-achievement discrepancies to failure to respond to validated treatment protocols. In *Frames of Reference for the Assessment of Learning Disabilities: New Views on Measurement Issues*, ed. G. Reid Lyon. Baltimore: Paul H. Brookes Publishing Co.

Berninger, V. W., Abbott, R. D., Zook, D., Ogier, S., Lemos-Britton, Z., and Brooksher, R. 1999. Early intervention for reading disabilities: Teaching the alphabetic principle in a connectionist framework. *Journal of Learning Disabilities* 32:491–503.

Blachman, B. A., Tangel, D. M., Ball, E. W., Black, R., and McGraw, C. K. 1999. Developing phonological awareness and word recognition skills: A two-year intervention with low-income, inner-city children. *Reading and Writing: An Interdisciplinary Journal* 11:239–73.

Bowers, P. G., Golden, J., Kennedy, A., and Young, A. 1994. Limits upon orthographic knowledge due to processes indexed by naming speed. In *The Varieties of Orthographic Knowledge I: Theoretical and Developmental Issues*, ed. V. W. Berninger. Dordrecht, The Netherlands: Kluwer Academic.

Bowers, P. G., Sunseth, N., and Golden, J. 1999. The route between rapid naming and reading progress. *Scientific Studies of Reading* 3:31–54.

Bryk, A. S., and Raudenbush, S. W. 1992. *Hierarchical Linear Models: Applications and Data Analysis Methods*. London: Sage.

Bryk, A. S., Raudenbush, S. W., and Congdon, R. T. 1996. *Hierarchical Linear and Nonlinear Modeling with the HLM/2L and HLM/3L Programs: Computer Program and Users Guide*. Chicago, IL: Scientific Software International, Inc.

Compton, D. L. 2000. Modeling the growth of decoding skills in first grade children. *Scientific Studies of Reading* 4:219–58.

Deno, S. L. 1985. Curriculum-based assessment: The emerging alternative. *Exceptional Children* 52:219–32.

Ehri, L. C. 1992. Reconceptualizing the development of sight word reading and its relationship to recoding. In *Reading Acquisition*, eds. P. B. Gough, L. C. Ehri, and R. Treiman. Hillsdale, NJ: Lawrence Erlbaum Associates, Publishers.

Ehri, L. C. 1998. Grapheme-phoneme knowledge is essential for learning to read words in English. In *Word Recognition in Beginning Literacy*, eds. J. L. Metsala and L. C. Ehri. Mahwah, NJ: Lawrence Erlbaum Associates, Publishers.

Ehri, L. C., and Soffer, A. G. 1999. Graphophonemic awareness: Development in elementary students. *Scientific Studies of Reading* 3:1–30.

Felton, R. H. 1993. Effects of instruction on the decoding skills of children with phonological-processing problems. *Journal of Learning Disabilities* 26:583–89.

Felton, R. H., and Pepper, P. P. 1995. Early identification and intervention of phonological deficits in kindergarten and early elementary children at risk for reading disability. *School Psychology Review* 24:405–14.

Fletcher, J. M., and Foorman, B. R. 1994. Issues in definition and measurement of learning disabilities. In *Frames of Reference for the Assessment of Learning Disabilities: New Views on Measurement Issues*, ed. G. Reid Lyon. Baltimore: Paul H. Brookes Publishing Co.

Foorman, B. R., Francis, D. J., Fletcher, J. M., Schatschneider, C., and Mehta, P. 1998. The role of instruction in learning to read: Preventing reading failure in at-risk children. *Journal of Educational Psychology* 90:37–55.

Foorman, B. R., Francis, D. J., Shaywitz, S. E., Shaywitz, B. A., and Fletcher, J. M. 1997a. The case for early reading intervention. In *Foundations of Reading Acquisition and Dyslexia: Implications for Early Intervention*, ed. B. Blachman. Mahwah, NJ: Lawrence Erlbaum Associates, Publishers.

Foorman, B. R., Francis, D. J., Winikates, D., Mehta, P., Schatschneider, C., and Fletcher, J. M. 1997b. Early intervention for children with reading disabilities. *Scientific Studies of Reading* 1:255–76.

Hatcher, P. J., and Hulme, C. 1999. Phonemes, rhymes, and intelligence as predictors of children's responsiveness to remedial reading instruction: Evidence from a longitudinal intervention study. *Journal of Experimental Child Psychology* 72:130–53.

Hatcher, P. J., Hulme, C., and Ellis, A. E. 1994. Ameliorating early reading failure by integrating the teaching of reading and phonological skills: The phonological linkage hypothesis. *Child Development* 65:41–55.

Invernizzi, M., Rosemary, C., Juel, C., and Richards, H. C. 1997. At-risk readers and community volunteers: A 3-year perspective. *Scientific Studies of Reading* 1:277–300.

Iversen, S., and Tunmer, W. E. 1993. Phonological processing skills and the Reading Recovery program. *Journal of Educational Psychology* 85:112–26.

Juel, C. 1988. Learning to read and write: A longitudinal study of 54 children from first through fourth grades. *Journal of Educational Psychology* 80:437–47.

Lovett, M. W., Borden, S. L., DeLuca, T., Lacerenza, L., Benson, N. J., and Brackstone, D. 1994. Testing the core deficits of developmental dyslexia: Evidence of transfer of learning after phonologically- and strategy-based reading training programs. *Developmental Psychology* 30:805–22.

Marston, D., Deno, S. L., Kim, D., Diment, K., and Rogers, D. 1995. Comparison of reading intervention approaches for students with mild disabilities. *Exceptional Children* 62:20–37.

McBride-Chang, C., Wagner, R. K., and Chang, L. 1997. Growth modeling of phonological awareness. *Journal of Educational Psychology* 89:621–30.

McCarthy, P., Newby, R. F., and Recht, D. R. 1995. Results of an early intervention program for first grade children at risk for reading disabilities. *Reading Research and Instruction* 34:273–94.

McCormick, S. 1995. *Instructing Students Who have Literacy Problems*. Englewood Cliffs, NJ: Merrill.

Olson, R. K., Wise, B., Ring, J., and Johnson, M. 1997. Computer-based remedial training in phoneme awareness and phonological decoding: Effects on the posttraining development of word recognition. *Scientific Studies of Reading* 1:235–54.

Perfetti, C. A. 1991. Representations and awareness in the acquisition of reading competence. In *Learning to Read: Basic Research and its Implications*, eds. L. Rieben and C. A. Perfetti. Hillsdale, NJ: Lawrence Erlbaum Associates, Publishers.

Perfetti, C. A. 1992. The representation problems in reading acquisition. In *Reading Acquisition*, eds. P. B. Gough, L. C. Ehri, and R. Treiman. Hillsdale, NJ: Lawrence Erlbaum Associates, Publishers.

Pikulski, J. J. 1994. Preventing reading failure: A review of five effective programs. *The Reading Teacher* 48:30–39.

Santa, C. M., and Høien, T. 1999. An assessment of Early Steps: A program for early intervention of reading problems. *Reading Research Quarterly* 34:54–79.

Scarborough, H. S., Ehri, L. C., Olson, R. K., and Fowler, A. E. 1998. The fate of phonemic awareness beyond the elementary school years. *Scientific Studies of Reading* 2:115–42.

Shanahan, T., and Barr, R. 1995. Reading Recovery: An independent evaluation of the effects of an early instructional intervention for at-risk learners. *Reading Research Quarterly* 30:958–96.

Shinn, M. R. 1989. *Curriculum-based Measurement: Assessing Special Children*. New York: Guildford.

Shaywitz, S. E., Shaywitz, B. A., Fletcher, J. M., and Escobar, M. D. 1990. Prevalence of reading disability in boys and girls: Results of the Connecticut longitudinal study. *Journal of the American Medical Association* 254:998–1002.

Snow, C. E., Burns, M. S., and Griffin, P. 1998. *Preventing Reading Difficulties in Young Children*. Washington, D.C: National Academic Press.

Torgesen, J. K., Wagner, R. K., and Rashotte, C. A. 1997. Prevention and remediation of severe reading disabilities: Keeping the eye in mind. *Scientific Studies of Reading* 1:217–34.

Torgesen, J. K., Wagner, R. K., Rashotte, C. A., Rose, E., Lindamood, P., Conway, T., and Garvan, C. 1999. Preventing reading failure in young children with phonological processing disabilities: Group and individual response to instruction. *Journal of Educational Psychology* 91:579–93.

Vellutino, F. R., Scanlon, D. M., Sipay, E. R., Small, S. G, Pratt, A., Chen, R., and Denckla, M. B. 1996. Cognitive profiles of difficult-to-remediate and readily re-mediated poor readers: Early intervention as a vehicle for distinguishing be-tween cognitive and experiential deficits as basic causes of specific reading disability. *Journal of Educational Psychology* 88:601–38.

Wagner, R. K., Torgesen, J. K., Rashotte, C. A., Hecht, S. A., Barker, T. A., Burgess, S. R., Donahue, J., and Garon, T. 1997. Changing causal relations between phonological processing abilities and word-level reading as children develop from beginning to fluent readers: A five-year longitudinal study. *Developmental Psychology* 33:468–79.

Wilkinson, G. 1993. *Wide Range Achievement Test-3*. Wilmington, DE: Jastak Associates.

Wolf, M., and Bowers, P. G. 1999. The double-deficit hypothesis for the developmental dyslexias. *Journal of Educational Psychology* 91:415–38.

PART III
Language Development
and Reading Disabilities

Both papers in this section raise questions about the possible consequences of early language difficulties for later reading achievement, and the relationship between language impairments and reading disorders. These questions are important because many preschoolers with specific language impairments (SLI) continue to have language-related problems during their school years. However, little longitudinal data on long-term outcomes is available.

Dr. Rescorla's paper is a follow-up study of the adolescent language and literacy skills of children who had been delayed in language development in their preschool years. Significant group differences at age 13 were found for verbal memory and reading. Her findings confirm prior evidence that early language problems continue into adolescence. In interpreting her findings, Rescorla raises the question of whether or not national norms on some tests are sensitive enough to assess reading and language problems in some children because her late-talkers achieved scores in the average-low average range (although the scores were significantly lower than the comparison group). Her findings also indicate that oral language problems persist to a greater extent than reading problems in children with SLI, thereby raising questions about the relationship between children with SLI and those with dyslexia.

Goulandris, Snowling, and Walker ask the question "Is dyslexia a form of specific language impairment?" In their longitudinal research, they compared three groups of 15 to 16 year old children on a number of oral and written language tasks. Two groups of children had childhood histories of SLI (those with resolved language difficulties and those with persistent language difficulties), and one group of children had dyslexia.

They matched the groups for age and nonverbal IQ with two groups of typically developing children (same age and younger). Among their findings were similarities in performance between children with dyslexia, and those with Resolved SLI and age matched controls on some oral language tasks. On reading, spelling, and nonword reading tasks, the dyslexics performed more poorly than the Resolved SLI group and as poorly as the Persistent SLI and younger controls. Both dyslexics and Resolved SLI group did poorly on phonological awareness tasks. The authors reject the hypothesis that dyslexia is a resolved form of specific language impairment but find support for the conclusion that SLI is a risk factor for reading disabilities. They suggest that both dyslexia and SLI children have phonological skill deficits but that dyslexics are better able to compensate by using higher-order language skills.

To date, there have been few long-term comparisons between children diagnosed as having specific reading difficulties and those with developmental language disorders. In these papers, the authors have begun to clarify the complex relationship between language and reading difficulties, and to examine the nature of language difficulties and their changes over time. Perhaps, as Goulandris, Snowling, and Walker suggest, SLI and dyslexia are not distinct conditions but, rather, exist on a "continuum of language disorder" (p. x (insert page).

Do Late-Talking Toddlers Turn Out to Have Reading Difficulties a Decade Later?

Leslie Rescorla

Bryn Mawr College
Bryn Mawr, Pennsylvania

Language and reading outcomes at age 13 were examined in a sample of 22 children who were late talkers as toddlers. The late talkers, all of whom had normal nonverbal ability and age-adequate receptive language at intake (24-to-31 months), were compared to a group of 14 typically developing children similar at intake on age, SES, and nonverbal ability. Late talkers had significantly poorer vocabulary, grammar, reading/spelling, and verbal memory skills at age 13, although as a group, they generally performed in the average range on most language and academic tasks. The findings suggest that slow early language development reflects a predisposition for slower acquisition and lower asymptotic performance in a wide range of language-related skills into adolescence.

INTRODUCTION

Delayed expressive language is the most common developmental problem for which young children are referred. Primary language delay—most commonly called Specific Language Impairment or SLI—is diagnosed when a child has normal hearing acuity, at least average nonverbal cognitive ability, and a significant delay in language development. To diagnose SLI, other disorders that have language delay as a symptom must be ruled

Annals of Dyslexia, Vol. 50, 2000

out (e.g., hearing impairment, mental retardation, and autism). A recent distinction is being made in the SLI field between late talkers, identified before age four, and preschool children with SLI, identified at age four or older (Rescorla and Lee 1999).

Many preschoolers with SLI go on to have continuing language impairments (reading/learning disabilities and/or emotional and behavioral problems) in later childhood (Aram, Ekelman, and Nation 1984; Bishop and Adams 1990; Rescorla and Lee 1999; Tallal 1988; Whitehurst and Fischel 1994). Even when they have caught up in their language skills by age five and one-half, preschoolers with SLI have lower scores than comparison children with normal language histories on many language and academic measures at age 15 (Stothard et al. 1998).

The literature suggests that late talkers have a better outcome than preschoolers with SLI (Paul 1996). Paul, Murray, Clancy, and Andrews (1997) found that late talkers had lower scores than comparison children at age seven in expressive language performance, but that they were no different in receptive language, reading, spelling, IQ, or phonological skills. Similarly, preliminary data presented from our ongoing longitudinal study (Rescorla and Dahlsgaard 1995) have indicated that most of the late talkers were functioning roughly in the normal range in language by the time they entered school, and that few appeared to be reading or language disabled by age eight or nine. On the other hand, the late talkers appeared to score consistently below typically developing comparison peers with normal language histories in many language, reading, and phonological tasks in the early school years.

The present study examined age 13 language and reading outcomes for 22 late talkers, and 14 comparison children from the cohorts followed to age nine by Rescorla and Dahlsgaard (1995). Our goal was to see whether the subclinical weaknesses in language and reading skills the late talkers manifested at age eight and nine had persisted into adolescence.

METHOD

PARTICIPANTS

The 22 late talkers (21 boys and 1 girl), whose age 13 outcome data are presented here, were a subset of a cohort of 40 toddlers (36 boys and 4 girls) identified with SLI at 24-to-31 months of age. Late talkers were recruited through newspaper advertisements, notices to pediatricians, and a local infant lab. All children came from middle- to upper middle-class white families. At intake, all the late talkers had to have a Mental Development Index score of greater than 85 on the Bayley Scale of infant development (Bayley 1969). They also needed to score within three months of chronological age on the Reynell Receptive Language Scale (which assessed comprehension of object labels and simple commands), and at least six months below chronological age on the Reynell Expressive Language Scale (which assessed object naming, vocabulary size, and production of phrases) (Reynell 1977).

Fourteen comparison children (all boys) have also participated in the age 13 follow-up to date. Comparison children were recruited in the same fashion as late talkers, had the same Bayley and Reynell Receptive Language Scale criteria, and had to have a Reynell Expressive Language Scale score within three months of chronological age. All participants in both groups met these selection criteria except for one late talker whose receptive language skills were four rather than three months delayed.

Table I contains the intake demographic information and test scores for both age 13 participant groups. These data look very similar to the intake scores for the full cohorts of 40 late talkers and 38 typically developing comparison children. The only respect in which these subsets are not fully representative of the original cohorts is that the age 13 comparison children seen thus far have a slightly higher mean Hollingshead (1975) SES score than the full cohort of comparison children (score of 60 as opposed to 56).

As can be seen in table I, the late talkers and the comparison children were essentially identical in age. There was a slight difference in SES score favoring the comparison children, but this was not significant at the $p < .01$ level, which is the appropriate standard for these intake scores given the number of variables analyzed.

The two groups were also fully comparable in their total scores on the 19 nonverbal Bayley items above the basal level (e.g., towering blocks, doing puzzles, drawing, and inserting pegs). The groups were significantly different in receptive language as measured by the Reynell Receptive Language Scale z-score, although the late talkers had fully normal receptive skills for their age. Of course, by design, there was a striking difference in Reynell Expressive Language Scale z-score between the two groups, with the late talkers on average at the 18 month age level in expressive language (a lag of more than eight months).

Table I. Intake Measures by Group			
	Late Talkers (LT)		Typically Developing (TD)
Intake Measures			
Intake Age in months	26.14	(2.30)	25.36	(.93)
Hollingshead Total	52.56	(13.30)	60.86	(5.72)
Bayley Nonverbal Raw Score	13.82	(2.56)	14.93	(3.83)
Reynell Receptive z-score	0.16	(0.51)	1.23	(0.45)***
Reynell Expressive z-score	−1.56	(0.29)	0.42	(0.45)***
LDS Vocabulary*	24.55	(25.82)	228.50	(71.45)***

*** $p < .001$ by independent means t-test

Finally, the late talkers had a mean reported vocabulary on Rescorla's (1989) Language Development Survey (LDS) of 24.55 words, in contrast to a vocabulary of 228.50 words for the comparison children. The LDS is a highly reliable and well-validated vocabulary checklist of 310 words (Rescorla 1989) on which a parent reports a toddler's expressive vocabulary and use of word combinations. All late talkers met Rescorla's (1989) language delay criterion of fewer than 50 words or no word combinations at 24 months.

All of the late talkers were seen for follow-up at ages three, four, and five. However, the earliest late talkers recruited were not tested on all the follow-up measures because some measures were added to the protocol after these youngsters had already been seen. Only a few of the 14 comparison children who have currently been followed to age 13 were seen between intake and age six, because most were recruited initially as a pilot group and not scheduled for visits at three, four, or five. Therefore, correlational analyses to examine early predictors of age 13 outcome were only done for the late talker group.

Preschool predictor measures included the Expressive One-Word Picture Vocabulary Test (EOWPVT) (Gardner 1981), a measure of single word expressive vocabulary, given at age three and four; the Test of Auditory Comprehension of Language-Revised (TACL-R) (Carrow-Woolfolk 1985), which measured word and sentence comprehension, given at age three; the Index of Productive Syntax (IPSYn) (Scarborough 1990) and mean length of utterance (MLU) calculated from a 100-utterance speech sample at age three and four; and the Patterned Elicitation Syntax Test (PEST) (Young and Perachio 1983), used at age five, which assessed grammatical skills using a sentence repetition paradigm. The number of late talkers for whom these scores were available ranged from 11 for the TACL-R to 22 for IPSyn and MLU at age three.

PROCEDURE

At age 13, participants were seen for a two-hour session during which a variety of language and academic measures were administered. These are briefly summarized below.

Wechsler Intelligence Scale for Children-Third Edition (WISC-III) (Wechsler 1991). The Block Design and Vocabulary subtests were administered to obtain quick estimates of nonverbal and verbal ability. In addition, Digit Span was given in order to examine verbal memory.

Wechsler Individual Achievement Test (WIAT) (Wechsler 1992). The Basic Reading and Spelling subtests were administered to assess word decoding and spelling skills.

Test of Written Language-Third Edition (TOWL-3) (Hammill and Larsen 1996). The Contextual Language, Contextual Conventions, and Story Construction subtests were scored from the adolescent's written narrative.

Test of Adolescent and Adult Language-Third Edition (TOAL-3) (Hammill et al. 1994). The Listening Vocabulary and Reading Vocabulary subtests assessed mastery of word meanings, and the Listening Grammar and Reading Grammar subtests tapped grammatical comprehension and sentence processing.

Clinical Evaluation of Language Fundamentals-Third Edition (CELF-3) (Semel, Wiig, and Secord 1995). The Formulated Sentences subtest assessed the ability to incorporate a target word into a grammatical and semantically relevant sentence, and the Recalling Sentences subtest tapped verbal memory.

Test of Language Competence-Expanded Edition (TLC) (Wiig & Secord 1989). On the Ambiguous Sentences subtest, the adolescent had to provide two interpretations for each stimulus sentence.

Qualitative Reading Inventory-II (QRI-II) (Leslie and Caldwell 1995). Each adolescent read a junior high school level passage about Peter the Great from the *QRI-II* and answered ten questions about it.

Test of Word Reading Efficiency (TOWRE) (Torgeson, Wagner, and Rashotte 1999). The Sight Word Efficiency and Phonemic Decoding Efficiency subtests of the TOWRE assessed automaticity of word and nonword decoding.

The child was asked to read as many items on a list of words (or nonsense words) as he could in 45 seconds. A pre-publication version of the TOWRE provided to the author by Torgeson was used in this study.

Pseudoword Repetition. This phonological task, modified by Scarborough from a procedure reported by Taylor, Lean, and Schwartz (1989), required immediate imitation of 30 multi-syllabic nonsense words such as "turskuhbassity." Poor nonword repetition is strongly associated with language and reading impairment (Bishop, North, and Donlan 1996).

RESULTS

DATA AGGREGATION

Principal components analysis was used to combine the various language and reading/writing measures into four factors and to derive factor scores. Group outcomes at age 13 were compared using t-tests on the four factor scores. Subsidiary analyses also compared the groups on the component measures comprising each factor. In addition, the number of children in each group showing below average performance on each standardized outcome measure was examined. The next set of analyses examined intercorrelations between the four age 13 factors. Finally, predictors of age 13 outcome from the preschool period were examined for the late talker group. Because many statistical tests were conducted, a significance criterion of $p < .01$ was adopted for all analyses.

AGE 13 FACTORS

The four factors generated by separate principal components analyses were all quite coherent and robust, as can be seen in the loadings of the various measures on their respective factors presented in table II.

Each set of component measures was highly associated with its core factor, with factor loadings ranging from .75 to .91. Correspondingly, each core factor accounted for between 62 percent and 75 percent of the variance in the component measure scores, indicating a high degree of common variance within the measures comprising a given factor. Except for Vocabulary with Verbal Memory, all correlations among factor scores were moderately strong and statistically significant (r .56 to .69, $p < .001$)

Table II. Age 13 Factor Scores		
Factor	Component Measures	Loadings
Vocabulary	WISC-III Vocabulary	.91
(75% of variance)	TOAL-3 Listening Vocabulary	.86
	TOAL-3 Reading Vocabulary	.83
Grammar	TOAL-3 Listening Grammar	.75
(62% of variance)	TOAL-3 Reading Grammar	.80
	CELF-3 Formulated Sentences	.76
	TLC Ambiguous Sentences	.83
Verbal Memory	WISC-III Digit Span	.84
(70% of variance)	CELF-3 Recalling Sentences	.88
	Pseudoword Repetition	.78
Reading	TOWRE Nonwords A	.90
(72% of variance)	TOWRE Nonwords B	.90
	TOWRE Words A	.89
	TOWRE Words B	.85
	WIAT Basic Reading	.80
	WIAT Spelling	.81
	QRI miscues	−.76
	QRI words/minute	.88

GROUP DIFFERENCES IN AGE 13 OUTCOME

Table III presents the mean factor z-score by group for the four age 13 factors, with negative scores representing performance below the mean factor score for the entire sample and positive scores representing the converse. The difference between the mean factor score of the two groups (see last column of table III) represents the effect size for that measure. An effect size of .80 or greater is commonly considered "large" (Cohen 1988).

As can be seen in table III, there were significant differences on all four factors at age 13. Effect sizes were large for the Grammar and Vocabulary factors, and somewhat weaker for the Verbal Memory and Reading factors.

Although the late talkers scored substantially below the typically developing comparison children on all four factors at age 13, it should be noted that their actual test performance on most measures was in the average range according to national norms. This can be seen in the mean scores for the individual

Table III. Outcome Factor Scores by Group				
	Late Talkers (LT)		Typically Developing (TD)	
Age 13 Factors	Score (SD)		Score (SD)	ES
Vocabulary Factor	−.32	(.99)	.51 (.81)**	.83
Grammar Factor	−.41	(.87)	.61 (.88)**	1.02
Verbal Memory Factor	−.29	(1.09)	.48 (.60)**	.77
Reading Factor	−.29	(.88)	.41 (1.05)*	.70
Age 13 Normed Measures	Score (SD)		Score (SD)	
WISC-III Vocabulary	11.09	(3.38)	14.57 (2.34)***	
WISC-III Block Design	11.41	(3.58)	14.71 (3.63)**	
WISC-III Digit Span	10.23	(3.57)	11.83 (2.02)	
TOAL-3 Listening Vocabulary	9.27	(3.41)	12.57 (2.47)**	
TOAL-3 Listening Grammar	7.73	(2.90)	10.43 (2.85)**	
TOAL-3 Reading Vocabulary	10.91	(3.39)	11.43 (3.86)	
TOAL-3 Reading Grammar	8.62	(4.49)	9.71 (3.63	
TLC Ambiguous Sentences	9.32	(3.29)	12.57 (2.44)**	
CELF-3 Formulated Sentences	8.73	(1.83)	11.43 (1.83)***	
CELF-3 Recalling Sentences	10.14	(2.59)	11.93 (2.23)*	
WIAT Basic Reading	103.59	(6.43)	111.57 (9.31)**	
WIAT Spelling	104.41	(12.35)	110.86 (10.62)	
TOWL-3 Contextual Conventions	11.59	(2.56)	10.71 (3.00)	
TOWL-3 Contextual Language	13.27	(3.21)	14.21 (3.42)	
TOWL-3 Story Construction	12.91	(2.41)	14.21 (1.48)	

* $p < .05$ ** $p < .01$ *** $p < .001$

measures for which standard scores were available as displayed in table III.

Late talkers scored in the average range on all three *WISC-III* subtests administered (Vocabulary, Block Design, and Digit Span), but significantly below the comparison children (with scores about one *SD* lower on Vocabulary and Block Design). On the *TOAL-3* Listening and Reading Vocabulary subtests, late talkers had scores in the average range (standard score of 10); they differed significantly from comparison peers in Listening Vocabulary but not Reading Vocabulary. Late talkers underperformed comparison peers in Listening Grammar but not Reading Grammar on the *TOAL-3*, and their score on Listening Grammar was somewhat below average (7.73). There was a substantial difference (one *SD*) between groups on the

TLC Ambiguous Sentences subtest, despite the fact that the late talkers performed in the average range. The late talkers also scored one *SD* below comparison peers on the *CELF-3* Formulated Sentences subtest, but the group difference on the *CELF-3* Recalling Sentences subtest was only marginally significant. The groups differed by about one-half *SD* on the *WIAT* Basic Reading subtest, although the late talkers scored in the average range. Finally, late talkers and comparison children did not differ on the three subtests of the *TOWL* or in the *WIAT* Spelling subtest, indicating comparable written language skills.

OUTCOMES FOR INDIVIDUAL CHILDREN

In the next analysis, scores of individual children on each normed measure at age 13 were examined. For purposes of this analysis, a child was considered delayed if he scored more than one *SD* below the mean. By this criterion, no child in either the late talker or the comparison group was a delayed reader on the WIAT Basic Reading subtest; furthermore, only one late talker scored below 85 on the *WIAT* Spelling subtest. One late talker scored below average on the *WISC-III* Vocabulary subtest, and two children in each group were delayed on the *TOAL-3* Reading Vocabulary subtest. On the *TOAL-3* Reading Grammar subtest, six late talkers and three comparison children showed delay (27 percent and 21 percent respectively).

A number of language measures did reveal weaker performance by the late talkers. For example, eight out of 22 (36 percent) late talkers had below average scores on the *TOAL-3* Listening Grammar subtest, compared to one out of 14 (7 percent) comparison children. The *TLC* Ambiguous Sentences, *TOAL-3* Listening Vocabulary, and *CELF-3* Formulated Sentences subtests appeared to be particularly problematic for the late talkers (five, six, and four delayed late talkers respectively, but no delayed comparison children). Interestingly, all three of these subtests require flexible manipulation of language, with the first two involving grasp of multiple meanings and the last necessitating construction of a sentence to incorporate a specific word and relate to a particular content. *WISC-III* Digit Span and *CELF-3* Recalling Sentences also appeared to be difficult for the late talkers (four and two late talkers were delayed, respectively, but no comparison children), suggesting weak verbal memory as a residual sign of early language delay.

Table IV. Correlations Between Preschool and Age 13 Outcome Measures for Late Talkers (N=22)

Preschool Measures	(N)	Age 13 Outcome Factors			
		Vocabulary	Grammar	Verbal Memory	Reading
		Correlations			
Reynell-E	(22)	.26	.35	.39	.23
Reynell-R	(22)	.48*	.43	.05	.20
EOWPVT-3	(14)	.65**	.51	.29	.42
TACL-R-3	(11)	.52	.60	.18	.51
IPSyn-3	(22)	−.02	.11	.34	.01
MLU-3	(22)	.03	.16	.28	.08
EOWPVT-4	(16)	.72**	.33	.12	.29
IPSYN-4	(21)	−.03	.42	.63**	.41
MLU-4	(21)	.04	.31	.52*	.54*
PEST-5	(19)	−.02	.53*	.66*	.20

*p < .05 ** < .01

PRESCHOOL PREDICTORS OF AGE 13 OUTCOME

The correlations between age two to five measures and age 13 outcomes for the late talker group appear in table IV.

Although many of these correlations were of moderate size (.50 and above), only a small number reached the $p < .01$ significance level, largely due to the small sample size (ranging from 11 to 22). Within this sample of late talkers, intake Reynell Expressive Language Scale scores were uniformly low, resulting in minimal correlations with age 13 outcomes. However, intake Reynell Receptive Language Scale score showed more variance and had moderate correlations (.48 and .43) with age 13 **Vocabulary** and **Grammar**, although neither met the $p < .01$ significance level. Age 3 receptive language on the *TACL-R* also had a moderate correlation with age 13 outcome (.52 with **Vocabulary**, .60 with **Grammar**, and .51 with **Reading**), but the small sample size reduced statistical significance. Age three and age four expressive naming skill (EOWPVT) significantly predicted age 13 **Vocabulary** (.65, .72). IPSyn and MLU at age four, the two grammatical measures, predicted **Verbal Memory** score at age 13 (.63, .52). Age four MLU also had a moderate correlation with age 13 **Reading**. Finally, an orally presented grammatical measure at age five, the PEST, was significantly correlated with age 13 **Grammar** and **Verbal Memory**.

DISCUSSION

The data reported here indicate that late talkers continued to score below typically developing comparison children with normal language histories on a variety of language and academic measures at age 13. Despite the fact that the late talkers scored in the average range on most age 13 measures, they performed less well on language and reading tasks than comparison children who had been similar at 24-to-31 months on SES and nonverbal cognitive ability. These results mirror those seen at age eight and nine for the cohorts from which these children were drawn. The results indicate that delayed expressive language development at age two is a risk factor for subclinical but nonetheless significant weakness in language-related skills into adolescence.

The fact that the late talkers in this study scored below comparison children on most measures while performing well within the average range raises the question of whether or not national norms are sufficiently sensitive to be used as a metric for assessing reading and language problems in youngsters from relatively affluent backgrounds. If children from upper middle SES backgrounds attend schools in which the norm is to perform one standard deviation or more above the national average on most standardized measures, then late talkers or other youngsters with mild residual learning problems may significantly underperform their peers while appearing to be average by national standards. This suggests that local norms need to be taken into account in assessing children's performance. In fact, many group-administered standardized test scores do just this by presenting a child's percentile rank relative to both national and local norms (e.g., suburban norms, independent school norms, and the like).

The findings of the present study are compatible with Paul's report (Paul, Murray, Clancy, and Andrews 1997) that the 84 percent of her late talker group who had "recovered" in language by age seven were still inferior to comparison children on a general expressive language scale. In contrast, her age seven late talkers were no worse than comparison children in reading and spelling. This may be due to the fact that the children in both groups were just developing early literacy skills at that age. As Rescorla (Rescorla and Dahlsgaard 1995) reported, their late talkers (the larger cohort from which the present sample was drawn) did not differ from comparison children in reading skills at age six or seven, but this difference was significant at ages 8 and 9.

The findings of the present study are also consistent with Bishop's follow-up of preschoolers with SLI. The 44 percent of her sample of four year olds with SLI who had made a good recovery in language by age five and one-half (Bishop and Adams 1990) were average on all language and reading measures at age 8 and one-half and not significantly different from comparison children. However, when Bishop and colleagues followed up her subjects at age 15 (Stothard et al. 1998), the age five "good outcome" children were significantly different from controls on four of the nine measures given (Sentence Repetition, Nonword Repetition, Spoonerisms, and a measure of reading and spelling). Their scores were in the range of 85-98 on the nine reading and language measures given, indicating that they were not significantly below average but were also not performing very well.

It is notable, furthermore, that Stothard (Stothard et al. 1998) found 48 percent of the age four children with SLI still diagnosable with SLI at age 15, whereas only 20 percent had significant reading/learning problems. This is consistent with our finding that the effect size for reading/spelling at age 13 was somewhat smaller than the effect sizes for vocabulary and grammar.

This pattern of language outcomes being worse than reading outcomes was also evident in the analysis of the outcomes of the individual late talkers in this study. The late talkers appeared to be most delayed in the language tasks that involved processing and mental manipulation of verbal information (TOAL-3 Listening Grammar and WISC-III Digit Span) and flexible manipulation and recombination of words and phrases (TLC Ambiguous Sentences, TOAL-3 Listening Vocabulary, and CELF-3 Formulated Sentences). Interestingly, they performed analogous tasks somewhat better when they could employ written text as a support (TOAL-3 Reading Grammar and Reading Vocabulary). Therefore, it appears to be the case that young children with early language delay are at higher risk for continuing language problems than for reading, writing, and spelling difficulties. Nonetheless, the adolescents who were slow to talk did score significantly below matched comparison children on a variety of reading tasks.

It is interesting to note that children with SLI tend to manifest more pronounced language problems than reading problems as they get older, whereas reading impaired/dyslexic children tend to have the opposite pattern. That is, dyslexic children manifest their primary disability in written language, but they typically manifest a variety of weaknesses in oral language skills as well. This suggests that oral and written language problems are highly interrelated, but not necessarily identical. Although many underlying component skills may be shared between the two systems, it appears that the hypothetical underlying deficit profile for reading disability may differ to some degree from that for SLI.

The high degree of intercorrelation between the four age 13 factors analyzed in this study indicates that there is much shared variance among reading, spelling, vocabulary, grammar, and verbal memory skills. This suggests the existence of what might be termed a general language "faculty," which consists of a complex collection of abilities that tend to be highly associated with one another but that can and do vary independently. This construct of a general language faculty is somewhat akin to the concept of *g* in the field of intelligence, namely a set of interrelated cognitive abilities. According to this formulation, both late talkers and children with SLI occupy a place on the general language ability continuum that is lower than that of typically developing children. Late talkers seem to be closer to average on this hypothetical language ability continuum than preschool children with SLI, as indicated by their generally more favorable outcomes.

The argument proposed here is that children with SLI have less optimal endowment for language than children with typical language histories. This argument is consistent with Leonard (1991), who suggested that specific language impairment was a "weakness" in the linguistic faculty rather than a true pathology. An additional component of the argument proposed here is that this weakness in the language faculty does not have a single source. Rather, it can arise from weaknesses in one or more of the many skills that subserve language, such as auditory perception, word retrieval, verbal working memory, motor planning, phonological discrimination, and the processing and utilization of grammatical rules. According to this argument, children with a primary reading disability have deficits in many of these same component skills, but they may also have other more domain-specific deficits (e.g., phonological awareness, cross-modal integration, visual processing and memory, and the like) that make them particularly likely to manifest problems with written language.

If late talkers and preschool children with SLI are at the lower end of the normal distribution in language skills, one would expect both groups to manifest slower development and poorer asymptotic performance. The data from the present study are consistent with this hypothesis, as are other recent findings in the literature. Furthermore, one would expect that language skills measured throughout the preschool period would be significantly associated with long-term outcome of the vocabulary, grammar, verbal memory, reading, and spelling skills that constitute aspects of general language ability. Just such a pattern was suggested in the results of this study, even when only the late talkers were analyzed, which restricted the range in the preschool period and reduced the sample size.

In sum, it is proposed here that young children who are significantly delayed in expressive language after age two have a predisposition for weak language abilities. The most mildly impaired outgrow their delay by age four, and those most severely impaired continue to have language problems for many years. All the children on this SLI continuum have slower language development than comparison children from the same backgrounds. Even the least impaired youngsters on this theoretical SLI continuum, namely late talkers and preschoolers with SLI who move into the average range in language by age five, continue to manifest significantly lower asymptotic performance across a wide variety of language and reading measures than comparison children with normal language histories who have comparable nonverbal abilities and SES backgrounds at intake.

There are several clinical implications of the research findings reported here. First, parents and practitioners can be confident that most late talkers will perform in the average range in most language skills by the time they enter school. For those late talkers whose language delay is so severe and persistent that they are diagnosable as SLI at age four, more than one-half will have a good language outcome by school age. In addition, parents and practitioners can anticipate that relatively few late talkers will develop into children with dyslexia or reading disability. On the other hand, they need to be aware that early language delay may well indicate some subclinical weakness in the component skills that serve language and reading. For this reason, it might be a good idea to provide late talkers with extra exposure to games and activities that may help to strengthen word retrieval, verbal memory, phonological discrimination, and grammatical processing.

ACKNOWLEDGMENTS

This research was supported by grants to the author from the Bryn Mawr College Faculty Research Fund and from the

National Institutes of Health (NICHD Area Grant 1-R15-HD22355-01; NIDCD R01-DC00807). The author wishes to thank the parents and children whose participation made this research possible.

Address correspondence to: Leslie Rescorla, Department of Psychology, Bryn Mawr College, 101 N. Merion Avenue, Bryn Mawr, Pennsylvania 19010. Telephone: 610-527-5190. email lrescorl@bryn-mawr.edu.

References

Aram, D., Ekelman, B., and Nation, J. 1984. Preschoolers with language disorders: 10 years later. *Journal of Speech and Hearing Research* 27:232–44.

Bayley, N. 1969. *The Bayley Scales of Infant Development*. New York: The Psychological Corporation.

Bishop, D. V. M., and Adams, C. 1990. A prospective study of the relationship between specific language impairment, phonological disorders and reading retardation. *Journal of Child Psychology and Psychiatry* 31:1027–50.

Bishop, D. V. M., North, T., and Donlan, C. 1996. Nonword repetition as a behavioral marker for inherited language impairment: Evidence from a twin study. *Journal of Child Psychiatry and Psychology* 37:391–403.

Carrow-Woolfolk, E. 1985. *Test of Auditory Comprehension of Language-R*. Allen, TX: DLM Teaching Resources.

Cohen, J. 1988. *Statistical Power Analysis for the Behavioral Sciences*, 2nd ed. Hillsdale, NJ: Lawrence Erlbaum Associates.

Gardner, M. F. 1981. *Expressive One-Word Picture Vocabulary Test*. Novato, CA: Academic Therapy Publications.

Hammill, D. D., Brown, V. L., Larsen, S. C., and Wiederholt, J. L. 1994. *Test of Adolescent and Adult Language - Third Edition*. Austin, TX: PRO-ED.

Hammill, D. D., and Larsen, S. C. 1996. *Test of Written Language - Third Edition*. Austin, TX: PRO-ED.

Hollingshead, A. 1975. Four-Factor Index of Social Status. New Haven, CT: Working paper.

Leonard, L. B. 1991. Specific language impairment as a clinical category. *Language, Speech, and Hearing Services in Schools* 22:66–68.

Leslie, L., and Caldwell, J. 1995. *Qualitative Reading Inventory-II* New York: Harper Collins.

Paul, R. 1996. Clinical implications of the natural history of slow expressive language development. *American Journal of Speech-Language Pathology* 5(2):5–21.

Paul, R., Murray, C., Clancy, K., and Andrews, D. 1997. Reading and metaphonological outcomes in late talkers. *Journal of Speech, Language, and Hearing Research* 40:1037–47.

Rescorla, L. 1989. The Language Development Survey: A screening tool for delayed language in toddlers. *Journal of Speech and Hearing Disorders* 54:587–99.

Rescorla, L., and Dahlsgaard, K. 1995. Reading and language outcomes at ages 5-to-8 for toddlers with specific expressive language impairment (SLI-E). Poster presented at the Biennial Meeting of the Society for Research in Child Development, Indianapolis, March, 1995.

Rescorla, L., and Lee, E. C. 1999. Language impairments in young children. In *Handbook of Early Language Impairment in Children: Volume I: Nature*, eds. T. Layton and L. Watson. Albany, NY: Delmar Publishing Company.

Reynell, J. K. 1977. *Reynell Developmental Language Scales*. Windsor: NFER.

Scarborough, H. S. 1990. Index of Productive Syntax. *Applied Psycholinguistics* 11:1–12.

Semel, E., Wiig, E. H., and Secord, W. A. 1995. *Clinical Evaluation of Language Fundamentals-Third Edition*. San Antonio: Psychological Corporation.

Stothard, S. E., Snowling, M. J., Bishop, D. V. M., Chipchase, B. B., and Kaplan, C. A. 1998. Language-impaired preschoolers: A follow-up into adolescence. *Journal of Speech, Language, and Hearing Research* 41:407–18

Tallal, P. 1988. Developmental language disorders. In *Learning Disabilities: Proceedings of the National Conference*, eds. J. F. Kavanaugh and T. J. Truss, Jr. Parkton, MD: York Press.

Taylor, H. G., Lean, D., and Schwartz, S. 1989. Pseudoword repetition ability in learning-diabled children. *Applied Psycholinguistics* 10:203–19.

Torgeson, J., Wagner, R., and Rashotte, C. 1999. *Test of Word Reading Efficiency (TOWRE)*. Austin, TX: PRO-ED.

Wechsler, D. 1991. *Wechsler Intelligence Scale for Children - Third Edition*. San Antonio, TX: Psychological Corporation.

Wechsler, D. 1991. *Wechsler Individual Achievement Test*. San Antonio, TX: Psychological Corporation.

Whitehurst, G. J., and Fischel, J. E. 1994. Early developmental language delay: What, if anything, should the clinician do about it? *Journal of Child Psychology and Psychiatry* 35(4):613–48.

Wiig, W. H., and Secord, W. 1989. *Test of Language Competence-Expanded Edition*. San Atnonio, TX: Psychological Corporation.

Young, E. C., and Perachio, J. J. 1983. *The Patterned Elicitation Syntax Test (PEST)*. Tuscon, AZ: Communication Skill Builders.

IS DYSLEXIA A FORM OF SPECIFIC LANGUAGE IMPAIRMENT? A COMPARISON OF DYSLEXIC AND LANGUAGE IMPAIRED CHILDREN AS ADOLESCENTS

Nata K. Goulandris,

University College London,
United Kingdom

Margaret J. Snowling

University of York,
United Kingdom

Ian Walker

Max Planck Institute of Cognitive Neuroscience,
Bennewitz, Germany

Two groups of adolescents with a childhood history of language impairment were compared with a group of developmentally dyslexic young people of the same age and nonverbal ability. The study also included two comparison groups of typically developing children, one of the same age as those in the clinical groups, and a younger comparison group of similar reading level to the dyslexic students. Tests of spoken and written language skills revealed that the adolescents with dyslexia were indistinguishable from those with resolved language impairments on spoken language tasks, and both groups performed at age-expected levels. However, both dyslexic readers and those with resolved specific language impairments showed deficits in phonological awareness. On written language tasks, a different pattern of performance was

Annals of Dyslexia, Vol. 50, 2000

apparent. In reading and spelling, adolescents with dyslexia performed only as well as those with persistent oral language impairments and younger controls. However, their reading comprehension was better. The theoretical and educational implications of these findings are discussed.

Specific language impairment (SLI) and developmental reading disorder (dyslexia) are usually considered two distinct conditions (e.g., DSM-IV, American Psychiatric Association 1994). The term dyslexia is usually used to describe a child who has a disorder of written language skills despite ostensibly normal oral language abilities, and there is general agreement that such children have specific phonological deficits (Snowling 1991). In contrast, the term specific language impairment is used to describe children who have problems with the acquisition of spoken language despite normal nonverbal ability (Bishop 1997). The language difficulties of SLI children tend to encompass a wide range of linguistic processes including vocabulary impairments and grammatical deficits (Leonard et al. 1987; Bishop and Leonard 2000).

However, many dyslexic children have a history of language difficulty (Rutter and Yule 1975) and it is common for children with language impairments to go on to have reading difficulties (Scarborough 1990; Tallal, Ross, and Curtiss 1989; van der Lely and Stollwerck 1996). Such findings suggest that the two disorders exist on a continuum of language disorder, both groups of children showing deficits in phonological awareness and phonological processing (Catts 1989, 1993, 1996; Stackhouse and Wells 1997). Within this view, dyslexia is conceptualized either as a mild form of language impairment, affecting only the phonological system, or as a residual problem that remains when oral language difficulties have resolved (Aram, Ekelman, and Nation 1984; Scarborough and Dobrich 1990).

An alternative interpretation of these findings is that language impairment is a risk factor for dyslexia (Snowling, Bishop, and Stothard 2000). According to this view, phonological skills are critical to reading development (Byrne et al. 1997; Share 1995) and, to the extent that children have phonological difficulties, they will be at risk of reading failure. However, whether or not they show specific reading difficulties/dyslexia depends on how this phonological deficit interacts with other cognitive and language skills (Snowling 2000). For children who have good semantic skills, a degree of compensation is possible (Nation and Snowling 1998), and it is likely that the common dyslexic profile of better reading comprehension than word-level decoding will ensue. However, children who have poor semantic or syntactic resources show a global delay in reading. Moreover, semantic difficulties compromise verbal IQ, and such children rarely receive a discrepancy-based definition of dyslexia. Therefore, a dyslexic outcome cannot be assumed for children with preschool language impairments. Indeed, it is likely that the characteristics of children who attract such a "diagnosis" will change with the age of the child, along with both the demands of reading at that stage in development and the teaching they have received. Consistent with this idea, Shaywitz et al. (1992) reported that different children from their epidemiological sample fulfilled criteria for specific reading retardation at different ages, and Snowling et al. (2000) reported that the prevalence of specific reading difficulties among children with a history of preschool language impairment increased from 6 percent to 24 percent between the ages of 8 and 15 years.

In light of the theoretical and clinical interest in this issue, it is surprising that there have been few direct comparisons of the reading and cognitive skills of children diagnosed as having specific reading difficulties and those with developmental language disorders. Our aim in the present study was to examine the notion of a continuum of language disorder directly by investigating the cognitive, linguistic, and literacy profiles of adolescents of school-leaving age who had a childhood history of either SLI or developmental dyslexia. To enable a rigorous comparison between these groups, they were compared with age- and reading-level matched controls of similar nonverbal ability. By including adolescents with either resolved or persistent oral language impairments, it was possible to address the following hypotheses:

1. Dyslexia is a resolved form of SLI. According to this hypothesis, children with dyslexia perform similarly to children with a preschool history of language impairment whose oral language difficulties have resolved but who have been shown to have residual phonological processing deficits (Bishop, North, and Donlan 1996; Stothard et al. 1998).

2. SLI is a risk factor for reading difficulties. According to this hypothesis, children with dyslexia have a qualitatively different profile from children with SLI because they have more specific phonological deficits and stronger vocabulary and comprehension skills.

METHOD

PARTICIPANTS

Three clinical groups of 15- to 16-year-old adolescents participated in this study, one with a childhood history of developmental dyslexia and two with a preschool history of specific
language impairment. The groups were matched for age and
nonverbal IQ and compared with two groups of normal readers, an age-matched group selected to be of the same level of
nonverbal ability, and a younger group selected as reading age-
matched controls for the dyslexics.

The dyslexic group consisted of 20 adolescents with childhood diagnoses of dyslexia, aged 14 years to 18 years 10
months, with a mean age of 15 years 9 months (SD = 15
months). Eighteen of the adolescents were drawn from a cohort
that had participated in a longitudinal study of developmental
dyslexia, approximately five years after their first assessment.
Initially, this group comprised 20 children ranging in reading
age from 6 to 8 years, all of at least average IQ, whose reading
performance lagged at least 18 months behind their chronological age (Snowling, Goulandris, and Defty 1996). The data we
had about the early language development of these children
was from parental reports. About one-third of parents reported
preschool language delays in their children.

Ninety percent of the original sample agreed to participate
in this follow-up; one refused on the grounds that he did not
wish to undertake any more tests and the other was unable to
attend because of illness. 12/18 of the childhood dyslexics still
met the criterion of 18 months below grade level. Two more
adolescents with dyslexia, both reporting long-standing reading
difficulties, were added at this stage according to the same selection criteria.

The participants with a history of speech and language difficulties were drawn from a sample originally recruited between
3:9 and 4:2 years of age by Bishop and Edmundson (1987).
Eighty-seven children (68 with SLI) participated in the study
and were assessed at 4, 4:6 and 5:6 years of age. At 5:6, 30 of
these children had resolved their language difficulties
(Resolved SLI), while the remaining 38 had persistent language
difficulties (Persistent SLI). The data presented in this paper
were collected as part of a follow-up of these groups of children
at 15 years, reported by Stothard et al. (1998). The resolved SLI
group comprised 19 children whose mean age at the time of the

assessment was 15 years 5 months (SD = 3 months), being those that matched the dyslexics on the basis of chronological age and Block Design score, a measure of nonverbal IQ. The persistent SLI group consisted of 20 children aged 15 years 7 months (SD = 4 months), selected from the 30 available to match on the basis of chronological age and Block Design score. The reading status of these children was not known prior to the study.

Nineteen normally developing readers whose mean age was 15 years 9 months (SD = 3 months) formed the age-matched comparison group (CA-controls). These children were drawn from the normative sample tested by Stothard et al. (1998) by performing a range match by nonverbal IQ and age to the dyslexics. Eighteen younger children with a mean age of 10 years 4 months (SD = 4 months) formed a second comparison group of normally developing readers. These children were selected to be of similar nonverbal ability to the dyslexics and to perform at a similar level to the dyslexic and the persistent SLI readers according to raw score on the Wechsler Objective Reading Dimensions test of basic reading (WORD; Wechsler 1993), a test of single-word reading.

Details of the participants are summarized in table 1. There were no significant differences between the groups for Block

Table I. Characteristics of adolescents with a history of dyslexia, specific language impairment, RA, and CA- controls.

	Dyslexic (n = 20)	Resolved SLI (n = 19)	Persistent SLI (n = 20)	Young Controls (n = 18)	Older Controls (n = 19)
Age (years)					
M	15.79 [a]	15.44 [a]	15.62 [a]	10.39[b]	15.68 [a]
SD	1.30	0.31	0.41	0.39	0.25
Block Design (Scaled Score)					
M	11.15 [a]	11.00 [a]	9.65 [a]	9.33 [a]	10.74 [a]
SD	2.89	3.30	2.74	2.00	2.45
Word reading (WORD)					
Mean SS	84.80 [a]	97.26[b]	85.20 [a]	102.22[b]	104.89[b]
SD	11.85	11.90	15.33	10.42	6.95

Note all F ratios are significant at the .001 level.

Means having the same superscript are not significantly different at the $p<.05$ level on Tukey or Games-Howell post hoc tests.

Design standard scores, showing that the groups were well-matched for nonverbal ability ($F[4,91] = 1.76$, $MSe = 7.39$).

TESTS AND PROCEDURES

The children were tested on a battery of tests designed to provide a broad characterisation of spoken and written language processing skills of the participants.

Nonverbal ability. The Block Design of the *Wechsler Intelligence Scale for Children - III*[UK] (Wechsler 1992) was administered as a measure of nonverbal ability. In this task, the child was asked to reconstruct two dimensional patterns using red and white blocks. This test is designed for use with children age 6 to 16 years and has a split-half reliability for children age 15 of .92.

Language skills. Receptive vocabulary. *The Long Form of the British Picture Vocabulary Scale (BPVS)* (Dunn, Dunn, Whetton, and Pintilie 1982) assesses receptive vocabulary. In this test, the child chose a picture from a selection of four that most closely matched the word spoken by the examiner. The test is standardized on children ranging in age from 3 to 17 years and has a split-half reliability for children aged 15-16 of.91.

Expressive vocabulary. This test comprised six easy items taken from the Snowling picture naming test (Snowling, van Wagtendonk, and Stafford 1988), and the first 24 items of the *Graded Naming Test* (McKenna and Warrington 1983). This composite measure provided a range of pictures thought suitable for a wide range of abilities.

Sentence processing. The *Clinical Evaluation of Language Fundamentals – Revised (CELF-R)* (Semel, Wiig, and Secord 1986) Recalling Sentences subtest was used to measure grammatical sensitivity. In this test, the child repeated a sentence of increasing length and syntactic complexity. This test is standardized for children age 5 to 18 and has a reliability for children age 15 to 16 of .80.

PHONOLOGICAL PROCESSING SKILLS

Nonword repetition. To assess children's ability to repeat unfamiliar words, we administered the *Children's Nonword Repetition Test (CN Rep)* (Gathercole et al. 1994). This test comprised 40 nonwords with 10 items of two, three, four, and five syllables (e.g., "ballop" and "blonterstaping"). The test-retest reliability for children in the 5 to 7 age range was .77. The nonwords were presented via audiotape to all the groups except the dyslexics, who repeated the nonwords after the experimenter. It was important to include nonword repetition because this test was thought to be too sensitive to underlying language difficulties (Bishop, North, and Donlan 1996).

Spoonerisms. Phonological awareness skills were examined using a version of a test devised by Perin (1983). In this test, the child had to transpose the initial sounds from the beginning of two spoken words (e.g., paddington bear > baddington pear; hot dogs > dot hogs). Eleven different two-word items were presented in this test. One point was allocated for each phoneme transposed correctly on condition that word order was respected. The maximum possible score on this test is 22. The test has an internal reliability for children age 15 to 16 of .79 (Stothard et al. 1998).

LITERACY SKILLS

The Wechsler Objective Reading Dimensions (WORD) (Wechsler 1993) was administered to provide measures of current literacy attainment. This test contains three subtests: Single Word Recognition, Spelling, and Reading Comprehension. All the subtests were entered into the analyses individually to investigate possible group differences. The *WORD* is standardized on children between the ages of 6 and 16 years and has a split-half reliability for children age 15 to 16 of .88 for reading, .91 for spelling, and .82 for reading comprehension.

Nonword reading. In this test, the participant read a set of 10 one-syllable and 10 two-syllable nonwords (e.g. "blem", "tegwop") from the *Graded Nonword Reading Test* (Snowling, Stothard, and MacLean 1996). Five more difficult nonwords (1 two- and 4 three-syllable nonwords, e.g., "pragendent") were added to increase the level of difficulty. This test has a split-half reliability for children age 15 to 16 of .77.

Nonword spelling. In order to examine the participants' ability to encode unfamiliar words, they spelled 20 one- and two- syllable nonwords. Written spellings were considered correct if all the sounds in the target were correctly represented regardless of which grapheme was selected.

All the children were tested individually in a single session, either at the university lab, their school, or their home.

RESULTS

The performance profile of the children from the three clinical groups and their age-matched controls across the test battery is shown in figure 1, expressed in terms of z scores relative to the mean and *SD* of the younger controls. A number of important differences in profile can be seen. First, the Persistent SLI group were impaired across all tasks and showed especially strong deficits in sentence and nonword repetition, whereas the Resolved SLI group showed only mild impairments for their age on spoken language tasks but poorer reading, spelling, and phonological awareness than their oral skills predicted. Second, the dyslexic children performed at the same level as those with Resolved SLI on tests of spoken language and in reading comprehension but they were impaired in reading, spelling, and phonological awareness.

As performance approached ceiling in the CA-control group on many of the tests administered, transformations were conducted on all variables that departed from normality or homo-

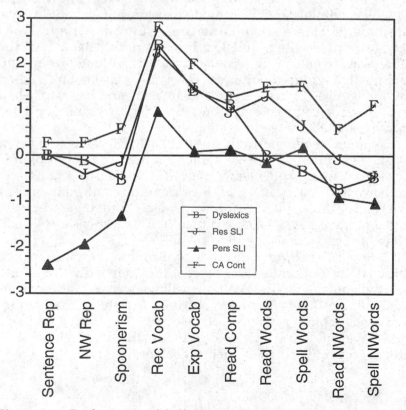

Figure 1.   *Performance of dyslexic, resolved SLI, persistent SLI, and CA-controls across tests of spoken and written language; scores are standardized against the mean and SD of RA-controls.*

geneity of variance (see Tabachnik and Fidell 1996). Reflect and square root transformations were applied to the following tests: Sentence Repetition, Nonword Repetition, *WORD* Spelling, *WORD* Comprehension, Nonword Reading, and Nonword Spelling. Reflect and logarithm transformations were applied to *WORD* Reading and Spoonerisms. However, as the results of the analyses using transformed data only differed marginally from those on raw data, analyses on raw data are reported here. Multivariate analyses of variance were conducted separately for the spoken and written language tests. Following these analyses, univariate ANOVAs and multiple comparisons were undertaken using Tukey's HSD for variables with homogeneous variances. When heterogeneity of variance was present, the Games and Howell post-hoc tests were applied. Since the present study had relatively low statistical power, effect sizes are reported relative to the mean and *SD* of the younger controls, to clarify marginal group differences.

Table II shows the performance of the three clinical groups and the two comparison groups across the spoken language and phonological processing tasks. The MANOVA on the language tests indicated that there were significant group differences across tasks $\Lambda(20, 289) = 7.14$, $p<.001$. The adolescents with dyslexia generally performed at the same level as the Resolved SLI group and the CA-controls, and were superior to the Persistent SLI group and younger controls. In turn, the Persis-tent SLI group scored below the level of the Resolved SLI group on most of the oral language tests.

Univariate tests showed that there were significant group difference in receptive ($F[4,91] = 21.56$, $MSe = 187.05$, $p <.001$) and expressive vocabulary ($F[4,91] = 14.46$, $MSe = 13.06$, $p <.001$). Post-hoc analyses demonstrated in the case of both receptive and expressive language that the adolescents with dyslexia performed at the same level as the Resolved SLI group and the CA-controls and better than the Persistent SLI and the younger controls. There were also significant group differences in Sentence Repetition ($F (4,91)=7.81$, $MSe=57.86$, $p<.001$). This time, Games and Howell post-hoc analyses revealed that the Persistent SLI group performed significantly less well than the other four groups, while there was no significant difference between the performance of the dyslexic, Resolved SLI, younger, and older controls.

There were significant group differences on both phonological tasks: (Spoonerisms: $F[4,91] = 7.25$, $MSe = 19.07$, $p <.001$; Nonword Repetition $F[4, 91] = 12.26$, $MSe = 21.51$,

Table II.   Mean scores on standardised and experimental spoken language tests for adolescents with a history of dyslexia, specific language impairment, RA- and CA- controls.

	Dyslexic (n = 20)	Resolved SLI (n = 19)	Persistent SLI (n = 20)	Young Controls (n = 18)	Older Controls (n = 19)
Receptive Vocabulary (BPVS)[1]					
M	122.90[a]	120.89[a]	104.60[b]	92.61[b]	127.84[a]
SD	12.03	14.87	15.06	12.58	13.53
Range	100-141	88-140	76-131	72-112	96-147
Expressive Vocabulary (Naming)[2]					
M	19.95[a]	20.11[a]	15.25[b]	15.00[b]	22.00[a]
SD	3.87	3.36	3.84	3.53	3.40
Range	13-26	13-26	9-24	7-21	15-27
Sentence Repetition[3]					
M	66.60	66.68	57.15	66.67	67.74
SD	6.54	6.51	11.67	4.00	6.79
Range	54-76	54-77	26-77	60-74	57-78
Nonword Repetition[4]					
M	33.50[a]	32.21[a]	25.90[b]	34.06[a]	35.16[a]
SD	3.85	4.28	6.88	4.20	2.85
Range	25-39	23-39	12-36	27-39	30-39
Spoonerisms[5]					
M	15.35[ac]	16.79[ab]	12.35[c]	17.38[ab]	19.53[b]
SD	4.22	3.63	6.63	3.79	2.12
Range	7-21	11-22	0-20	8-22	15-22

Note all F-ratios are significant at .001 level.

Means having the same superscript are not significantly different at the $p<.05$ level on Tukey or Games and Howell post hocs.

[1] Raw score   [2] Maximum = 30   [3] Maximum = 25
[4] Maximum = 40   [5] Maximum = 24

$p < .001$). Post-hoc analyses revealed that on the Spoonerisms task, CA-controls performed at a higher level than the adolescents with dyslexia and the Persistent SLI group. The Resolved SLI made more errors than the CA-controls but the difference just missed significance ($p = .058$). The three clinical groups did not differ from one another but performed at the same level as younger controls. The analysis of between-group differences in nonword repetition revealed that the dyslexics, the Resolved SLI group, and the two sets of controls performed at a comparable level which was higher than that achieved by the Persistent SLI group. However, a range effect here may have obscured true group differences. It is notable that, in terms of absolute level of performance, both adolescents with dyslexia and those with Resolved SLI scored less well than controls some five years younger (effect sizes were -.13 and -.43, respectively).

The performance of the groups across the literacy tasks is shown in table III. MANOVA on these tests indicated that there was a significant main effect of group, $\Lambda(20, 290) = 5.34$, $p < .001$, confirmed by univariate analyses on all the written language tasks. Importantly, follow-up tests revealed a different picture of group differences to that seen on the spoken language measures. There were significant main effects of group in single word reading ($F[4, 91] = 8.59$, $MSe = 35.64$, $p < .001$ and spelling ($F[4,91] = 11.60$, $MSe = 25.14$, $p < .001$). In the case of single word reading, the dyslexic group were impaired for their age and performed at the same level as the Persistent SLI group and the younger controls without a history of language delay. The Resolved SLI group read more words correctly than the Persistent SLI and the dyslexic groups, although this latter difference failed to reach conventional levels of significance ($p < .08$). In spelling, the adolescents with dyslexia once again performed at the same level as the Persistent SLI group and the younger controls. Their performance was significantly below that of the Resolved SLI and the CA-control groups.

There were also significant main effects of group for nonword reading ($F [4, 91] = 7.06$, $MSe = 23.12$, $p < .001$) and for nonword spelling ($F[4, 91] = 10.30$, $MSe = 9.95$, $p < .001$). In nonword reading, the three clinical groups and the younger controls performed at a statistically similar level, but it is clear that those with Resolved SLI had a less severe impairment (effect sizes were -.09 for Resolved SLI, -74 for dyslexics, and -.92 for Persistent SLI). Indeed, only the dyslexics and Persistent SLI performed significantly less well than CA-controls. The dyslexics also performed at a comparable level to the Persistent SLI and younger controls on nonword spelling. Once again, the resolved SLI group attained scores between those of the adolescents with dyslexia and the CA-controls and between-group differences were marginally significant ($p < .063$). Effect sizes were -.47 for dyslexics, -.45 for Resolved SLI and –1.04 for Persistent SLI.

Table III. **Mean scores on written language tests for adolescents with a history of dyslexia, specific language impairment, RA- and CA-controls.**

	Dyslexic (n = 20)	Resolved SLI (n = 19)	Persistent SLI (n = 20)	Young Controls (n = 18)	Older Controls (n = 19)
Single word reading					
(WORD: Raw)					
M	41.85[a]	48.84[a]	41.00[a]	41.94[a]	50.21[b]
SD	6.54	5.13	8.23	5.53	2.90
Range	26-49	31-52	22-52	31-49	40-53
Spelling					
(WORD raw)					
M	30.70[a]	35.68[bc]	33.25[ab]	32.44[ac]	40.05[c]
SD	5.15	5.23	6.09	4.98	3.01
Range	20-40	27-46	22-43	22-38	33-47
Reading Comprehension					
(WORD raw)					
M	28.80[a]	28.00[a]	24.25[b]	23.67[b]	29.58[a]
SD	3.85	3.64	4.60	4.67	4.09
Range	22-35	18-34	13-30	14-30	18-35
Nonword Reading[1]					
M	16.85[ab]	20.00[ab]	16.00[a]	20.44[ab]	23.16[b]
SD	4.25	5.08	6.55	4.85	2.12
Range	6-22	6-25	4-25	5-25	17-25
Nonword Spelling[1]					
M	12.75[abc]	15.32[bcd]	11.15[a]	14.06[c]	17.11[d]
SD	2.90	2.89	4.56	2.80	1.94
Range	5-17	9-19	1-18	9-18	11-20

Note all F-ratios are significant at .001 level.

Means having the same superscript are not significantly different at the $p<.05$ level on Tukey or Games and Howell post hocs.

[1.] Maximum = 25

Finally, a significant main effect of group was also found on the reading comprehension subtest ($F[4, 91] = 8.01$, $MSe = 17.49$, $p <.001$). In this case, the dyslexic readers showed no impairment and gained comparable scores to those with Resolved SLI and CA-controls. The Persistent SLI and younger control groups did significantly less well but in line with each other.

DISCUSSION

The comparison of adolescents with childhood diagnoses of dyslexia and specific language impairment revealed similarities as well as differences between the groups on tests of spoken and written language processing. Interestingly, differences between adolescents with dyslexia and those with Resolved and Persistent SLI turned on the kind of processing domain tapped by the various tasks with which they were assessed. Dyslexic readers were indistinguishable from age-matched controls and those with resolved language problems on oral language tasks tapping vocabulary and grammatical sensitivity, arguably, measures of general language competence. However, both adolescents with dyslexia and those with Resolved SLI did less well than expected for their age on Spoonerisms, a test requiring explicit phonological awareness. A similar pattern of results was seen for nonword repetition, although group differences did not reach conventional level of significance. On all of these oral language measures, the group with Persistent SLI were impaired for their age and, at best, performed only as well as younger children some five years their junior.

On tests of written language, the profile of the groups revealed a somewhat altered perspective. Despite the fact that the dyslexic group were indistinguishable from the Resolved SLI group on spoken language tasks, they were more impaired in reading, spelling, and nonword reading. Indeed on all these tasks, they performed as poorly as those with Persistent SLI and younger controls, confirming the severity of their written language disorder. On basic tests of reading and spelling, the performance of the group with Resolved SLI was slightly impaired in relation to age-matched controls, and they were almost as poor as adolescents with dyslexia in nonword spelling. In the introduction, we posed two different hypotheses about the relationship between dyslexia and SLI. These results force us to reject a strong version of the hypothesis that dyslexia is a form of Resolved SLI. Although the dyslexic readers performed like those whose early language difficulties had resolved on tests of oral language, they did demonstrably less well on tests of reading and spelling. On these tests, they performed more like those with persisting problems, although their reading comprehension was better. Arguably, a better characterization of the group similarity is that the group with Resolved SLI has residual phonological processing difficulties that affect their ability to spell nonwords but they have developed literacy skills in the normal range.

Our second hypothesis was that SLI is a risk factor for reading difficulties. The shared difficulties encountered by both the Resolved SLI and dyslexic group on the Spoonerisms task and in nonword spelling are consistent with this idea. However, the fact that the Resolved SLI group avoided reading failure is not easily accommodated within this view. The implication would be that children with Resolved SLI have a greater capacity to compensate for phonological weaknesses during the course of reading development than children with dyslexia. Nation and Snowling (1998) have argued that dyslexic children can learn to read by relying on global strategies underpinned by vocabulary for word recognition, despite persisting nonword reading deficits (Rack, Snowling, and Olson 1992). It seems unlikely that the Resolved SLI group could do this more effectively than those in the dyslexic group because they were indistinguishable from them on the spoken language tasks administered.

An alternative hypothesis is that dyslexic children carry the same risk of dyslexia as language-impaired children who have phonological deficits. However, dyslexic readers also have some, as yet unidentified, additional impairment. A candidate area of difficulty would be in creating links between print and pronunciation, a difficulty that goes beyond phonology per se. A number of recent theories suggest just such a deficit in dyslexia in developing word-specific orthographic representations (Wolf and Bowers 1999; Wimmer, Mayringer, and Landerl 1998).

It is important to note that the present study departs from others that have compared language-impaired and dyslexic children in the age of the sample tested. Kamhi and Catts (1986) investigated groups of much younger children, age 6 to 8 years, and it is relevant to note that our Resolved SLI group would not have filled the criteria for language impairment at this stage. Figure 2 shows the profile of the dyslexic group against that of those with preschool language impairment at four years (i.e., pooling data from the Resolved and Persistent SLI groups). When viewed in this way, the profiles of the two groups are strikingly similar; while the adolescents with dyslexia had more significant spelling problems and better developed reading comprehension, both groups showed deficits in phonological awareness and in the use of phonological reading and spelling strategies.

These findings provide some confirmation for the hypothesis posed above. Therefore, dyslexic and SLI children carry the same risk of dyslexia, namely phonological deficits. It seems, however, that dyslexic children use higher-order language skills as a compensatory resource (as revealed by their superior read-

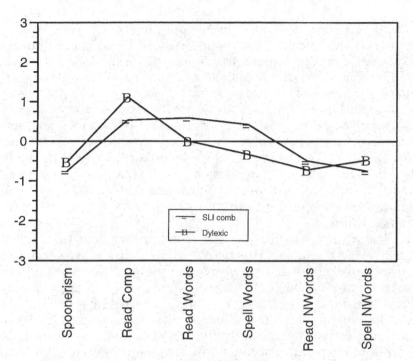

Figure 2.   *Performance of dyslexic children relative to the whole*
sample of adolescents who had a language impairment at
4 years (SLI combined).

ing comprehension). A consequence of their greater reliance on
context is that they develop less well-specified orthographic
representations than those who rely less on top-down processing to learn to read, such as language-impaired children.

When sampling differences are taken into consideration, it is
clear that the present findings align well with those of Kamhi
and Catts (1986) who found that dyslexic children and those
with persisting language impairments both performed poorly
on phonological processing tasks and in nonword reading.
However, the superior performance of the group with Resolved
SLI confirms the view that the age at which oral language impairments resolve is an important predictor of prognosis.

A limitation of the present study was that the numbers of
children classified into the three clinical groups were small.
Indeed, the results differ somewhat from those language-
impaired children from whom we selected the present groups
(Stothard et al. 1998). The lower statistical power in the present
study means that between–group performance differences frequently failed to reach conventional levels of significance

although there were distinct trends pointing to nonword reading and spelling deficits in those with Resolved SLI. These findings point to diagnostic issues surrounding the definition of dyslexia and lead us to be cautious about our interpretation. We suggest that the concept of a dyslexic spectrum may be one with considerable clinical utility that circumvents the issue of fuzzy category boundaries. We propose that a dimension of phonological processing impairments is at the core of this spectrum (cf. Stanovich and Siegel 1994). The impact of these impairments will be modified both by language processing resources outside of the phonological domain (Nation and Snowling 1998), more general cognitive resources such as processing speed, and aspects of attention control.

The findings of the present study make clear that, when considering the factors that place a child at risk of dyslexia, it is important to take a developmental view of the demands of learning to read. In particular, it is necessary to consider how language difficulties impact on children's reading development at different stages, placing them at differential risk of dyslexia. Learning to read is an interactive process that draws not only on phonology, but also on other language resources as well (Plaut et al. 1996). As others have argued, language impairment places a child at risk of reading failure, but a dyslexic outcome is not the only scenario for children from this population. An interaction of their language strengths and weaknesses will determine their outcome, which will be more favorable in the context of appropriate intervention (Snowling 1996).

ACKNOWLEDGMENTS

This study was carried out with support from Wellcome grant 040195/Z/93/A to the second author. Ian Walker was supported by a Wellcome Vacation scholarship. We thank Sue Stothard and Dorothy Bishop for help at various stages in the research and Janice Brown, who assisted in data collection supported by a vacation award from the Nuffield Foundation.

Address correspondence to: Margaret J. Snowling, Department of Psychology, University of York, York YO10 5DD (mjs19@york.ac.uk); Dr. Nata Goulandris, Department of Human Communication Science, University College London, (a.goulandris@ucl.ac.uk); Dr. Ian Walker, Max Planck Institute of Cognitive Neuroscience (MEG group), D-04828 Bennewitz, Germany (walker@cns.mpg.de).

References

American Psychiatric Association. 1994. *Diagnostic and Statistical Manual of Mental Disorders IV*. Washington, DC: American Psychiatric Association.

Aram, D., Ekelman, B., and Nation, J. 1984. Preschoolers with language disorders: 10 years later. *Journal of Speech and Hearing Research* 27:232–44.

Bishop, D. V. M. 1997. *Uncommon Understanding*. Hove: Psychology Press.

Bishop, D. V. M., and Edmundson, A. 1987. Language impaired 4-year-olds: Distinguishing transient from persistent impairment. *Journal of Speech and Hearing Disorders* 52:156–73.

Bishop, D. V. M., and Leonard, L. C. 2000. *Speech and Language Impairments: From Research to Practice*. Hove: Psychology Press.

Bishop, D. V. M., North, T., and Donlan, C. 1996. Nonword repetition as a behavioural marker for inherited language impairment: Evidence from a twin study. *Journal of Child Psychology and Psychiatry* 37:391–403.

Byrne, B., Fielding-Barnsley, R., Ashley, L., and Larsen, K. 1997. Assessing the child's and the environment's contribution to reading acquisition: What we know and what we don't know. In *Foundations of Reading Acquisition and Dyslexia: Implications for Early Intervention*, B. Blachman, ed. Mahwah, NJ: Lawrence Erlbaum Associates.

Catts, H. W. 1989. Defining dyslexia as a developmental language disorder. *Annals of Dyslexia* 39:50–64.

Catts, H. W. 1993. The relationship between speech language and reading disabilities. *Journal of Speech and Hearing Research* 36:948–58.

Catts, H. W. 1996. Defining dyslexia as a developmental language disorder: An expanded view. *Topics in Language Disorders* 16(2):14–29.

Dunn, L. M., Dunn, L. M., Whetton, C., and Pintilie, D. 1982. *British Picture Vocabulary Scale*. Windsor, England: NFER-Nelson.

Gathercole, S. E., Willis, C., Baddeley, A. D., and Emslie, H. 1994. The children's test of nonword repetition: A test of phonological working memory. *Memory* 2:103–27.

Kamhi, A. G., and Catts, H. W. 1986. Toward an understanding of developmental language and reading disorders. *Journal of Speech and Hearing Disorders* 5:337–47.

Leonard, L., Sabbatini, L., Leonard, J., and Volterra, V. 1987. Specific language impairment in children: A cross-linguistic study. *Brain and Language* 32:233–52.

McKenna, R., and Warrington, E. K. 1983. *Graded Naming Test*. Windsor, England: NFER-Nelson.

Nation, K., and Snowling, M. J. 1998. Individual differences in contextual facilitation: Evidence from dyslexia and poor reading comprehension. *Child Development* 69:996–1011.

Perin, D. 1983. Phonemic segmentation and spelling. *British Journal of Psychology* 74:245–57.

Plaut, D. C., McClelland, J. L., Seidenberg, M. S., and Patterson, K. 1996. Understanding normal and impaired word reading: Computational principles in quasi-regular domains. *Psychological Review* 103:56–115.

Rack, J., Snowling, M., and Olson, R. 1992. The non-word reading deficit in dyslexia: A review. *Reading Research Quarterly* 27:28–53.

Rutter, M., and Yule, W. 1975. The concept of specific reading retardation. *Journal of Child Psychology and Psychiatry* 16:181–97.

Scarborough, H. 1990. Very early language deficits in dyslexic children. *Child Development* 61:1728–43.

Scarborough, H., and Dobrich, W. 1990. Development of children with early language delay. *Journal of Speech and Hearing Research* 33:70–83.

Semel, E., Wiig, E. K., and Secord, W. 1986. *The Clinical Evaluation of Language Fundamentals-Revised*. New York: The Psychological Corporation.

Share, D. 1995. Phonological recoding and self-teaching: Sine qua non of reading acquisition. *Cognition* 55:151–218.

Shaywitz, S. E., Escobar, M. D., Shaywitz, B. A., Fletcher, J. M., and Makugh, R. 1992. Evidence that dyslexia may represent the lower tail of a normal distribution of reading ability. *New England Journal of Medicine* 326:145–50.

Snowling, M. J. 1991. Developmental reading disorders. *Journal of Child Psychology and Psychiatry* 32:49–78.

Snowling, M. J. 1996. Annotation: Contemporary approaches to the teaching of reading. *Journal of Child Psychology and Psychiatry* 37:139–48.

Snowling, M. J. 2000. Language and literacy skills. Who is at risk and why? In *Speech and Language Impairments: From Research to Practice*, D. V. M. Bishop and L. C. Leonard, eds. Hove: Psychology Press.

Snowling, M. J., Bishop, D. V. M., and Stothard, S. E. 2000. Is pre-school language impairment a risk factor for dyslexia in adolescence? *Journal of Child Psychology and Psychiatry 41*, 587–600.

Snowling, M. J., Goulandris, N., and Defty, N. 1996. A longitudinal study of reading development in dyslexic children. *Journal of Educational Psychology* 88(40):653–69.

Snowling, M. J., Stothard, S. E., and MacLean, J. 1996. *Graded Nonword Reading Test*. Bury St. Edmunds, England: Thames Valley Test Company.

Snowling, M., Van Wagtendonk, B., and Stafford, C. 1988. Object naming deficits in developmental dyslexia. *Journal of Research in Reading* 11(2):67–85.

Stackhouse, J., and Wells, B. 1997. *Children's Speech and Literacy Difficulties*. London: Whurr Publishers.

Stanovich, K. E., and Siegel, L. S. 1994. The phenotypic performance profile of reading-disabled children: A regression-based test of the phonological-core variable-difference model. *Journal of Educational Psychology* 86:24–53.

Stothard, S. E., Snowling, M. J., Bishop, D. V. M., Chipchase, B., and Kaplan, C. 1998. Language impaired pre-schoolers: A follow-up in adolescence. *Journal of Speech, Hearing and Language Research* 41:407–18.

Tabachnick, G., and Fidell, L. 1996. *Using Multivariate Statistics* (3rd ed.). New York: Harper Collins College Publishers.

Tallal, P., Ross, R., and Curtiss, S. 1989. Family aggregation in specific language impairment. *Journal of Speech, Hearing and Language Research* 27:987–98.

Van der Lely, H., and Stollwerk, L. 1996. A grammatical specific language impairment in children. An autosomal dominant inheritance? *Brain and Language* 52:484–504.

Wechsler, D. 1992. *Wechsler Intelligence Scale for Children - Third Edition*. UK. New York: Psychological Corporation.

Wechsler D. 1993. *The Wechsler Objective Reading Dimensions (WORD)*. New York: Psychological Corporation.

Wimmer, H., Mayringer, H., and Landerl, K. 1998. Poor reading: A deficit in skill-automatization or a phonological deficit? *Scientific Studies of Reading* 2:321–40.

Wolf, M., and Bowers, P. G. 1999. The double deficit hypothesis for developmental dyslexia. *Journal of Educational Psychology* 91:154–68.

PART IV
Reading and
Foreign Language Learning

In June 1999, the British Dyslexia Association (BDA), in cooperation with IDA and the European Dyslexia Association, held a conference on bilingualism, multilingualism, and dyslexia, including the study of modern foreign languages. For the first time educators from around the world gathered together to examine thorny questions about the effects of language problems in the native tongue on learning a second or third language, similarities and differences between languages and their effect on at-risk learners, and crosslinguistic transfer of linguistic rules. Part IV presents three views on dyslexia and learning a foreign language: the perspective of researchers on bilingualism; that of an adult dyslexic who struggled to learn French; and a case study report of two students with characteristics of hyperlexia who studied a foreign language.

In the first article, Geva and her colleagues report on dyslexia among children for whom English is a second (foreign) language (ESL). They examine risk factors for reading difficulties over two years in ESL children in comparison to children for whom English is their first language. Their results indicate the importance of phonological awareness and rapid naming for bilingual learners, and support research findings on children's learning to read their first language.

The second article by Charlann Simon provides a personal perspective on learning a foreign language, that of a speech-language specialist who has training in English as a Second Language and is herself dyslexic. Simon describes her process of learning French as a dyslexic from both professional and personal perspectives. She provides useful tips to teachers of foreign languages, including the advice that teachers be flexible in their expectations and help students to identify their language strengths. The author urges teachers to structure the foreign language for dyslexics and to help them understand the task at hand by directly teaching metacognitive strategies.

In the third article, Sparks and Artzer present the first study of its kind on hyperlexia and foreign languages. They provide an in-depth case study of two adolescents whose progress the first author has been following since the students were in grade school. Both students were reading words accurately before the age of five. One student meets the accepted criteria for hyperlexia; the other presents some hyperlexic behaviors. Common to both, however, is unusual strength in reading words accurately early in life. The authors make a case for their conclusion that word recognition extends across alphabetic orthographies (i.e., the students also exhibited strengths in word recognition and relative weaknesses in comprehension in Spanish).

The articles add to a growing body of literature on the relationship between native and foreign language learning in relation to individuals with dyslexia.

Understanding Individual Differences in Word Recognition Skills of ESL Children

Esther Geva

Zhoreh Yaghoub-Zadeh

Barbara Schuster

University of Toronto
Toronto, Ontario, Canada

This paper focuses on the extent to which the development of ESL (English as a Second Language) word recognition skills mimics similar trajectories in same-aged EL1 (English as a First Language) children, and the extent to which phonological processing skills and rapid naming can be used to predict word recognition performance in ESL children. Two cohorts of Grade 1 ESL and EL1 primary-level children were followed for two consecutive years. Results indicated that vocabulary knowledge, a measure of language proficiency, and nonverbal intelligence were not significant predictors of word recognition in either group. Yet, by considering individual differences in phonological awareness and rapid naming, it was possible to predict substantial amounts of variance on word recognition performance six months and one year later in both language groups. Commonality analyses indicated that phonological awareness and rapid naming contributed unique variance to word recognition performance. Moreover, the profiles of not at-risk children in the EL1 and ESL groups were similar on all but the oral language measure, where EL1 children had the advantage. In addition, EL1 and ESL profiles of children who had word-recognition difficulty were similar, with low performance on rapid naming and phonological

Annals of Dyslexia, Vol. 50, 2000
ISSN 0736-9387

awareness. Results indicate that these measures are reliable indicators of potential reading disability among ESL children.

EDUCATIONAL ISSUES IN THE ASSESSMENT OF READING DISABILITIES AMONG IMMIGRANT ESL CHILDREN

There is a growing concern over the ability of the educational system to meet the needs of the increasingly diverse multiethnic, multilingual classroom. Prominent among these needs is the acquisition of literacy skills. In recent years, researchers have begun to challenge simplistic notions about the development of English as a Second Language (ESL)[1] literacy skills, including the notion that second language (L2) oral proficiency can be used as a chief index of L2 reading. An injudicious adoption of first language (L1) based reading models to explain the development of ESL reading has also been questioned, as has the argument that accurate assessment of reading difficulties among L2 learners cannot be achieved without evaluating performance in the L1, or without first ensuring adequate L2 proficiency.

In response to the criticism that placement in special education is often related to socioeconomic, linguistic, and cultural factors rather than to psychoeducational factors (Cummins 1991; Ogbu 1978; Ortiz and Ramirez 1989), and a growing awareness that educational difficulties may reflect normal linguistic and acculturation trajectories, well-intentioned professionals and school officials have avoided diagnosing ESL learners as LD for a number of years. One positive outcome of this growing sensitivity has been the development of alternative, culturally sensitive assessment procedures (e.g., Campione 1989; Cole 1996; Dao 1991; Duran, 1989; Figueroa 1989; Gavillan-Torres 1983; Oller and Damico 1990; Feuerstein 1979) and a growing awareness that assessment in the child's L1 may be more accurate and informative. Assessment in the L1 is, however, often not feasible because of a lack of trained professionals and appropriate assessment tools (Geva 2000a; Sattler 1992). Moreover, with time,

---

[1] The term ESL is used in Canada to refer to individuals whose L1 is not English, who live in an English-speaking environment, and gradually develop their English oral and written language proficiency. The term L2 may be used interchangeably with the term ESL. The term bilingual is used in this paper to refer to children who concurrently develop their oral and literacy skills in two languages.

immigrant children begin to lose their L1 proficiency. As a result, even when assessment tools and trained professionals are available, the L1 norms are not useful as benchmarks for assessment and evaluation.

As is the case with EL1 (English as a First Language) learners, some ESL learners may read with difficulty, not because they have not gained sufficient ESL proficiency, but because they have problems with decoding skills. Yet there is a dearth of research on literacy acquisition in language minority children (August and Hakuta 1997). In particular, there is little systematic research on normal and delayed development of word recognition skills in ESL children. A controversial area in reading research and practice concerns the extent to which ESL and minority children can be successful in acquiring reading skills for the first time in a second language in the absence of reading skills in the L1 (Fitzgerald 1995; Snow, Burns, and Griffin 1998). At this point, there is also very little solid research evidence concerning the belief that instruction designed to ensure the attainment of some (unspecified) level of L2 oral language proficiency should precede the introduction of instruction designed to teach various reading skills in the L2 (Fitzgerald 1995).

There is some research, however, that pertains to the development of basic reading skills in bilingual children (e.g., Comeau et al. 1999; Durgunoglu, Nagy, and Hancin-Bhatt 1993; Geva and Siegel 2000; Geva and Wade-Woolley 1998; Geva, Wade-Woolley, and Shany 1993, 1997; Gholamain and Geva 1999). This research has shown that young school children can learn to decode and spell words without apparent difficulty, even when their oral L2 proficiency is still developing. This research suggests that normally achieving children should not experience persistent difficulties in acquiring basic reading skills. Furthermore, like L1 children, some L2 learners may have a specific learning disability involving word recognition skills, and the common practice of delaying assessment and remediation for a number of years until language proficiency develops may lead to cumulative deprivation. It is necessary to develop ways of minimizing overidentification and underidentification of ESL learners who also may be at-risk of being reading disabled. To achieve this, it is first necessary to identify the developmental trajectories associated with various reading components in ESL learners. It is also necessary to study the correlates and precursors of early development of basic reading skills among ESL children and to examine the extent to which the development of basic word recognition skills in ESL children is bootstrapped to ESL oral proficiency and to underlying cognitive-linguistic processes.

LINGUISTIC-COGNITIVE COMPONENT PROCESSES AND READING DEVELOPMENT IN EL1 AND ESL CHILDREN

Phonological awareness. An extensive body of research literature on L1 reading skills development has shown that learning to read requires mastering the system by which print encodes oral language (Adams 1990). This entails established letter-name knowledge (Chall 1996; Ehri 1991) and various phonological processing skills (Adams 1990; Wagner, Torgesen and Rashotte 1994). There is consensus among researchers concerned with the development of reading skills in Ll that phonological awareness is related to the onset of reading skills and the ability of beginning readers to break the orthographic code (e.g., Adams 1990; Ehri 1991; Liberman, Shankweiler, and Liberman 1989; Stanovich 1992; Wagner and Torgesen 1987). Various aspects of phonological processing measured prior to the onset of formal reading instruction appear to be good predictors of later reading achievement (e.g., Bradley and Bryant 1985; Gough, Juel, and Griffith, 1992; Scarborough 1990; Tunmer, Herriman, and Nesdale 1988; Vellutino and Scanlon 1987). Deficits in the representation, retrieval, or analysis of phonological information are associated with persistent problems in the acquisition of word identification and decoding skills (e.g., Share et al. 1984; Stanovich 1992). In addition, there is reasonable agreement among researchers that over time the relationships between phonemic skills and reading are mutually enhancing (e.g., Goswami and Bryant 1990; Morais, Alegria, and Content 1987; Wagner et al. 1994).

Of the various aspects of phonological processing skills studied in the L1-based research literature, only one aspect—phonological awareness—has received considerable attention in the research on L2 young learners. A handful of studies focusing on normally achieving bilingual children (e.g., Bruck and Genesee 1995; Cisero and Royer 1995; Comeau et al. 1999; Durgunoglu, Hancin-Bhatt, and Nagy 1993; Geva and Wade-Woolley 1998; Geva, Wade-Woolley and Shany 1993; Wade-Woolley, and Siegel 1997) have demonstrated that phonological awareness skills can transfer cross-linguistically, and predict word recognition and spelling development in L1 and L2. Some of these studies (e.g., Comeau et al. 1999; Durgunoglu, Nagy, and Hancin-Bhatt 1993;

Geva and Siegel 2000; Gholamain and Geva 1999) have shown that general linguistic proficiency in the L2 was only marginally useful in predicting word recognition and decoding skills even though L2 oral proficiency has been shown to be important in predicting L2 reading comprehension (Geva and Ryan 1993; Verhoeven 1994, in press).

These research findings suggest that phonological awareness might be a good predictor of the development of word recognition skills in ESL children who are developing concurrently their oral and written skills in a language other than their home language (Chall 1996; Snow, Burns, and Griffin 1998). Moreover, poor phonological awareness may be indicative of reading disability among ESL children as well. To date, this question has not been studied systematically in the context of ESL learners. Available research evidence on L1–L2 transfer would suggest that performance on phonological awareness tasks in L1 and L2 is positively correlated. From a theoretical perspective, the logic is that what transfers between L1 and L2 (as shown by Comeau et al. 1999; Geva 2000b) is the child's growing understanding that words can be divided into constituents that can be manipulated in various ways through deletion, transposition, and reassembly. This awareness does not have to be learned separately in each language although certain constituents may be more difficult to manipulate because of negative transfer from L1 (Fowler 1991; Geva, Wade-Woolley, and Shany 1993; Wang and Geva 1999). This discussion suggests that it should be possible to measure reliably phonological awareness in ESL children, that phonological awareness in ESL learners is related to word recognition skills, and that it will be predictive of reading disability among ESL learners as well.

Phonological memory.   There is no general consensus among researchers as to whether or not phonological memory tasks have value in predicting individual differences in reading skills, apart from that attributed to phonological awareness. In a series of longitudinal studies, Wagner and Torgesen and their colleagues (e.g., Torgesen, Wagner, and Rashotte 1994; Wagner, Torgesen, and Rashotte 1994; Wagner et al. 1997) conclude that while both phonological memory and phonological awareness appear to be tapping a common underlying phonological processing component, only phonological awareness explains unique variance in word-level reading. Gottardo, Stanovich, and Siegel (1996) found that phonological memory contributed only a small proportion of variance to word recognition, although it explained a considerable amount in reading comprehension. On the whole, the L1-based research evidence suggests that phonological memory and phonological awareness tap a common phonological ability. Establishing whether phonological memory and phonological awareness are similarly associated with word recognition skills in L1 and L2 learners is critical to an understanding of the similarities and differences between reading skills in EL1 and ESL children.

Only a handful of researchers have examined the role of phonological memory in children learning to read in an L2. These studies, all concerned with bilingual children (e.g. Geva and Siegel 2000; Geva and Ryan 1993; Gholamain and Geva 1999), show that short-term verbal memory measures such as digit span and lexical repetition predict individual differences in word recognition and reading comprehension. These studies also suggest that individual differences in phonological memory can predict performance cross-linguistically.

It may be reasonable to hypothesize that individual differences in phonological short-term memory would be predictive of individual differences in word recognition skills of ESL learners, but it is not clear whether their contribution would be unique or whether phonological memory and phonological awareness tap a common phonological ability.

Naming speed.   Poor readers can be distinguished from good readers in that they have difficulty with naming and labeling objects. This difficulty has been noted when the task involves serial naming or uses a discrete item paradigm (Fawcett and Nicolson 1994). Researchers such as Denckla and Rudel (1976) and Wolf and Obregon (1992) have shown that speed of naming objects, colors, and letters differentiated good and poor readers using a task called Rapid Automatized Naming, or RAN.

There is research evidence that the relationship between RAN and word reading decreases with age for normally achieving children (Wagner et al. 1997; Walsh, Price, and Gillingham 1988; Wolf 1991). Korhonen (1995) reported that slow naming persists in children with reading disabilities. In related research, Manis et al. (1996) showed that the relationship between RAN and reading was significant only for poor readers, not for good readers. They argue that because good readers are more likely to have automatized word recognition skills, the association of word recognition and naming speed is lower in this group than among the poor readers.

Although general findings indicate that poor readers have a deficit in naming speed, there is disagreement among researchers as to the extent to which rapid automatized naming is an aspect of phonological processing or is distinct from phonological processes. Researchers working within the phonological core deficit framework characterize poor readers as having deficits in various aspects of phonological processing such as phonological awareness, phonological coding in working memory, and in the retrieval of phonological codes from long-term memory (e.g., Wagner and Torgesen 1987; Wagner, Torgesen, and Rashotte 1994; Wagner et al. 1997). They argue that the deficit in rapid naming in poor readers reflects an inability to retrieve phonological codes from a long-term store. Researchers such as Bowers and Wolf and their colleagues (e.g., Bowers and Wolf 1993; Bowers 1995; Felton et al. 1987; Wolf and Bowers 1999) acknowledge the importance of phonological processes in word recognition but argue that slow naming speed is also an important characteristic of some poor readers, and that this deficit does not arise from deficient phonological processing. The latter group of researchers has proposed the "double deficit hypothesis," according to which, some readers are poor at phonological processing, others are primarily poor in naming speed, and some have a deficit in phonological processing as well as in naming speed. Bowers and Wolf (1993) maintain (a) that rapid automatized naming tasks measure a core deficit that is distinct from phonological processing; (b) that the deficit in naming reflects a dysfunction in the precise timing mechanism necessary for establishing unitized orthographic and phonological codes; and (c) that it reflects problems in accessing phonological codes from visual input.

Wagner et al. (1997) explain that with increasing skill and practice, beginner readers become more fluent and their word recognition skills become automatized, resulting in a decrease in variability in naming speed, and, therefore, in a decrease in the role of rapid automatized naming in explaining variance on word recognition. This explanation is highly relevant for the study of underlying cognitive processes driving the development of word recognition skills in the L2. For example, evidence from adult-based research on lexical decision suggests that even if they are as accurate as their L1 counterparts, adult L2 learners are not as fast (Segalowitz and Hebert 1990; Segalowitz, Poulsen, and Komeda, 1991). One study of research on ESL graduate students included rapid naming (Nassajizavareh and Geva 1999) and showed that it was a significant predictor of accurate word recognition, pseudoword decoding, and reading comprehension. Another study involving bilingual Farsi-English primary-level children (Gholamain and Geva 1999) showed that rapid naming predicted accurate word and pseudoword reading cross-linguistically.

To date, no studies have focused on the extent to which rapid automatized naming predicts word-based reading skills in ESL children. Based on the notion of L1–L2 transfer at the level of underlying cognitive-linguistic skills, it is reasonable to hypothesize that two processes may compound the role of rapid naming in L2. First, L2 learners are likely to be slower than L1 learners in naming items with which they are familiar because being L2 means that lexical access processes are slower (Segalowitz, Poulsen, and Komeda 1991; Wade-Woolley and Geva 1999). At the same time, an individual differences perspective suggests that some ESL learners may be slower while others may be faster. These differences may relate less closely to differences in language proficiency and more closely to underlying differences in the ability to access and activate phonological codes accurately and efficiently. This analysis led us to hypothesize that rapid naming would be a good predictor of accurate word recognition among ESL children as it is for EL1 children.

We also wished to examine whether ESL learners would improve their performance over time. This hypothesis naturally follows the notion that with schooling and increased automaticity in word recognition, rapid naming in ESL children would become more automatized. Concomitantly, it would seem reasonable to hypothesize that even if one detected an increase in naming speed in the EL1 group, it would not be dramatic since the EL1 children would be accessing codes in their first language.

In addition to the research questions raised above, we also wished to contribute to the debate about the extent to which rapid naming primarily taps a deficit in the ability to retrieve phonological codes from a long-term store, or whether it is primarily an index of difficulties in the precise timing mechanism necessary for establishing unitized orthographic codes. To evaluate these alternatives, one must examine the extent to which naming speed and phonological processes are independent of one another in predicting word recognition skills.

The objectives of the research reported here were threefold:

1. to examine the extent to which the development of ESL word recognition skills mimics the development of similar trajectories in same-aged EL1 children;
2. to determine the extent to which, over and above the role of language proficiency, various aspects of phonological processing skills (e.g., phonological memory,

phonological awareness) and rapid naming predict individual differences in word recognition; and

3. to examine, from a developmental perspective, the utility of these underlying skills in predicting EL1 and ESL word recognition skills over time.

METHOD

SAMPLE

ESL and EL1 participants were drawn from 10 public schools in three multiethnic areas of metropolitan Toronto. Altogether, children came from 41 classes. In these schools, one finds in the same classroom immigrant children who come from a variety of ethnic and linguistic backgrounds. Our sample consisted of immigrant children from three ethnic groups: South Asian, Chinese, and children drawn from the same schools who were born in Canada and spoke English as their first language (EL1). The South Asian group consisted of children from Punjabi, Gujerati, Hindi, Urdu, and Tamil backgrounds. The Chinese group consisted of children from Mandarin or Cantonese backgrounds. The majority of children from the South Asian backgrounds attended schools in two districts, and the majority of children from the Chinese backgrounds attended schools in the third district. Children in the ESL group came to Grade 1 with varying levels of ESL proficiency. Most children in the Chinese group attended Chinese heritage classes on the weekend.[2] There were two cohorts in the sample, as children were recruited in the same schools in two consecutive years. Of the total EL1 sample, 56 percent of the children were in Cohort 1 and 44 percent in Cohort 2. Of the total ESL sample, 45 percent were in Cohort 1 and 55 percent in Cohort 2.

At the onset of the project, the ESL group consisted of 248 children (54 percent females and 46 percent males). The EL1 group consisted of 100 children (61.5 percent females and 38.5 percent males). The mean age of the ESL group at Time 1 (spring of Grade 1) was 81 months, and the mean age of the EL1

---

[2] The two-hour heritage language programs take place once a week, outside school. Attendance in heritage classes is not compulsory. In such programs, children may be exposed to some instruction in the L1 as well as to a curriculum intended to maintain children's familiarity with their culture of origin. Teachers are not necessarily qualified to teach in regular schools. Often, these classes take place in places of worship.

group at Time 1 was 83 months. The ages ranged from 75 to 91 months in both the EL1 and ESL groups. Only children with parental consent participated in the study. Consent forms were sent out in English to the EL1 children, and in the respective home languages and English to the families of the ESL children. As is the case in any longitudinal study, there was attrition in the sample. By Time 3 (spring of Grade 2), there were 70 participants in the EL1 group and 200 participants in the ESL group.

It was not possible to interview parents about home literacy and the extent to which the native language was used at home due to language barriers, budgetary constraints, and reluctance by the school districts to allow access to parents. Information about children's ethnic and linguistic background was established through school records. This information was cross-validated during interviews with classroom teachers. Children who were recent newcomers and had not lived in an English-speaking country for at least four months at the onset of Grade 1 were not included in the sample. This precaution was taken to ascertain that children who were included had exposure to the rudiments of language and literacy instruction.

In English-speaking Canada, school-aged children who are recent arrivals from a non-English-speaking country typically attend school-based ESL classes for up to two years. In the school districts where the study was conducted, ESL instruction typically occurs in daily, 30- to 40-minute sessions with groups of three to five children. All have similar levels of language proficiency, but not necessarily the same L1. Teachers with ESL specialist training conduct these classes. ESL tutoring focuses on the development of English (oral and written) or readiness for literacy skills. Besides the ESL tutoring, new immigrant children attend regular classrooms, where all instruction takes place in English. (French instruction begins in Grade 4.) Classroom teachers provide appropriate adaptations to the curriculum. This ESL support is provided on a withdrawal basis. Before entering Grade 1, the majority of children in the sample (with the exception of newcomers) attended senior kindergarten (SK), a three-hour daily program mandatory for the five to six age group. No ESL programming is available in SK and the focus is on the development of cognitive, language, school readiness, and social skills.

Two-thirds (69 percent) of the 41 teachers involved spoke English as their L1 and almost one-third (31 percent) of the teachers spoke another language. In addition to English, other languages included Portuguese, Gujarati, French, Italian,

Chinese, Korean, Dutch, German, and Urdu. The teaching experience of teachers in participating classes ranged from one to twenty-two years, and 44 percent had an ESL Specialist certificate (that is, they took courses directed at methods for teaching English to ESL children).

The participating teachers used a variety of instructional approaches to teaching reading and writing skills, the role of oral language, and top-down processes in literacy acquisition. In some schools, teachers introduced literacy and enhanced oral language concomitantly (Willows 1998; Cunningham and Allington 1994). In other schools, the focus was more on a "whole language" approach, with less systematic instruction of decoding skills and grapheme-phoneme correspondences.

PREDICTOR MEASURES

Nonverbal intelligence. Children completed the *Matrix Analogies Test* (*MAT*) (Naglieri 1989), a measure of nonverbal intelligence. In this test, children are presented with an illustration of an incomplete visuo-spatial matrix and asked to complete it by locating the missing piece among five or six patterned segments. The test consists of four subtests (pattern completion, reasoning by analogy, serial reasoning, and spatial visualization), each of which consists of 16 matrices. Testing within each subtest is discontinued after four consecutive errors.

Receptive vocabulary. The *Peabody Picture Vocabulary Test-Revised* (*PPVT-R*) (Dunn and Dunn 1981) is a measure of receptive vocabulary. The child is shown four pictures on a page (e.g., "dog," "brush," "chair," and "car") and then asked to point to one item (e.g., "Can you point to the picture of a chair?"). The test consists of 175 words of increasing difficulty. The test is discontinued when the child responds incorrectly to six items in a block of eight questions. PPVT-R has been shown to be a good measure of oral language proficiency in L2 learners, and it correlates positively with other indices of oral language proficiency (Geva and Petrulius-Wright 2000).

Phonological awareness. Phonological awareness was measured with a task adapted from the *Auditory Analysis Task* developed by Rosner and Simon (1971). In this segmentation-deletion task, children had to delete syllables or phonemes and indicate what the resultant word is (e.g., "Say 'meat.' Now say it without the /m/.") Methodological considerations guided us in adapting this task to the ESL population. In particular, it was necessary to minimize the possible confounding of language proficiency with performance on a phonological awareness task. Our primary concern was that many of the original words. or the resultant words on the original *Auditory Analysis Task,* are words not likely to be familiar to young ESL children (e.g., "Say 'stale.' Now say it without the /t/.) The items on the adapted task were all high frequency words, and the resultant words after the child deleted the phoneme or syllable were also high-frequency words. Of the 25 items on the task, four involved syllable deletion and the remainder required phoneme deletion. Four practice items preceded the administration of the test items. Children discontinued the test after five consecutive errors. Scoring involved calculating the total number of items for which the target phonemes or syllables were correctly deleted. The Cronbach α was 0.91 at Time 1 and 0.92 at Time 2.

Phonological memory. Pseudoword repetition tasks are often used to measure phonological memory. The rationale for using a pseudoword-based phonological memory task is that it requires children to repeat phonological strings that do not relate to the English lexicon. In this study, an additional precaution included developing and using a Hebrew pseudoword repetition task. The Hebrew Pseudoword Repetition task is similar in structure to the one developed by Gathercole et al. (1994). However, the task used by Gathercole includes pseudowords that comply with English morphology (Snowling, Chiat, and Hulme 1991). The 22 pseudowords used in the Hebrew phonological memory measure follow Hebrew rules of morphology (e.g., "eklah", "lesharnegolim") and should be challenging to EL1 and ESL children alike. The total number of correctly repeated pseudowords was calculated for each child. The Cronbach α was 0.77 at Time 1 and 0.74 at Time 2.

Rapid automatized naming. The *Rapid Automatized Naming task (RAN),* developed by Denckla and Rudel (1976), was used to measure speed of rapid serial naming. In this continuous naming task, children were asked to name five letters as fast as they could. Each letter appeared 10 times in random order. The child's time (in seconds) to name all the letters on the board was used as the speed measure. Prior to administering the RAN, the child was asked to name each of the five letters in order to ascertain familiarity with the letters. The RAN was not administered to children who could not name all five letters without assistance.

DEPENDENT MEASURES

Word Recognition. Two tasks assessed children's ability to identify accurately words out of context. The Word Recognition subtest of the *Wide Range Achievement Test-Revised (WRAT-R)* (Jastek and Wilkinson 1984) was one measure. In this standardized task, the child is asked to read a list of 42 isolated words. The list starts with simple words (e.g., "cat," "book") and progresses to more difficult and less frequent words (e.g., "horizon," "itinerary"). The test terminates when a child reads incorrectly ten consecutive words. Words on the *WRAT-R*, which is a diagnostic test, become long and difficult very quickly. On the other hand, the 16 items on an experimental word identification task (e.g., "dogs," "teeth," "flying") were all high frequency words. There was no stop procedure for this task, and children had to read all 16 words. The Cronbach α on this task at Time 3 was 0.92. Subsequent data analyses indicated that the two measures were highly correlated at each testing time ($r = 0.84$, $r = 0.83$, and $r = 0.72$ at Time 1, Time 2 and Time 3, respectively in the EL1 sample; $r = 0.88$, $r = 0.86$, and $r = 0.72$ at Time 1, Time 2, and Time 3, respectively, in the ESL sample). Due to these high correlations, we created a new combined index. The Word Identification score (WID) is the sum of the child's scores on the *WRAT-R* and the experimental word recognition task.

PROCEDURES

The research reported here is a component of a larger, multiyear longitudinal project, assessing the development of various components of oral language and literacy skills of ESL children (Geva 2000a). We report on results pertaining to the performance of children on the (WID) task at three points in time: the spring of Grade 1 (Time 1), fall of Grade 2 (Time 2), and spring of Grade 2 (Time 3). The nonverbal intelligence test was measured at Time 3. The phonological awareness and phonological memory tasks, *RAN*, and the *PPVT-R* were measured at Time 1 and Time 2. We examined the role that these cognitive and linguistic skills, measured at Time 1 and Time 2, play in predicting word recognition skills of EL1 and ESL children at the end of Grade 2 (Time 3).

Graduate students in psychology or education tested children individually in a quiet setting. It is important to point out that in order to avoid bias associated with using norms standardized on samples not representative of the ESL sample (i.e., *WRAT-R, PPVT-R*), we based the analyses on raw scores (rather than being converted to percentile or standard scores). At the same time, in order to account for the developmental factor, in all the analyses we treated age (in months) as a covariate.

RESULTS

DEVELOPMENT OF WORD RECOGNITION AND COMPONENT PROCESSES IN EL1 AND ESL CHILDREN

Table I summarizes the EL1 and ESL means and standard deviations of the cognitive, linguistic, and reading measures. Results of t-tests on age and MAT showed that EL1 and ESL students were not significantly different on either index. To examine the effects of language group and development over time on the predictor measures and the dependent measure, we conducted analyses of covariance with repeated measures (ANCOVA) separately for *PPVT-R*, phonological memory, phonological awareness, *RAN*, and WID. Language group (EL1 versus ESL) was the between factor, and time the within (repeated) factor. We covaried age in each of the analyses. Age was a significant covariate only for *PPVT-R* ($p < .05$).

Table I. Means and Standard Deviations (in parentheses) for EL1 and ESL Groups of Dependent and Independent Measures.

	Time 1[a]		Time 2[b]		Time 3[c]	
	EL1	ESL	EL1	ESL	EL1	ESL
	($n = 100$)	($n = 248$)	($n = 77$)	($n = 240$)	($n = 70$)	($n = 200$)
WID	16.63	16.82	20.29	20.27	26.27	26.74
(0-58)	(9.03)	(10.51)	(9.24)	(9.84)	(8.00)	(8.41)
MAT[a]	—	—	—	—	98.57	96.84
(standard score)	—	—	—	—	(9.67)	(12.27)
Age	—	—	88.03	87.26	—	—
(months)	—	—	(3.67)	(3.69)	—	—
PPVT-R	75.71	57.94	80.13	64.29	—	—
(0 - 175)	(13.71)	(17.57)	(13.56)	(15.63)	—	—
PM	13.03	12.10	14.79	12.77	—	—
(0 - 27)	(4.64)	(4.49)	(4.47)	(4.34)	—	—
PA	10.00	9.61	10.62	11.72	—	—
(0 - 25)	(4.26)	(5.08)	(5.05)	(6.09)	—	—
RAN	37.95	57.94	39.66	34.01	—	—
(seconds)	(12.34)	(17.57)	(15.83)	(11.58)	—	—

Note. [a] = Scores at the end of grade one; [b] = Scores at the beginning of grade two; [c] = Scores at the end of grade two; WID = Word Identification Task; MAT = Matrix Analogies Test; PPVT-R = Peabody Picture Vocabulary Test-Revised; PM = Phonological Memory Test; PA = Phonological Awareness Test; RAN = Rapid Automatized Naming

As might be anticipated, the language group main effect (EL1 versus ESL) was significant on *PPVT-R*, $F(1, 227) = 68.58$; $p < .001$, indicating that the EL1 children had better knowledge of English vocabulary than ESL children. The ANCOVAs revealed also that the effect of time was significant for *PPVT-R*, $F(1, 228) = 62.10$, $p < .001$. Finally, the group by time interaction was also significant, $F(1, 228) = 11.42$; $p < .001$. This interaction reflects the fact that the improvement on vocabulary was more pronounced in the ESL group than in the EL1 group.

The ANCOVAs revealed that the language group main effect (EL1 vs. ESL) was significant for phonological memory, $F(1, 177) = 6.53$; $p < .01$, as was the effect of time, $F(1, 178) = 4.97$; $p < .05$. The interaction of group by time was not significant for phonological memory. In other words, performance at a later time was significantly higher when compared to earlier performance in both language groups; and there was an EL1 advantage.

The ANCOVAs revealed that the language group main effect (EL1 versus ESL) was not significant for phonological awareness but the effect of time was significant $F(1, 228) = 24.38$; $p < .001$. The group by time interaction was significant for phonological awareness, $F(1, 228) = 7.57$; $p < .01$. Again this interaction reflects the more pronounced improvement from Time 1 to Time 2 in the ESL group than in the EL1 group.

As for *RAN*, the language group main effect (EL1 versus ESL) was significant, $F(1, 225) = 8.19$; $p < .01$, but the effect of time was not significant. The group by time interaction was significant for *RAN*, $F(1, 226) = 9.31$; $p < .01$. This interaction reflects the fact that there was a substantial EL1 advantage at Time 1. However, by Time 2, the group difference on *RAN* disappeared.

There was no group main effect on word identification. At the same time the ANCOVAs revealed that the effect of time (i.e., Time 1, Time 2, and Time 3) was significant $F(2, 456) = 323.19$; $p < .001$. Post-hoc comparisons showed that in both language groups the improvement from Time 1 to Time 2 and from Time 2 to Time 3 was significant ($p < .001$). Overall, the significant group by time interactions reflected the fact that improvement over time was always more pronounced in the ESL group in the EL1 group.

LONGITUDINAL PREDICTORS OF WORD RECOGNITION IN EL1 AND ESL CHILDREN

To investigate the contribution of predictor variables to performance on the word identification task, we conducted two sets of hierarchical multiple regression analyses separately for the EL1 and ESL groups. In each case, WID at Time 3 was the dependent variable. In one analysis, Time 1 variables were predictors. In the second analysis, Time 2 variables were predictors. This approach enabled us to examine the utility of predicting word recognition at the end of Grade 2 on the basis of performance on the predictor variables one year earlier (i.e., Time 1) and six months earlier (i.e., Time 2). To control for the effects of age and cognitive ability, age in months and Time 3 nonverbal intelligence scores were entered first (Step 1) in each of the analyses. In each analysis, *PPVT-R* was entered in a second step. Phonological memory, phonological awareness, and *RAN* were entered one at a time in subsequent steps.

As can be seen in tables II and III which provide a summary of the regression analyses, neither age nor nonverbal intelligence contributed significantly to the performance on WID. This was true for EL1 and ESL groups alike. *PPVT-R* was not a significant predictor of WID in either language group. Phonological memory explained 15 percent ($p < .05$) of the variance for the EL1 group at Time 1, but was otherwise not signifi-

Table II. Hierarchical Regression Analysis Predicting Word Identification Performance at Time 3 (end of grade 2) in EL1 and ESL Groups, with Vocabulary, Phonological Memory, Phonological Awareness, and Rapid Naming at Time 1 (end of grade 1) as Independent Variables.

Variables	EL1			ESL		
	R^2	ΔR	T	R^2	ΔR	T
Step 1	.15	.15		.10	.10	
Age			−.83			−.33
MAT			1.92			1.38
Step 2						
PPVT-R	.19	.04	.24	.16	.06	1.08
Step 3						
PM	.34	.15	3.20**	.21	.05	.95
Step 4						
PA	.45	.11	2.16*	.42	.37	4.77***
Step 5						
RAN	.68	.23	−5.80***	.58	.16	−8.75***

Note. MAT = Matrix Analogies Test; PPVT-R = Peabody Picture Vocabulary Test-Revised; PM = Phonological Memory Test; PA = Phonological Awareness Test; RAN = Rapid Automatized Naming

* $p < .05$, ** $p < 01$, *** $p < .001$

Table III. Hierarchical Regression Analysis Predicting Word Identification Performance at Time 3 (end of grade 2) in EL1 and ESL Groups, with Vocabulary, Phonological Memory, Phonological Awareness, and Rapid Naming at Time 2 (beginning of grade 2) as Independent Variables.

Variables	EL1			ESL		
	R^2	ΔR	T	R^2	ΔR	T
Step 1	.12	.12	—	.13	.13	—
Age			.17			-.08
MAT			.45			.90
Step 2						
PPVT-R	.17	.05	.75	.17	.04	1.41
Step 3						
PM	.26	.09	1.17	.19	.02	1.16
Step 4						
PA	.43	.17	3.65***	.50	.31	9.39***
Step 5						
RAN	.59	.16	-4.99***	.63	.13	-7.87***

Note. MAT = Matrix Analogies Test; PPVT-R = Peabody Picture Vocabulary Test-Revised; PM = Phonological Memory Test; PA = Phonological Awareness Test; RAN = Rapid Automatized Naming

* $p < .05$, **$p < 01$, ***$p < .001$

cant. Both phonological awareness and *RAN* were significant contributors at Time 1 and Time 2 for both EL1 and ESL groups. That is, regardless of language group, performance on phonological awareness and *RAN* at the end of Grade 1 and at the beginning of Grade 2 predicted significantly individual differences in WID at the end of Grade 2. Altogether, performance at Time 1 and Time 2 on phonological awareness and *RAN* explained significantly 34 percent and 33 percent, respectively, of the variance on WID at Time 3 in the EL1 group. In the ESL group, performance on the phonological awareness and *RAN* at Time 1 and Time 2 explained 53 percent and 44 percent of the variance, respectively, on WID at Time 3.

The hierarchical regression analyses indicate whether phonological memory, phonological awareness, and *RAN* are significant predictors of word recognition skills in EL1 and ESL. The purpose of the commonality analysis was to assess the overlapping variances between these three measures in predicting word recognition skills. The procedure of commonality analysis allows for closer examination of the unique and shared variances contributed by a number of independent variables to a predicted outcome measure (see Kerlinger and Pedhazur 1973). For example, in the present context, commonality analysis can help to clarify the proportion of the variance unique to the phonological processing measures, *RAN*, and the amount of variance shared by all possible combinations of these variables. This procedure can help to evaluate the extent to which phonological memory, phonological awareness, and rapid naming are tapping the same underlying phonological processing skill. We carried out this analysis separately for EL1 and ESL groups in order to examine whether the unique variance accounted for by each predictor variable is different in EL1 and ESL learners.

Tables IV and V summarize the unique and shared variances for all predictor variables (after partialling out nonverbal intelligence) for both EL1 and ESL groups. As would have been expected from the regression analyses, *PPVT-R* and phonological memory explained negligible unique variance (less than 1 percent) on WID in either language group at any time. On the other hand, phonological awareness and *RAN* contributed a noticeable proportion of the unique variance to WID in both language groups. Interestingly, the amount of unique variance in WID explained by phonological awareness and *RAN* varied for the EL1 and ESL groups. Compared to the ESL group, *RAN* explained a larger amount of unique variance in word identification scores for EL1 at both Time 1 and Time 2 (Time 1: 19 percent for EL1 versus 12 percent for ESL; Time 2: 23 percent for EL1 versus 16 percent for ESL). The pattern reversed in the case of phonological awareness. The unique variance associated with phonological awareness was higher for the ESL group than the EL1 group at both Time 1 and Time 2 (Time 1: 18% for ESL versus 9 percent for EL1; and Time 2: 8 percent for ESL versus 3 percent for EL1). In sum, both phonological awareness and *RAN* are significant predictors of WID for EL1 and ESL groups at earlier stages of learning to read. However, phonological awareness skills appear to play a more important role for ESL children than *RAN*. In later stages of learning to read, *RAN* appears to account for a larger proportion of the unique variance on WID than phonological awareness in the ESL group. As for shared variances, the largest amount of shared variance was between phonological awareness and *RAN* (EL1: 8 percent at Time 1; 9 percent at Time 2; ESL: 14 percent at both Time 1 and Time 2). The shared variance between *RAN* and phonological memory was meaningful only for EL1 (11 percent at Time 1 and 5 percent at Time 2). As can be noted in tables IV and V, all the other shared variance terms among predictor

Table IV. Commonality Analysis Predicting Word Identification (end of grade 2) Performance in EL1 and ESL subjects, with Oral and Phonological Measures at Time 1 (end of grade one) as Predictor Variables.

| | Predictor Variables | | | | | | | |
| | PPVT-R | | HRP | | PA | | RAN | |
	EL1	ESL	EL1	ESL	EL1	ESL	EL1	ESL
Unique Variance	.000	.003	.002	.020	.027	.080	.229	.160
Variance in Common								
PPVT-R, PM	.001	.003	.001	.003				
PPVT-R, PA	.001	.013			.001	.013		
PPVT-R, RAN	.013	-.002					.013	-.002
PA, PM			.007	.009	.007	.009		
PM, RAN			.109	-.008			.109	-.008
PA, RAN					.077	.137	.077	.137
PPVT-R, PM, PA	-.002	.008	-.002	.008	-.002	.008		
PPVT-R, PM, RAN	-.013	-.001	-.013	-.001			-.013	-.001
PM, PA, RAN			.050	.041	.050	.041	.050	.041
PPVT-R, PA, RAN	.020	.005			.020	.005	.020	.005
PPVT-R, PM, RAN, PA	.002	.020	.002	.020	.002	.020	.002	.020
Total unique + common	.022	.049	.156	.092	.182	.313	.487	.352

Note. PPVT-R = Peabody Picture Vocabulary Test-Revised; PM = Phonological Memory Test; PA = Phonological Awareness Test; RAN = Rapid Automatized Naming

Table V. Commonality Analysis Predicting Word Identification (end of grade 2) Performance in EL1 and ESL subjects, with Oral and Phonological Measures at Time 2 (beginning of grade 2) as Predictor Variables.

| | Predictor Variables | | | | | | | |
| | PPVT-R | | HRP | | PA | | RAN | |
	EL1	ESL	EL1	ESL	EL1	ESL	EL1	ESL
Unique Variance	.004	.004	.009	.006	.087	.175	.186	.116
Variance in Common								
PPVT-R, PM	.003	.002	.003	.002				
PPVT-R, PA	.005	.009			.005	.009		
PPVT-R, RAN	.000	.000					.000	.000
PA, PM			.002	.002	.002	.002		
PM, RAN			.046	.005			.046	.005
PA, RAN					.089	.141	.089	.141
PPVT-R, PM, PA	.003	.004	.003	.004	.003	.004		
PPVT-R, PM, RAN	.008	.003	.008	.003			.008	.003
PM, PA, RAN			.026	.014	.026	.014	.026	.014
PPVT-R, PA, RAN	.004	.009			.004	.009	.004	.009
PPVT-R, PM, RAN, PA	.012	.008	.012	.008	.012	.008	.012	.008
Total unique + common	.039	.039	.109	.044	.228	.362	.371	.296

Note. PPVT-R = Peabody Picture Vocabulary Test-Revised; PM = Phonological Memory Test; PA = Phonological Awareness Test; RAN = Rapid Automatized Naming

variables were extremely low, often explaining less than 1 percent of the variance.

PROFILES OF EL1 AND ESL NORMALLY ACHIEVING AND AT-RISK CHILDREN

This section focuses on an examination of the extent to which the developmental profiles of EL1 and ESL children who are normally achieving or at-risk for reading disability are similar. The at-risk group consisted of children whose scores on the WID at Time 3 were at least one standard deviation below the mean (of the total sample). The normally achieving group consisted of children whose WID scores at Time 3 were at least −.75 standard deviation below the mean.

Figures 1 and 2 illustrate the Z-score profiles of EL1 and ESL groups who were either at-risk or normally achieving. Figure 1 includes predictor variable scores at Time 1 and figure 2 includes predictor variable scores at Time 2. In addition, to facilitate a visual comparison of the profiles, each figure includes the mean nonverbal intelligence Z-scores and the mean WID Z-scores at Time 1, Time 2, and Time 3. The profile of EL1 and ESL groups with no difficulties in word recognition were similar. Likewise, the profiles of EL1 and ESL groups who had difficulties with word recognition skills resembled each other. Both at-risk groups had low phonological awareness scores and were slow on the RAN. Both normally achieving groups had comparable phonological awareness scores and performed within the normal range on the RAN. The nonverbal intelligence means of the at-risk groups were slightly lower than those of the normally achieving groups. Regardless of reading level, scores on the PPVT-R were lower in the ESL groups than in the EL1 groups.

DISCUSSION

In considering the results of the research findings, the first aspect to underscore is that the participants formed two groups: one group of children with English as L1 and another group of children whose mother tongue was not English, but who were gradually improving their proficiency in English. Performance on the PPVT-R confirms information provided by the respective schools about the language status of these children. Moreover,

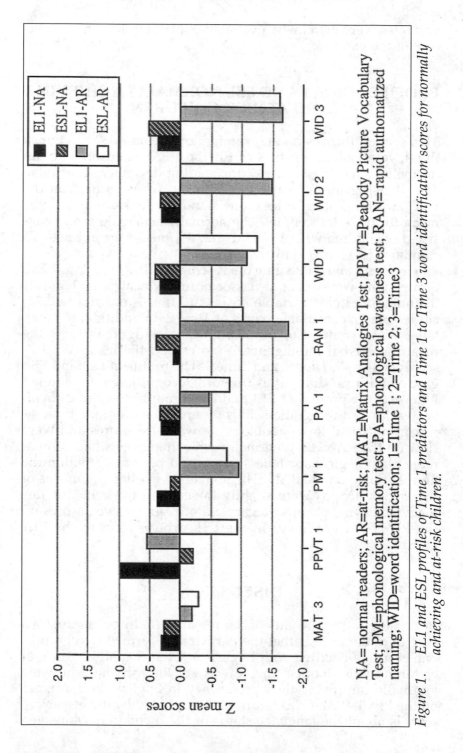

Figure 1. EL1 and ESL profiles of Time 1 predictors and Time 1 to Time 3 word identification scores for normally achieving and at-risk children.

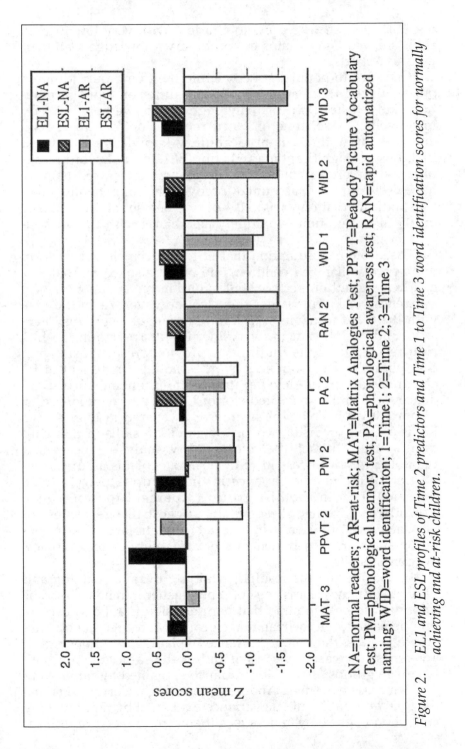

NA=normal readers; AR=at-risk; MAT=Matrix Analogies Test; PPVT=Peabody Picture Vocabulary Test; PM=phonological memory test; PA=phonological awareness test; RAN=rapid automatized naming; WID=word identificaiton; 1=Time1; 2=Time 2; 3=Time 3

Figure 2.   EL1 and ESL profiles of Time 2 predictors and Time 1 to Time 3 word identification scores for normally achieving and at-risk children.

the ESL children who came to Grade 1 with very low English skills showed bigger gains in vocabulary knowledge than their L1 counterparts.

Contrary to popular beliefs, while the two groups differed on language proficiency, they did not differ on word recognition skills. Instead, in each language group, we note a steady improvement over time on word recognition. The regression analyses show that when vocabulary knowledge is entered first, it is not significant in predicting EL1 and ESL word recognition skills once phonological awareness and rapid naming have been taken into account. Moreover, the commonality analyses indicate that only 0.0 to 0.4 of one percent of the variance on word recognition is uniquely associated with the vocabulary measure.

Based on an assumption that ESL children should perform more poorly than EL1 children, one might also expect that EL1 children should outperform ESL children on the phonological awareness task. This is not the case, however. As is the case with the word recognition task in both language groups, there is a steady improvement over time. Results pertaining to EL1 children replicate the findings of previous research showing that phonological awareness is an essential component of L1 children's ability to develop grapheme-phoneme correspondence skills and a good predictor of L1 word recognition skills. Importantly, phonological awareness measured in English, the L2, is a good predictor of word recognition skills in ESL children as well. In fact, the commonality analysis reveals that phonological awareness in ESL learners explains a larger proportion of the unique variance in that group (8 percent to 18 percent) than in the EL1 group (3 percent to 9 percent). Considered together, these results suggest that regardless of oral language proficiency, individual differences in word recognition skills are closely tied to the availability of phonological awareness skills.

In considering the results pertaining to rapid naming and phonological awareness, we note some general trends. First, it is important to bear in mind that both are significant and explain unique variance in each language group. Moreover, in both language groups, the unique variance explained by phonological awareness increases over time, and at the same time, in both language groups, the unique variance explained by rapid naming decreases over time. Another interesting observation is that the total amount of unique variance explained by rapid naming and phonological awareness is rather similar. For example, at

Time 1, the total unique variance of these two measures accounts for about 26 percent of the variance in the EL1 group and 24 percent in the ESL group. At Time 2, the total unique variance of these two measures accounts for about 27 percent of the variance in the EL1 group and about 29 percent in the ESL group. In addition, in both language groups, rapid naming and phonological awareness also share substantial amount of variance. In this respect, then, underlying processes in EL1 and ESL children mirror each other.

However, even though the total unique variance associated with rapid naming and phonological awareness is rather similar across the groups, the relative role played by each of these variables in explaining individual differences in word identification is not identical. Instead, in the ESL group, phonological awareness plays a more important role than it does in the EL1 group. Conversely, rapid naming plays a more important role in EL1 learners than in the ESL group. This observation also is true when we consider the combined effect of the unique and shared variance associated with rapid naming and phonological awareness.

These observations suggest that similar but not completely identical processes underlie the development of word recognition skills in children who are learning to read in their L1, and their classmates who are learning to speak English and read English concurrently. As noted by Chall (1996), children who learn to read and speak English at the same time cannot rely to the same extent on their familiarity with components of the language such as the phonology, vocabulary, and grammatical structures. It is this point that underlies the concern voiced by various educators about the need to allow ESL children to develop their language proficiency before their exposure to reading skills. At the same time, L1–L2 research on transfer of phonological skills and rapid naming and their role in the development of word recognition and spelling of bilingual children (e.g., Comeau et al. 1999; Dorgunoglu, Nagy, and Hancin-Bhatt 1993; Geva, Wade-Wooley and Shany 1993; Gholamain and Geva 1999; Wade-Woolley, and Siegel 1997) suggests that this concern is not fully warranted. From a theoretical perspective, such findings suggest that what drives this transfer is an underlying cognitive factor common to both L1 and L2 (Cummins 1984; Geva and Ryan 1993; Geva 2000b). In line with the available research on bilingual children, the current research results suggest that individual differences in phonological processes and rapid naming are underlying prerequisite skills that drive the development of word recognition skills in primary-level ESL children.

One might ask how these ESL children come to develop their phonological awareness skills. We might consider two complementary explanations, each of which deserves further study. One explanation is that children already possess those skills in their L1 and are able to transfer those skills to the L2, once they have had enough opportunity to begin to learn to speak and read in English, the L2. In addition, it is likely that these skills are, in fact, enhanced in the context of the preschool (SK) program. Even though the current research does not shed additional light on these possibilities, the results indicate that it is possible to assess ESL children's phonological awareness and rapid naming; individual differences on these skills are predictive of later development of word recognition skills in English, the L2.

Moreover, it appears that once the phonological skills are better established, these ESL learners may gradually improve the speed with which they can carry out naming tasks. This is exactly what we note in our research; while there is no change in naming speed in the EL1 group from Time 1 to Time 2, there is a significant increase from Time 1 to Time 2 in the speed with which the ESL group could carry out the letter naming task.

As noted in the introduction, there is some controversy in the research literature with regard to the extent to which rapid automatized naming is an aspect of phonological processing or is distinct from phonological processes. Results of the commonality analysis show that while rapid naming shares variance with phonological awareness, it also accounts for a substantial amount of unique variance in word recognition. This finding suggests that while rapid naming invokes phonological processes, it also invokes a basic naming speed component that is independent of phonological processes (Wolf and Bowers 1999). These findings provide research evidence for the theoretical position taken by Wolf and Bowers and their colleagues, and, at the same time extend it to ESL learners.

It is also interesting to speculate about theoretical underpinnings concerning the differences in the amount of shared variance between rapid naming and phonological awareness in each language group. Recall that this shared variance is much more considerable in the ESL group (14 percent) than it is in the EL1 group (8 percent). We propose that perhaps these EL1-ESL differences reflect the fact that in ESL learners, the effect of underlying processes is more global; that is, the effect of various component processes is less specific. It is possible that with increased language proficiency, these underlying processes gradually become more specialized and domain-specific. This is a hypothesis worth exploring in future research.

The pattern of results involving phonological memory is different from the one noted for phonological awareness. The phonological awareness task can be thought of as a working memory task, as children have to manipulate phonemes and keep track of the product of these manipulations in memory. The present results indicate that while a task with fewer demands on working memory, such as the pseudoword repetition task, is not predictive of word recognition, a phonological awareness task with greater working memory demands is predictive of reading ability among ESL children.

It is clear that by considering individual differences on phonological awareness and rapid naming, it is possible to explain a substantial amount of variance on word recognition in both language groups. Moreover, performance on word recognition skills at the end of Grade 2 can be predicted by performance on these measures at the end of Grade 1 as well as in early Grade 2. In general, then, in spite of their L2 status, normally developing ESL learners should not experience too much difficulty in developing word recognition skills, and the long-term performance on word recognition can be predicted by early performance on rapid naming and phonological awareness in both language groups. These findings have important ramifications for early assessment of at-risk status. There is ample research evidence that implicates these measures in EL1 children. The present study indicates that, in spite of the absence of fully developed proficiency in the L2, it is feasible to use these measures as reliable indicators of potential reading disability among ESL children.

CONCLUSIONS

An emerging model of reading development in L2 learners needs to capture the dynamic interplay between oral language and literacy development. This is important theoretically and clinically. Researchers, classroom teachers, curriculum developers, and clinicians need to better understand what the prerequisite skills for successful literacy development in L2 learners are, as well as the time frame within which it may be feasible to assess these skills.

Results of the present study suggest that (a) phonological awareness and rapid naming can be useful in predicting the development of basic reading skills in ESL children; (b) that notwithstanding children's ESL status, the development of ESL word recognition skills can be understood and predicted by the availability of prerequisite cognitive-linguistic skills; and (c) that individual differences on such prerequisite skills can be indicative of smooth or problematic acquisition of ESL reading skills. It follows that, as with EL1 children, some ESL learners may have a specific learning disability involving word recognition skills. This at-risk status can be identified even when full oral proficiency has not been attained yet, and the well-intentioned common practice of delaying assessment and remediation for a number of years may be overcautious and lead to cumulative deprivation and the withholding of access to remedial interventions. These in turn may result in the emergence of more complex problems over time.

ACKNOWLEDGMENTS

The research reported here was supported by a SSHRC grant # 410--96-0851 and a Block Transfer Grant from the Ontario Ministry of Education to the first author. We wish to thank Barbara Schuster and Robindra Sidhu for their invaluable input throughout this project. We also extend our thanks to the teachers, students, and staff who participated in the project.

Address correspondence to: Esther Geva, Ph.D., Professor, Department of Human Development and Applied Psychology, OISE, University of Toronto, 252 Bloor West, Toronto, Ontario, Canada, M5S 1V6. Email: egeva@oise.utoronto.ca.

References

Adams, M. J. 1990. *Beginning to Read: Thinking and Learning About Print.* London: MIT Press.

August, D., and Hakuta, K. Eds. 1997. *Improving Schooling for Language-Minority Students: A Research Agenda.* Committee on Developing a Research Agenda on the Education of Limited English Proficient and Bilingual Students - Board on Children, Youth and Families. National Academy Press, Washington, DC.

Bowers, P. G. 1995. Tracing symbol naming speed's unique contributions to reading disabilities over time. *Reading and Writing: An Interdisciplinary Journal* 7:189–216.

Bowers, P. G., and Wolf, M. 1993. Theoretical links among naming speed, precise timing mechanisms and orthographic skill in dyslexia. *Reading and Writing: An Interdisciplinary Journal* 5:69–85

Bradley, L., and Bryant, P. E. 1985. *Rhyme and Reason in Reading and Spelling.* Ann Arbor: University of Michigan Press.

Bruck, M., and Genesee, F. 1995. Phonological awareness in young second language learners. *Journal of Child Language* 22:307–27.

Campione, J. C. 1989. Assisted assessment: A taxonomy of approaches and an outline of strengths and weaknesses. *Journal of Learning Disabilities* 22:151–65.

Chall, J. S. 1996. *Stages of Reading Development* (2nd ed.). Orlando, FL: Harcourt Brace College Publishers.

Cisero, C. A., and Royer, J. M. 1995. The development and cross-language transfer of phonological awareness. *Contemporary Educational Psychology* 20:275–303.

Cole, E. 1996. Immigrant and refugee children and families: Supporting a new road traveled. In *Dynamic Assessment for Instruction: From Theory to Application*, ed. M. Luther. Toronto: Captus University Publication.

Comeau, L., Cormier, P., Grandmaison, E., and Lacroix, D. 1999. A longitudinal study of phonological processing skills in children learning to read in a second language. *Journal of Educational Psychology* 91:29–43.

Cummins, J. 1984. *Bilingualism and Special Education: Issues in Assessment and Pedagogy.* England: Multilingual Matters.

Cummins, J. 1991. Language development and academic learning. In *Language, Culture and Cognition*, eds. L. M. Malavé and G. Duquette. Clevedon, England: Multi-cultural Matters.

Cunnigham, P. M., and Allington, R. L. 1994. *Classrooms That Work.* New York: Harper Collins.

Dao, M. 1991. Designing assessment procedures for educationally at-risk southeast Asian-American students. *Journal of Learning Disabilities* 24:594–601.

Denkla, M. B., and Rudel, R. G. 1976. Rapid 'automatized' naming (R. A. N.): Dyslexia differentiated from other learning disabilities. *Neuropsychologia* 14:471–79.

Dunn, L. M., and Dunn, L. M. 1981. *Peabody Picture Vocabulary Test-Revised.* Circle Pines, Minnesota: American Guidance Service.

Duran, R. P. 1989. Assessment and instruction of at-risk Hispanic students. *Exceptional Children* 56:154–58.

Durgunoglu, A. Y., Nagy, W. E., and Hancin-Bhatt, B. J. 1993. Cross-language transfer of phonological awareness. *Journal of Educational Psychology* 85:453–65.

Ehri, L. C. 1991. Learning to read and spell words. In *Learning to Read: Basic Research and Its Implications*, eds. L. Rieben and C. A. Perfetti. Hillsdale, NJ: Lawrence Erlbaum Associates.

Fawcett, A. J., and Nicolson, R. I. 1994. Naming speed in children with dyslexia. *Journal of Learning Disabilities* 27:641–46.

Felton, R. H., Wood, F. B., Brown, I. S., and Campbell, S. K. 1987. Separate verbal memory and naming deficits in attention deficit disorder and reading disability. *Brain and Language* 31:171–84.

Feuerstein, R. 1979. *Dynamic Assessment of Retarded Performance: The Learning Potential Assessment Device, Theory, Instrument, and Techniques.* Baltimore: University Park Press.

Figueroa, R. A. 1989. Psychological testing of linguistic-minority students: Knowledge gaps and regulations. *Exceptional Children* 56:145–52.

Fitzgerald, J. 1995. English-as-a-second-language reading instruction in the United States: A research review. *Journal of Reading Behavior* 27:115–52.

Fowler, A. E. 1991. How early phonological development might set the stage for phoneme awareness. In *Phonological Processes in Literacy*, eds. S. Brady and D. Shankweiler. Hillsdale, NJ: Lawrence Erlbaum Associates.

Gathercole, S. E., Willis, C., Baddeley, A. D., and Emslie, H. 1994. The children's test of nonword repetition: A test of phonological working memory. *Memory* 2:103–27.

Gavillan-Torres, E. 1983. Issues of assessment of limited English proficiency students and of truly disabled children in the United States. In *Bilingualism and Language Disability*, ed. Niklas Miller. San Diego: College Hill Press, Inc.

Geva, E. 2000a. Issues in the assessment of reading disabilities in L2 children - beliefs and research evidence. *Dyslexia*, in press.

Geva, E. 2000b. L1–L2 transfer and orthographic specificity? Evidence from phonological processing and rapid automatized naming in young bilingual readers. Under review.

Geva, E., and Petrulius-Wright, J. 2000. The role of oral language proficiency in the reading development of L1 and L2 primary level children. Under review.

Geva, E., and Ryan, E. B. 1993. Linguistic and cognitive correlates of academic skills in first and second languages. *Language Learning* 43:5–42.

Geva, E., and Siegel, L. 2000. Orthographic and cognitive factors in the concurrent development of basic reading skills in two languages. *Reading and Writing: An Interdisciplinary Journal* 12:1–30.

Geva, E., and Wade-Woolley, L. 1998. Component processes in becoming English-Hebrew biliterate. In *Literacy Development in a Multilingual Context: Cross-cultural Perspectives*, eds. A. Y. Durgunoglu and L. Verhoeven. Mahwah, NJ: Lawrence Erlbaum Associates.

Geva, E., Wade-Woolley, L., and Shany, M. 1993. The concurrent development of spelling and decoding in different orthographies. *Journal of Reading Behavior* 25(4):383–406.

Geva, E., Wade-Woolley, L., and Shany, M. 1997. The development of reading efficiency in first and second language. *Scientific Studies of Reading* 1:119–44.

Gholamain, M., and Geva, E. 1999. The concurrent development of word recognition skills in English and Farsi. *Language Learning* 49:183–217.

Goswami, U., and Bryant, P. 1990. *Phonological Skills and Learning to Read*. Hove, UK: Erlbaum.

Gottardo, A., Stanovich, K. E., and Siegel, L. S. 1996. The relationships between phonological sensitivity, syntactic processing, and verbal working memory in the reading performance of third-grade children. *Journal of Experimental Child Psychology* 63:563–82.

Gough, P. B., Juel, C., and Griffith, P. L. 1992. Reading, spelling and the orthographic cipher. In *Reading Acquisition*, eds. P. B. Gough, L. C. Ehri, and R. Treiman. Hillsdale, NJ: Lawrence Erlbaum Associates.

Jastek, S., and Wilkinson, G. S. 1984. *Wide Range Achievement Test (WRAT-R)*. Wilmington, DE: Jastak Associates Inc.

Kerlinger, F. N., and Pedhazur, E. J. 1973. *Multiple Regression in Behavioral Research*. New York: Holt, Rinehart, and Winston.

Korhonen, T. 1995. The persistence of rapid naming problems in children with reading disabilities: A nine-year follow-up. *Journal of Learning Disabilities* 28:232–39.

Liberman, I., Shankweiler, D., and Liberman, A. 1989. The alphabetic principle and learning to read. In *Phonology and Reading Disability: Solving the Reading Puzzle*, eds. D. Shankweiler and I. Liberman. Ann Arbor, MI: University of Michigan Press.

Manis, F. R., Seidenberg, M. S., Doi, M. L., McBride-Chang, C., and Patterson, A. 1996. On the basis of two subtypes of developmental dyslexia. *Cognition* 58:157–95.

Morais, J., Alegria, J., and Content, A. 1987. The relationships between segmental analysis and alphabetic literacy: An interactive view. *Cahiers de Psychologie Cognitive* 7:415–38.

Naglieri, J. 1989. *Matrix Analogies Test*. New York: The Psychological Corporation.

Nassajizavareh, H., and Geva, E. 1999. Cognitive and linguistic processes in adult L2 readers. *Applied Psycholinguistics* 20:241–67.

Ogbu, J. U. 1978. *Minority Education and Caste.* New York: Academic Press.

Oller, J. W., and Damico, J. S. C. 1990. Theoretical considerations in the assessment of LEP students. In *Limiting Bias in the Assessment of Bilingual Students,* eds. Hamayan and Damico. Austin, TX: PRO-ED.

Ortiz, A. A., and Ramirez, B. A. Eds. 1989. *School and the Culturally Diverse Exceptional Student: Promising Practices and Future Directions.* Reston, VA: ERIC Clearinghouse on Handicapped and Gifted Children.

Rosner, J., and Simon, D. 1971. The auditory analysis test: An initial report. *Journal of Learning Disabilities* 4:40–48.

Sattler, J. M. 1992. Assessment of ethnic minority children. In *Assessment of Children* (3rd Edition), ed. J. M. Sattler, San Diego: Jerome M. Sattler, Publisher, Inc.

Scarborough, H. 1990. Very early language deficits in dyslexic children. *Child Development* 61:1728–43.

Segalowitz, N., and Hebert, M. 1990. Phonological recoding in the first and second language reading of skilled bilinguals. *Language learning* 40:503–38.

Segalowitz, N., Poulsen, C., and Komeda, M. 1991. Lower level components of reading skill in higher level bilinguals: Implications for reading instruction. *Association Internationale de Linguistique Appliquee (AILA) Review* 8:15–30.

Share, D. L., Jorm, A. F., Maclean, R., and Matthews, R. 1984. Sources of individual differences in reading acquisition. *Journal of Educational Psychology* 76:1309–24.

Snow, C. E., Burns, M. S., and Griffin, P. Eds. 1998. *Preventing Reading Difficulties in Young Children.* National Academy Press: Washington, DC.

Snowling, M., Chiat, S., and Hulme, C. 1991. Words, nonwords and phonological processes: Some comments on Gathercole, Willis, Emslie, and Baddeley. *Applied Psycholinguistics* 12:369–73.

Stanovich, K. E. 1992. Speculations on the causes and consequences of individual differences in early reading acquisition. In *Reading Acquisition,* eds. P. B. Gough, L. C. Ehri, and R. Treiman. Hillsdale, NJ: Lawrence Erlbaum Associates.

Torgesen, J. K. 1988. Studies of children with learning disabilities who perform badly on memory span tasks. *Journal of Learning Disabilities* 21:605–12.

Torgesen, J. K., Wagner, R. K., and Rashotte, C. A. 1994. Longitudinal studies of phonological processing and reading. *Journal of Learning Disabilities* 27:276–86.

Tunmer, W. E., Herriman, M. L., and Nesdale, A. R. 1988. Metalinguistic abilities and beginning reading. *Reading Research Quarterly* 23:134–58.

Vellutino, F. R., and Scanlon, D. 1987. Phonological coding and phonological awareness and reading ability: Evidence from a longitudinal and experimental study. *Merrill-Palmer Quarterly* 33:321–63.

Verhoeven, L. 1994. Transfer in bilingual development. The linguistic interdependency hypothesis revisited. *Language Learning* 44:381–415.

Verhoeven, L., in press. Components in early second language reading and spelling. *Scientific Studies of Reading.*

Wade-Woolley, L., and Geva, E. 1999. Processing inflected morphology in second language word recognition: Russian-speakers and English-speakers read Hebrew. *Reading and Writing: An Interdisciplinary Journal* 11:321–43.

Wade-Woolley, L., and Geva, E. in press. Processing novel phonemic contrasts in the acquisition of L2 word reading, *Scientific Studies of Reading.*

Wade-Woolley, L., and Siegel, L. S. 1997. The spelling performance of ESL and native speakers of English as a function of reading skills. *Reading and Writing: An Interdisciplinary Journal* 9:387–406.

Wagner, R. K., and Torgesen, J. K. 1987. The nature of phonological processing and its causal role in the acquisition of reading skills. *Psychological Bulletin* 101: 192–212.

Wagner, R. K., Torgesen, J. K., and Rashotte, C. A. 1994. Development of reading-related phonological processing abilities: New evidence of bi-directional causality from a latent variable longitudinal study. *Developmental Psychology* 30:73–87.

Wagner, R. K., Torgesen, J. K., Rashotte, C. A., Hecht, S. A., Barker, T. A., Burgess, S. R., Donahue, J., and Garon, T. 1997. Changing relations between phonological processing abilities and word-level reading as children develop from beginning to skilled readers: A 5-year longitudinal study. *Developmental Psychology* 33:468–79.

Walsh, D. J., Price, G. G., and Gillingham, M. G. 1988. The critical but transitory importance of letter naming. *Reading Research Quarterly* 23:108–22.

Wang, M., and Geva, E. 1999. The Development of Spelling in Chinese ESL Children. Paper presented at the Society for Scientific Study of Reading, April, Montreal.

Willows, D. 1998. Early systematic phonics in balanced literacy classrooms: Overview of two large scale investigations. Paper presented at the National Reading Conference, Austin, TX.

Wolf, M. 1991. Naming speed and reading : The contribution of the cognitive neurosciences. *Reading Research Quarterly* 26:123–41.

Wolf, M., and Bowers, P. G. 1999. The double-deficit hypothesis for the developmental dyslexias. *Journal of Educational Psychology* 91:415–38.

Wolf, M., and Obregon, M. 1992. Early naming deficits, developmental dyslexia, and a specific deficit hypothesis. *Brain and Language* 42:219–47.

Dyslexia and Learning a Foreign Language: A Personal Experience

Charlann S. Simon

Speech-Language Pathologist & ESL Specialist
Tempe, Arizona

Individuals with dyslexia can expect to have difficulties learning a second language since second language learning builds on native language learning. The factors that have a negative impact on learning one's native language have a similar impact on learning a foreign language (e.g., difficulties with phonemic awareness, retrieving and processing linguistic information, working memory, metalinguistic explanations, stabilizing sound-symbol relationships). This participant observer report provides (1) a brief review of research on how dyslexia complicates learning a second language; (2) a description of how dyslexia has affected my educational experiences; (3) a description of personal experiences learning a foreign language between 1992–1998; and (4) recommendations for individuals with dyslexia who are faced with fulfilling a foreign language requirement and for their foreign language instructors.

DYSLEXIA AND LEARNING A FOREIGN LANGUAGE : A PERSONAL EXPERIENCE

This paper is written from my perspective as a speech-language professional with dyslexia. My purpose is to describe my personal experiences in learning a foreign language to educators, fellow dyslexics, and parents of children with dyslexia, and to recount strategies I employed to pass foreign language courses

Annals of Dyslexia, Vol. 50, 2000
ISSN 0736-9387

successfully. I believe that my 30 years of clinical experience as a speech-language pathologist combined with my experiences in researching relationships between intact communication skills and academic performance (Simon 1998a; 1995; 1994; 1991; 1987; 1984; Damico and Simon 1993), have been significant assets in helping me to analyze my learning difficulties and to compensate for linguistic barriers that otherwise might have impeded success.

Neither the descriptions of my academic challenges nor the specific types of problems I have experienced in completing foreign language courses should be interpreted as "typical." Dyslexia is a complicated language-based learning disorder. The reader should bear in mind that this report is a participant-observer case study, based on the belief that reflections on personal experiences complement scientific investigations of how dyslexia affects linguistic pursuits. "Student voices" research provides unique insights that are a valuable addition to scientific data bases when creating strategies for mentoring others (Commeyras 1995; Dahl 1995; Fink 1998; Gerber 1994) and suggesting policy changes (Murphy 1992). Experimental research studies, looking for commonalties across individuals, provide balance to participant-observer reports. Research and personal experience can be powerful and compatible partners as we search for relevant assessment and intervention procedures that help people with dyslexia meet societal expectations with limited stress and maximum success.

DYSLEXIA AND LEARNING A FOREIGN LANGUAGE

Students with dyslexia frequently find they are unable to fulfill high school and college foreign language requirements (Cohen 1983; Ganschow and Sparks 1993; Ganschow, Sparks, and Schneider 1995; Pompian and Thum 1988). In a review of research on the characteristics of students who have difficulty learning foreign languages, Ganschow, Sparks, and Javorsky (1998) cite a number of studies (many of them their own) documenting how one's native language learning facility affects one's potential for learning a foreign language. In addition, they found similarities between the linguistic profiles of students who fell into the "high risk" category on foreign language aptitude tests and subsequently did poorly in foreign language courses, and students who had a history of language disabilities, including difficulty in learning to read. Both groups had difficulties making connections between phonology and orthography and remembering and applying spelling rules. The researchers concluded that students who did poorly in foreign languages had a collective profile of weaknesses similar to the profile typically described for students with dyslexia.

Students who have undue difficulties meeting foreign language requirements may not have been formally diagnosed as being dyslexic or learning disabled (LD), or possessed academic records marked by repeated failures. For example, Dinklage (1971) reported that certain students who had been accepted at Harvard and who obtained overall GPAs of 3.5 or higher had failed to fulfill their foreign language requirement at the university. However, in reviewing the educational histories of such students, he found that many had experienced learning difficulties in earlier grades that were similar to dyslexia (e.g., difficulties with learning to read and spell, letter/symbol reversals, sound confusion, poor discrimination of sounds and syllables in words, and poor verbal memory). Later, Dinklage (1987) noted that a high IQ and periodic remedial assistance had helped some students to compensate in earlier grades for their language disabilities. Levine (1987) suggested that some children with relatively mild—albeit significant—language disabilities may have learned to comprehend and express themselves in their native language because they had been overexposed to it. These same students, however, also may have encountered more noticeable difficulties when they attempted to master a second language.

Ganschow et al.'s (1998) findings, together with the observations of Dinklage (1971) and Levine (1987), support the Linguistic Coding Differences Hypothesis (Sparks, Ganschow, and Pohlman 1989; Sparks and Ganschow 1991). This hypothesis, derived from native language reading research by Vellutino and Scanlon (1986), states that one's skill in three native language components or "codes"—phonological/orthographic (sound-symbol), syntactic (grammatical), and semantic (vocabulary, meaning)—serves as the foundation for learning a foreign language successfully. Initially, the hypothesis grew out of case study research on 22 college-age students who had sought course substitutions for their foreign language requirement after having experienced unusual learning difficulties (Sparks, Ganschow, and Pohlman 1989). It has since been confirmed by numerous empirical studies. (For a review of this research, see Ganschow, Sparks, and Javorsky 1998.) Their research has produced the following general observations:

- The efficiency of one's native language skill plays a large part in the success or failure of foreign language learning.
- Difficulties with phonology/orthography and syntax in one's native language are likely to negatively affect one's performance in the foreign language classroom.
- Most foreign language difficulties do not seem to be at the semantic level.
- Lack of motivation and high anxiety are likely to be the consequences rather than causes of foreign language learning problems (Ganschow et al 1995, p. 78).

Ganschow and colleagues (1998) have found that: (1) foreign language learning difficulties can be placed on a continuum; (2) it is unlikely a distinct entity such as a "foreign language learning disability" exists; and (3) most poor foreign language learners do not exhibit language deficits, but exhibit significant language differences in their skills when compared to good foreign language learners. In addition, Sparks, Ganschow, and Pohman (1989) found differences in the nature of linguistic coding deficits between those students who experienced immediate difficulties in the first or second semester courses (i.e., 101 or 102) and those whose difficulties appeared later in the sequence of foreign language requirements (i.e., 201 or 202). In particular, those who had relatively intact phonological coding skills, but who had syntactic and/or semantic problems, did not encounter major difficulties before the second year of language. Specific problems in the native language reappeared as specific problems in the foreign language.

Phonological working memory deficits also have a negative impact on both first and second language learning (Sparks, et al. 1989, 1997; Service 1992). Gathercole and Baddeley (1993) use the term "working memory" to describe the short-term memory system involved in the temporary processing and storage of information, such as language:

Close links have been established between children's phonological memory abilities and both their native language vocabulary knowledge and their second-language learning. It also appears that the poor vocabulary growth associated with both developmental language disorders and specific reading impairments may be attributable to deficits of phonological working memory in these children (p. 67).

Although this complex area of research cannot be covered here fully, selected notations will set the stage for the description of foreign language learning difficulties that are presented in a later section of this paper.

In 1984, Vallar and Baddeley reported one of the earliest neuropsychological studies to show how working memory deficits affect linguistic processing. They hypothesized that the severe and highly specific phonological working memory deficits that were displayed by a young woman (PV) who had suffered a stroke could be attributed to "a damaged phonological store" that led to poor retention of linguistic material presented auditorily. PV did not seem to use subvocal rehearsal to maintain decaying representations in the phonological store, nor did she recode visually presented material into phonological form. In experimental trials, she showed "very poor immediate memory span for nonwords, failing to repeat any nonwords containing more than two syllables and her learning of unfamiliar phonological material was correspondingly severely impaired" (Gathercole and Baddeley 1993, p. 45). These working memory deficits had a significant impact on long-term phonological learning because of the superficial manner in which phonological material had been stored. Interestingly, PV was more successful on linguistic processing tasks when she was able to link phonological information with either semantic or orthographic information.

Linguistic processing deficits have also been observed in phonological recoding tasks used in studies of reading disabilities. Ehri (1992) describes these tasks as "translating letters into sounds by application of letter-sound rules and then recognizing the identities of words from their pronunciation" (p. 107). Not surprisingly, Sparks et al. (1997) found that one's phonological recoding skills were a key predictor of foreign language proficiency.

In a three-year study of Finnish children who were learning English, Service (1992) studied how phonological and working memory skills affect foreign language learning. Using a research design heavily influenced by the work of Baddeley and his associates, she tested children's pseudoword repetition skills in Finnish (e.g., haiska, hinto) and in English (e.g., punger, dreplet), as well as their abilities to recall "letter strings" in each language (e.g., aaduttaja, bicessary) that were rapidly presented on flash cards. All pseudowords conformed with Finnish and English linguistic rules. She found the following:

The quality of pronunciation in an auditory pseudoword repetition task, as well as the accuracy of spelling in a visual delayed copying task with pseudowords, was correlated with elementary foreign-language learning [in children age 9 to 12 years old]....As all new foreign words are initially foreign-sounding non-words, the inability to create sufficiently distinctive or durable traces of them in the phonological store could prevent their long-term memory learning . . . (1992, p. 45).

According to Service, for individuals with poor phonological memory skills, unsuccessful attempts to parse sentences may hinder the acquisition of foreign language vocabulary and learning of larger language units.

Considering the research conclusions of Service (1992) and those of Ganschow, Sparks, and Javorsky (1998), one should not dismiss the role of aptitude for learning a foreign language. The key to success for individuals who have linguistic coding differences and/or poor phonological memory skills might lie in having the good fortune of being in an educational context that acknowledges differences in aptitude and provides a variety of instructional approaches. In such an environment, students with dyslexia can choose to work with an instructor whose theoretical approach helps them compensate for their lack of foreign language learning aptitude. Foreign language programs, where aptitude is a consideration and a menu of instructional methods is available, are relatively recent and not necessarily pervasive. Many students may have failed foreign language courses over the past two decades because the "naturalistic" teaching approaches that were in vogue at the time did not meet their instructional needs.

The hypothesis that linguistic aptitude may explain why some individuals do well and others of equal intelligence fail foreign language courses is not new (Carroll 1962, 1973). However, during the 1970s and 1980s, the theories of "second language acquisition" researchers dominated foreign language instruction (Sparks 1995). Linguists who subscribed to Noam Chomsky's (1959) theory of innate cognitive capacity for learning language(s) (Krashen 1982; Ellis 1985; Gass and Selinker 1994) have deemphasized differences in aptitude. "The mind is endowed with linguistic universals that enable us to formulate rules from the verbal sounds we hear" (Crawford 1991, p. 100). From the perspective of second language acquisition researchers, a person will learn a second language naturally if exposed to sufficient comprehensible input (Krashen 1982; Crawford 1991). One's success in naturally acquiring the structural rules of a foreign language rests in the richness of the language acquisition context and the pedagogical style rather than student aptitude (Ellis 1985; Gass and Selinker 1994).

Crawford (1991) states that "perceptive [foreign language] educators have long recognized the potential of more natural approaches to language acquisition" (p. 99), and cites the immersion techniques used by Maximilian Berlitz who emphasized oral language and avoided translation. Berlitz encouraged students to think in the second language and to learn grammar inductively. According to Ellis (1985), students can develop skills in a foreign language through learning (i.e., a conscious process that focuses attention on language structure) or acquisition (i.e., a process similar to the way one subconsciously internalizes grammatical rules while consciously pursuing meaning). Gass and Selinker (1994) summarize the basic tenets of the language acquisition position: (1) all languages are equally easy to learn; (2) all normal children learn language in roughly the same way and within the same time frame; and (3) any inherent differences that might affect second language learning should have also affected native language learning (pp. 233–34). The focus here is primarily on the influence of individual affective and personality variables (Gardner 1985; Ehrman 1990; Krashen 1982) and one's learning strategies (Oxford 1990) on learning a foreign language.

Language acquisition theories of how one learned a foreign language dominated the 1980s. Therefore, foreign language instructors moved away from direct instruction on grammar rules (Savignon 1987) at the same time reading teachers emphasized "the wholeness of language" (Goodman 1986), rather than the analysis of the phonological structure. Now, many foreign language teachers conclude that students need a balanced approach to learning that combines direct instruction on language structure with realistic communication interactions. Chen (1995) represents the viewpoint that comprehensible input alone is insufficient.

For Krashen (1982), subconscious acquisition of comprehensible input in a low-anxiety context plays a pivotal role in developing language fluency; he sees the learning of grammar as useful only as a "monitor" and not an utterance-initiator. This theoretical claim is counter-intuitive and contrary to the personal experiences of numerous language teachers . . . (p. 58).

Earlier studies support Chen's conclusions. For example, Long (1983) examined twelve studies dealing with the effects of instruction (learning) and exposure (acquisition), and she concluded that formal instruction in grammar did make a difference. Likewise, Scott (1989), analyzing data from oral and written tests taken by students of French, found that students who had received direct instruction on language structure performed better overall than those with whom implicit methods of instruction had been used. Zhenhui (1999) suggests that cultural factors can play a significant role in determining the most effective foreign language teaching methods. For example, Chinese students generally show great interest in language structures and linguistic details because accuracy is very important to them. Zhenhui emphasizes a balance between accuracy and fluency by providing realistic scenarios in which students can practice specific English structures and learn to accept errors as part of the learning process.

Like Zhenhui, Chen (1995) suggests a method of foreign language instruction that incorporates the best features of an acquisition model and the best features of a learning model. Specifically, ". . . explicit grammar knowledge is realized through contextualized language practice in communicative activities in which rules of use are presented in discourse contexts" (p. 60). Reading specialists (Chall 1997; Adams 1997) and speech-language pathologists (Chaney 1990) have made similar recommendations for balancing "code emphasis" and "meaning emphasis" approaches to reading.

In the 1990s I completed a master's degree in ESL, and throughout the course work I debated professors who subscribed to a "one-size-fits-all" approach to teaching English. Professors were aligned with Gass and Selinker (1994) who proposed that all children can learn a second language naturally if they are exposed to "comprehensible input" (Krashen 1982) and are taught to read through whole language methodologies (Goodman 1986). Professional and personal experiences motivated me to argue against the indirect language teaching methods the professors recommended. First, as a speech-language pathologist, I could not discount the role of individual differences in language learning. It was unlikely that individuals with language-based learning disabilities (dyslexia) would learn a foreign language in roughly the same way and within the same time frame as individuals with typical language learning capabilities. Secondly, my personal experiences with dyslexia convinced me that a structured learning format provides the type of focused practice within a communication context that persons with dyslexia need to learn accurate pronunciation and a variety of language structures. Since language learning is not a natural process for some of us, direct instruction and repetition supply the support needed to develop greater accuracy, fluency, and confidence in our first or second languages.

Native English speakers with dyslexia are not alone in their difficulty learning a foreign language. Foreign language teachers who teach English have reported on how the learning characteristics of their students with dyslexia differ from those of their classmates. For example, Michaelides (1990) has found that for most of his Greek students who are learning English, the main sources of error are a temporary interference from the mother tongue (e.g., word order) and interlanguage (i.e., unstable structures in the target language). However, for the students with dyslexia, interference seems to persist for a prolonged period of time and may never disappear. Similarly, Lescano (1995) has observed that his English students with dyslexia have perception difficulties and tend to ignore details (e.g., plural forms) in spoken and written language. Instead of focusing attention on linguistic details, the students with dyslexia tend to focus on overall comprehension and production in both their native language and English. Lescano recommended that foreign language instructional programs for students with dyslexia utilize the five channels of sensory perception.

In the 1990s, research in reading and foreign language learning has provided compelling evidence supporting the principles of direct instruction for individuals with dyslexia who are learning to move from oral to written language (Chaney 1990) or from the native language to a foreign language. Sparks et al. (1991) found that Orton-Gillingham multisensory methods were a successful alternative to the "natural" communication approaches used by many foreign language educators for students who have weaknesses in oral and written native language skills that affect foreign language learning. Ganschow, Sparks, and Schneider (1995) reported that the level of language analysis ability (i.e., metalinguistic skills) that a student brings to a foreign language course is a critical factor. This was certainly true in my experience. I have honed my metalinguistic skills through clinical experiences and research on assessment of language disabilities (Simon 1984, 1986, 1989, 1998b; Damico and Simon 1993). These metalinguistic skills helped me in a number of ways: (1) being comfortable with linguistic terminology; (2) recognizing examples of grammatical structures and patterns of sentence construction; (3) analyzing what I did not understand about French language structure, so I could ask clarification questions; and (4) organizing linguistic data in preparation for exams.

A PERSONAL NEXUS: DYSLEXIA AND A FOREIGN LANGUAGE REQUIREMENT

Dyslexia consistently impaired my ability to function in school, starting at the kindergarten level when teachers reported that I did not follow directions and did not perform at a level commensurate with my potential (Simon 1999). In first grade, I failed to learn phonics and was transferred into a "look-say" basal program in second grade, at which time I began to experience some success. By fourth grade, I had developed a strong sight vocabulary that permitted me to complete assignments but not excel. Specific areas of difficulty during my early school years included:

- directionality (e.g., confusing polar opposites such as left/right or vertical/horizonal and using mirror writing);
- phonics principles (e.g., phonemic awareness, symbol/sound relationships, syllabication, decoding multisyllable words, spelling rules);
- metalinguistic tasks (e.g., comprehending directions for math or grammar assignments, grammar analysis, citing structural or spelling rules);
- math facts and application (e.g., retaining math facts despite an unusual amount of drill, acquiring basic operational procedures used in calculation, learning Roman numerals, and understanding word problems);
- comprehension and short-term memory (e.g., recalling facts presented orally or in print, repeating multisyllable words); and
- completing work within the time allotted. In one form or another and depending upon the context, each of these problems persists today. In her study of adult dyslexics, Fink (1998) reported on some of my experiences.

My high school counselor, witnessing my struggles with "symbol laden courses" (e.g., algebra, shorthand, and Spanish), advised me to attend a community college for one year and then transfer. With this plan, I needed only one year of science, math, and foreign language to graduate. At the community college, I visited the reading lab daily to improve reading speed and comprehension. However, at Northwestern University I was still unable handle the amount of reading assigned and did not know how to organize information for study, so I was placed on academic probation twice. In graduate school, when I finally was able to arrange my own schedule, I began to excel academically. During the 1960s, I acquired a bachelor's degree in speech and theater and a master's degree in speech-language pathology without encountering a foreign language requirement. My luck evaporated in 1992 when I was in the process of acquiring a second master's degree. It was at that time that I heard the words I was dreading: "In the ESL master's program you will need six hours of a foreign language."

To complete the ESL program's foreign language requirement, I enrolled in French 101 and 102 in two, five-day-a-week, back-to-back summer sessions in 1992. I correctly anticipated that second language acquisition would require a significant portion of my "linguistic hard drive," so I did not schedule any other classes and allotted five to seven hours a day for study. The instructor in French 101 had a nonthreatening teaching style and used a text that had explanations of grammatical rules in English. While the course was challenging and I needed to make it a full-time job, I was able to succeed. French 102, however, was extraordinarily stressful. I had a different instructor, the text was in French, and the comprehension of course content rested on recall of French 101 principles.

I applied metalinguistic skills I had developed as a speech-language pathologist to analyze language patterns, and metacognitive strategies I had taught LD students to analyze difficulties and develop compensatory strategies. Without these professional skills to analyze the linguistic content and learning demands, I doubt that I would have passed French 102 during the 1992 summer session. I outlined each chapter, reorganized content, and made one-page charts displaying key grammatical patterns. During exams, I relied on my strong visual skills to recall this information for reference. The desk top or the floor became a computer screen as I displayed the visual memory of my charts. For example, I "cracked" the verb code while studying for French 102 finals, summarized this information, and shared copies of it with fellow students. I also gave a copy to the instructor to demonstrate that I "knew" the information, regardless of how poorly I might apply this knowledge on the exam! (Should the reader be interested in seeing this chart, please contact me directly.)

Over the next six years, I continued to retake 100-level courses and studied for three to four weeks in France each summer. I developed a passionate interest in learning French because I felt "at home" in Paris and wanted to be able to communicate. In 1997–1998, I finally ventured into French 201 and 202. In May 1998, prior to the French 202 final, the instructor said to our class, "Here is something that will help you study the verb system," and she distributed the handout that I had created six years earlier to pass the French 102 final. Although the handout was titled "Simon's Summary of French Verbs," the instructor was surprised that I was the author, and for good reason. She knew how I had struggled with the verb system, showing absence of automaticity on some verb structures and lingering confusion about others. That is, there was (and still is) a "Grand Canyon gap" between my French linguistic competence (at a metalinguistic level) and my performance (as a speaker, listener, reader, and writer).

I no longer tell the truth about how long I have studied French because people cannot comprehend how I could have studied since 1992 and have so little proficiency. In the fall semester of 1999, I took French 264 (readings on, and discussion of, French culture) from the same professor with whom I had taken my first semester of French (French 101). She observed that while my comprehension had improved significantly since 1992, it was a puzzle to her that I still struggled so severely with spoken and written language. I could not fluently retrieve basic structures or pronunciation patterns to communicate my thoughts in classroom discussions, so I tended to speak in sentence fragments and phrases that would be typical of first year students.

Making the distinction between language competence (what one *knows* about a language) and language performance (what one can *do* with a language) (Gass and Selinker 1994) has been critical in sustaining my motivation to learn French. By keeping in mind this differentiation, I reduce my frustration about the gap between what I know about the French language after seven years of study and what I am able to retrieve for spontaneous use: When one is dyslexic, there is always a gap between what one knows and what one can do. Learning a foreign language provides one more example of this discrepancy.

A SELF-REPORT OF FOREIGN LANGUAGE LEARNING DIFFICULTIES: APPLYING THE LINGUISTIC CODING DIFFERENCES HYPOTHESIS

In this section, I present examples of difficulties I have experienced in past French courses and continue to experience to some degree after seven years of study. My learning has displayed the plateau in foreign language acquisition that foreign language teachers have reported in their students with dyslexia (Michaelides 1990; Lescano 1995). For example, I have been placed at the "low intermediate level" on entrance exams for summer classes in France for the past three years, despite continuous study at community colleges during the academic year.

I draw on marginal notes I have written in French texts over the past seven years to provide specific examples of difficulties and attitudes toward learning, helpful instructor behaviors, and study techniques. I am presenting a subjective analysis of my foreign language difficulties that is pertinent to this case study rather than a synthesis of research on the most common errors English speakers make when learning French. My goal is to have these examples serve as "the data" of this study, so the reader will be able to generate hypotheses and design future research to further investigate foreign language learning in persons with dyslexia.

The types of difficulties I have experienced are in keeping with the difficulties researchers have reported when studying the foreign language learning experiences of students with dyslexia. These problems include difficulty making sound/symbol connections, remembering and applying spelling and grammar rules, "parsing" spoken language, and drawing on phonological working memory to repeat words and phrases. Immersion experiences do not help me acquire and store linguistic rules because I cannot simultaneously listen for key words that aid comprehension and analyze language structure. Other critical pedagogical variables include the text that is used, the size of the class and where I sit, the instructor's willingness to use the board to write French structures and use English to clarify course content, and the rate and clarity of the instructor's speech. I have great difficulty comprehending the speech of instructors who are not native speakers of either French or English. Even accented English is difficult for me to understand.

Throughout my marginal notes over the past seven years, there are two consistent comments: (1) "There are no constants!"; and (2) "There are too many details to remember!" Intellectually, I know that linguistic principles are subject to the laws of relativity. For example, the same word can be a verb in one sentence and a noun in the next (e.g., He is *running* /*Running* is a popular sport) and languages have homophones (e.g., *rite* and *right*). As a learner with dyslexia, however, I search for "linguistic anchors" and get confused and frustrated by "linguistic relativity." When I see language written down, I am better able to understand phonological and syntactic details and analyze the interacting linguistic components.

There is, however, a significant downside to seeing the language in writing. Being "sight word-oriented," I find that a change in visual input is confusing. An example is the transformation of *Il y a* (There is/are) (pronounced eel-yuh) into the interrogative form, *Y a-t-il* (Is/Are there?) pronounced (E-ah-teel). I easily recognize *Il y a* at the semantic, syntactic, and phonological levels; *Y a-t-il* seems as if it is a structure from a different language. On the surface, this appears to be a syntactic coding problem. It is, however, the visual configuration of *letters* in *Y a-t-il* that lacks immediate meaning and affects pronunciation when reading aloud (e.g., I tend to say "why-ah-til"). My inclination is to place a configuration of *letters* into memory rather than a configuration of *sounds*, which affects syntactic and semantic coding (Gathercole and Baddeley 1993; Service 1992).

Following are specific examples of my foreign language difficulties separated into one of three categories: phonological, syntactic, and semantic (similar to what Sparks et al. propose in their Linguistic Coding Differences Hypothesis. While the categorical placements are not "pure," they do serve an organizational function. For example, one could argue that most difficulties are phonological at the core; structural and semantic concepts are lost in "the mush" of the speech stream (Service 1992). Vowels, in particular, are difficult for individuals with language disorders to identify and repeat (Post, Foorman, and Hiscock 1997). Both receptive and expressive phonological coding tasks are challenging for people with dyslexia. For example, Das, Mishra, and Kirby (1994) found that tasks demanding simultaneous use of phonological coding and articulation correctly identified children with dyslexia with up to 80 percent accuracy. For those of us with dyslexia, then, retaining a sequence of sounds in a novel multisyllable word or short phrase, and then repeating the sequence accurately, is nearly impossible. Recently, I have found that my knowledge of French syntax helps me predict linguistic content and increases the probability that I can repeat a phrase consisting of six to eight syllables. To provide the reader with an indication of which examples of difficulties in learning French are particularly unusual, I solicited an evaluation of them from a native French-speaking university professor with twenty-five years of experience in linguistics research and foreign language teaching (Ossipov 1999). I have marked an asterisk next to highly atypical, persisting difficulties even after seven years of motivated study.

PHONOLOGICAL CODING DIFFICULTIES

Phonological coding difficulties have an impact on auditory discrimination of sound elements, auditory blending of and memory for sound elements, understanding the sound/symbol code, spelling, and sustained attention to auditory information. Phonological processing deficits affect phonological, syntactic, and semantic coding. As enumerated in Catts (1989), these deficits include:

- encoding of speech sound information in long-term memory;
- use of phonological codes in working memory;
- retrieval of phonological information from long-term memory;
- production of complex phonological sequences; and
- awareness or sensitivity to the speech sound structure of the language (p. 54).

Manifestations of my continuing difficulties with phonological coding and related cognitive processes include the following:

    I.   Oral Language

        *A. I cannot remember and consistently apply phonological rules (i.e., "stabilize" sound/symbol relationships), which interferes with "anchoring" pronunciation of content and structural vocabulary. I tend to approximate rather than hit the target pronunciation, especially with vowels. According to native French instructors, my phonology is significantly less developed than my syntax which might explain why I am frequently asked to repeat what I have said. Specific examples include:

            (1) spelling aloud;

            (2) pronouncing core vocabulary (e.g., days of the week, months, numbers) and conjugated verbs;

            (3) applying *liaison* rules, even at the novice level (i.e., smoothly connecting one word

to the next according to phonological rules, instead of creating phonological boundaries by thinking of a sentence as word + word + word).

B. Since my phonological working memory is poor, I have difficulty repeating and then storing the pronunciation of words and phrases, which slows acquisition of French. I have found that accuracy of repetition is linked to the number of syllables within the word or phrase; each syllable is like a number in a digit span test. To compensate, I first must write words as I hear them (e.g., *réveillé* [arise in the morning] becomes *ray vay yeah.*). I must use a series of English vowel/consonant combinations or short words (*yeah*) because I do not have fluent recall of the International Phonetic Alphabet (IPA) nor the accent marks in French. Any symbol system (e.g., IPA, shorthand, Roman numerals, pronunciation marks) is a problem to remember or use. Examples of poor retention and repetition of auditorily presented linguistic material include:

*(1) *Words* with more than two or three *syllables* fade from memory once I begin to articulate them, with vowels particularly susceptible to distortion.

(2) *Phrases* of five to seven *syllables* containing a combination of familiar and unfamiliar content and/or structure words similarly overload my memory; if a phrase includes a large, highly familiar "syntactic chunk" (words that always appear together), then recall of pronunciation is easier.

*(3) Longer *phrases* (i.e., eight to ten syllables) that contain familiar content and structure words are subject to distortion (even after I hear one or two repetitions of the stimulus) because I must simultaneously hold in memory the sequence of words and the pronunciation of each word.

*C. Conversation or television news is "mush" because I cannot parse the speech stream (i.e., detect word boundaries as a listener), especially in a language like French that stresses *liaison* .

D. I cannot detect subtle changes in the phonemic structure of words that carry linguistic information (e.g., inflectional markers for tense, number, and gender at the end of words); therefore, doing audiotaped homework is tedious and usually filled with errors.

II. Written Language

*A. Reading French is problematic because I do not retain French sound/symbol relationships, including the meaning and the names of accent marks (e.g., é, è, ç, ê). Although the purpose of accent marks is to clarify pronunciation, to me they represent additional annoying linguistic details. Specific examples of difficulties include:

(1) reading the alphabet or phonograms (e.g., *ai, ou, eau*) aloud;

(2) remembering changes in pronunciation resulting from liaison (an interaction between phonological and syntactic rules) when reading text aloud (e.g., *elle est* [she is] is pronounced like the two alphabet letters L and A; in the sentence *Elle est actrice* [she is an actress], there is liaison between *est* and *actrice* which results in /t/ being attached to the initial vowel in *actrice*). I would note, however, that according to Ossipov (1999), *consistent* use of liaison can be somewhat of a challenge for many nonnative speakers (both with and without dyslexia).

*B. I continue to confuse English and French sound/symbol relationships. That is, I fail to approach a configuration of letters in French words as representing French sounds. When I read French, I revert to English sound/symbol rules. This phonological/orthographic instability creates persisting problems, such as:

(1) pronouncing words that are orthographic/semantic cognates of English but

not phonological cognates (e.g., *date* [daht] or *théâtre* [tay-ah-tre]);

(2) recoding and reading aloud vowels and vowel-consonant combinations that differ from English sound/symbol rules (e.g., *soirée* [swah ray]; *maillot* [my-yoh]);

(3) remembering differences between the visual appearance and pronunciation rules for a letter sequence (e.g., *parlent*, where the *-ent* is not pronounced); for me, visual input is more powerful than linguistic rule-governed information;

C. Learning to say a word and learning to spell it are two separate processes. In spelling, I revert to learning a series of "sight words" by visualizing the letter sequence, just as I have done in English. Specific types of spelling difficulties include:

*(1) words that differ from English sound/symbol rules (e.g., *lit* [bed], is pronounced [lee]);

*(2) words with contiguous vowels (e.g., *ceux* or *liaison*);

(3) words for which gender/number changes produce spelling changes (e.g., *nouvel, nouvelle, nouveau* [new]).

SYNTACTIC CODING DIFFICULTIES.

Syntactic coding difficulties affect understanding of grammatical rules, oral and written construction of grammatical sentences, tenses, appropriate word usage, prefixes and suffixes, and mechanical rules. Short-term memory for structured language and verbal flexibility are also affected. Since phonological memory deficits frequently affect the application of syntactic skills, it is difficult to isolate purely syntactic coding difficulties from those with underlying phonological coding difficulties. For example, Mann, Cowin, and Schoenheimer (1989) found that the use of a phonetic memory code was important for sentence comprehension and that misperception of spoken sentences was due to a processing limitation of working memory rather than insufficient knowledge of syntax. Expressively, I find that trying to coordinate multiple linguistic elements simultaneously such as structure, vocabulary, and pronunciation, and articulate a meaningful utterance within a normal time frame, overloads my memory and cognitive organization. Specific examples of difficulties are the following:

I. Oral Language

*A. I cannot remember, retrieve, or apply simultaneously multiple grammar rules such as tense, number, and gender markers when formulating statements or questions. The verb system, in particular, remains a blur when I try to retrieve it. When I engage in discourse, I feel like a clown trying to juggle too many plates. According to Ossipov (1999), experiencing "system breakdown" like this occurs for most people only when they are fatigued.

*B. Combining structural units is problematic for me as a listener and as a speaker (e.g., eliding words [*la + automobile –> l'automobile*] or forming contractions [à +le–>au]). (See Written Language, point B, for more detail about the nature of this difficulty.)

*C. Forming questions can be particularly difficult. In addition to the declarative sentence rules (e.g., for gender, number, tense), there are interrogative rules to remember for addition and permutation of structures (e.g., *L'autobus, quand arrive-t-il?* [When does the bus arrive?]). Fortunately, there are alternative methods of question formation.

II. Written Language

*A. I lack linguistic flexibility (i.e., being able to play with the language), which is problematic when instructors assign textbook exercises requiring sentence deletions, additions, or permutations. The same type of linguistic inflexibility that makes it impossible for me to speak pig Latin inhibits my ability to change French statements into questions or to arrange a series of phrases into a statement or question. A model demonstrating the requisite structural change is not really helpful because I process each grouping of words as *new* linguistic data rather than as another opportunity to apply the *same* linguistic rules. Examples of difficult workbook assignments include:

(1)   changing a phrase (e.g. *le nombre de personnes dans la famille* [the number of persons in the family]) into a question that requires additions or changes to the pool of words provided (*Combien de personnes sont dans votre famille?* [How many people are in your family?]);

(2)   substituting one syntactic form for another, when given an instruction such as *Substituez le verbe être au verbe avoir et changez la phrase* (Substitute the verb *to be* with the verb *to have* and change the sentence); although I understand the principle and the *modele—Mon nez est long* (My nose is long)/ *J'ai un long nez* (I have a long nose)—I cannot implement it in the remaining exercises;

(3)   sequencing a list of words or phrases into a sentence and making appropriate tense and/or number modifications (e.g., *Boris Becker/gagner/matches de tennis/la plupart de* –> *Boris Becker gagne la plupart de ses matches de tennis* [Boris Becker wins most of his tennis matches]).

*B.   To create a cohesive, grammatically accurate sentence—as a speaker or writer—it is necessary both to plan ahead (e.g., determine the gender and/or number of nouns before selecting articles) and to keep in memory what one has already said or written so that tense, number, and gender markers are consistent. I cannot seem to move beyond a word + word + word orientation, which results in agrammatical spoken and written sentences. I expect words to be constant sound or visual units; when structural units are combined, both the sound and appearance are altered dramatically. Adding to processing and selection difficulties, is the inconsistency of combination rules. Specific examples include:

(1) The masculine and plural partitive articles are combined (*de* + *le*–>du ; *de* + *les*–>*des*)[some/any of the]), but not the feminine (*de* + *la*) (e.g., *de* + *le*–>*du beurre* [some butter] but *de la crème* [some cream]);

(2) The masculine and plural contracted definite articles are combined (*à* +*le* >*au* ; *à* + *les* >*aux*) [to the] , but not the feminine (à la) (e.g., *Je vais au cinema* [I'm going to the movies] but *Je vais à la plage* [I'm going to the beach]; for both partitive articles and contracted definite articles, one must think ahead to the gender and/or number of the noun and become accustomed to the altered sound and appearance of the combined structure (e.g., *aux* [oh]) compared to its constituent structures *à* +*les* [*ah*+*lay*]);

(3) Eliding two elements (when there is a juxtaposition of vowels) in either spoken or written French (*que* + *il* –>*qu'il*) is normally an error related to "monitoring content rather than a form error" (Ossipov 1999), but I find it also to be the result of rigidly thinking word + word + word;

(4) Forming written questions requires special "linguistic vigilance" to retrieve and monitor all of linguistic details; to revisit an earlier example (*L'autobus quand arrive-t-il?*), one must retrieve the appropriate interrogative adverb (*quand*), remember the gender of *l'autobus* (masculine), elide the article (*le*) because *autobus* begins with a vowel, invert the subject and verb (*il arrive*), and insert /t/ plus two hyphens (to separate two vowels).

SEMANTIC CODING DIFFICULTIES.

Semantic coding difficulties affect vocabulary knowledge and word retrieval, semantic referencing of noun/pronoun relationships or synonyms, understanding of multiple-meaning words, inferences, understanding and use of cohesive ties, and management of both narrative and expository language formats. Sparks (1995) reported that semantic coding difficulties were the least likely to be an *immediate* barrier to foreign language learning. At the same time, when analyzing peaks and dips in overall performance on a battery of tests, semantic coding difficulties clustered with phonological and syntactic coding difficulties in students who had difficulty learning a foreign language. Likewise, Service (1992) found an association between students' nonword repetition skill and their achievement in learning foreign language vocabulary, and this association was linked to phonological working memory. These findings support those of Koda (1992), that knowledge of both lower-level (i.e., phonological and syntactic) and higher-level (i.e., semantic) language elements impact the quality of one's overall performance in foreign language courses.

Not surprisingly, the word retrieval problems I have in English resurface in French and are even more severe. Due to my many years of experience as an English speaker and writer (as well as to my extensive use of metalinguistic skills as a speech-language pathologist), I have choices in the selection of English words and structures. Unfortunately, this "menu of linguistic options" that supports comprehension and formulation does not exist for me in French. I frequently see the semantic coding difficulties listed above in English-speaking students on my speech-language pathology caseload, and I see them in myself during French language experiences. Specific examples of difficulties include:

I. Oral Language

    A.   Just because a word has been *learned* does not mean it will be *available*. I have word retrieval problems in both French and English.

   *B.   Segmenting the speech stream is a particular problem, so what a speaker says is frequently not what I "hear." I misinterpret details as well as the general idea being expressed (which can actually be quite amusing).

   *C.   Common idiomatic expressions used in syntactic constructions impede my comprehension (e.g., *faire* [to make/do] *Faites-vous du sport*? [Do you play sports?]. For example, use of *jouer* [to play] would result in a direct translation.

*D. Except in sentences that include cohesive ties that speakers vocally emphasize to signal a transition in thought (e.g., *donc* [therefore]), I lose connections in meaning that are supplied by syntax.

E. Comprehension of pronouns in "running speech" is almost impossible. Since all nouns have gender, an object is referred to as *elle* [she] or *il* [he]. I associate those words with female/male and therefore I assume that the discussion is about a person. When pronouns replace entire phrases (in spoken or written language), meaning evaporates for me.

II. Written Language

*A. I confuse English sight words with French words (e.g., *pain* [bread] or *as* [has]); one language actively competes with the other for attention, thus slowing and/or impairing my comprehension.

B. Looking at digits and transforming them into words as I read aloud (or comprehending an oral presentation of digits presented as words) is a task which epitomizes cognitive-linguistic gymnastics and is therefore exceedingly difficult for me (e.g., 1999–> *mil neuf cent quatre-vingt-dix-neuf* or *dix-neufcentquatre-vingt-dix-neuf*). I am not alone in my struggle, however, as translating numbers into a non-dominant language tends to be difficult for most people (Ossipov 1999).

*C. The nuances of words from less concrete parts of speech (e.g., adverbs of time, prepositions, pronouns) fade in and fade out. I cannot seem to anchor the meaning of many structural words. This is more of a problem in writing than in reading, where I can rely on context for semantic support.

*D. Frequently, I cannot decode multisyllablic printed words that divide at the end of a line. Division of words has always been problematic for me, but this problem intensifies when I read French because I am decoding at a basic level. Being sight-word oriented, I expect to see a complete semantic unit (i.e., a word); when the visual image is fragmented due to space restrictions, it also fragments comprehension because I see two separate collections of letters as two separate words. It is as if my brain stops processing at the end of each line and begins again on the next line. In French, I usually need to write all letters of a divided word together before I can recognize the word.

*E. I am still struggling with *decoding* French. I read word + word + word, the same behavior researchers have observed in poor readers whose laborious decoding interferes with comprehension. I must allot sufficient time to first decode structure and vocabulary before I begin reading for comprehension (i.e., rereading passages four or five times).

F. Some comprehension challenges that are severe in oral language (e.g., cohesive ties and multiple-meaning words) are more moderate in written language, because I carefully monitor comprehension, use contextual clues to clarify meaning, and reread until I understand. However, culling meaning from long, complex sentences is extremely difficult for me. I cannot remember earlier phrases long enough to connect them to subsequent phrases.

*G. Metalinguistic passages in textbooks are semantic challenges. For approximately two years of study, I could not understand explanations about French grammar when these were presented in French. Using the foreign language to talk about the foreign language (i.e., a metalinguistic text passage) was complete overload. If the teacher presented the same information in English, my background enabled me to grasp basic principles. However, it took almost five years before I really began to retain more abstract grammatical rules such as those governing pronouns and verb conjugation. I remember having experienced similar difficulties understanding explanations about English grammar as an elementary and high-school student.

FOREIGN LANGUAGE REQUIREMENT WAIVERS

Foreign language courses are predictably problematic to students with dyslexia, but how easy should it be for them to "petition out" of foreign language? Sparks, Philips, and Ganschow (1996) suggest that universities establish rigorous criteria for foreign language waivers. Learning a foreign language is difficult for many people. When I felt terribly discouraged, it was helpful to remember that some aspects of foreign language comprehension are more difficult than others for everyone. In other words, I tried to avoid attributing all my difficulties to dyslexia or assuming that I was the only one who was not "getting it." According to Sparks, Philips, and Javorsky (1998), the key distinction between students with at-risk profiles who do or do not pass a foreign language course may be the degree of perseverance exhibited by those who succeed and the adoption of good study habits. Brown-Azarowicz, Stannard, and Goldin (1992) add to these factors a realistic appraisal of the amount of time it takes to acquire a new symbol system. Sparks, Phillips, and Ganschow (1996) suggest that advisors counsel students with a history of language learning difficulties to enroll in foreign language courses early in their college career rather than in their junior or senior years.

For most people with dyslexia, passing a foreign language course requires an extraordinary commitment because dyslexic students tend to have particular weaknesses in the types of learning skills that a foreign language course demands. I would, nonetheless, concur with Sparks, Philips, and Ganschow (1996) that students with LD should at least attempt foreign language courses. I agree with Brown-Azarowicz, Stannard, and Goldin (1992, p. 15) who say: "Your aptitude for foreign languages is far less crucial to your success than your attitude."

Being successful requires being creative and strategic (e.g., enrolling in only a foreign language course at a community college). In my opinion, however, one year of foreign language is sufficient both to help students with dyslexia develop stronger linguistic skills and to enable them to "get by" in another language. Other university learning opportunities are equally if not more valuable, and the amount of psychological stress dyslexics experience to complete a second year of foreign language is simply not commensurate with the payoff. Creative problem-solving might include searching for a college that requires not more than one year of foreign language for graduation or taking course substitutions during the second year in settings where two years of foreign language are required.

STRATEGIES FOR LEARNING A FOREIGN LANGUAGE

Gerber and Reiff (1991) and Reiff, Gerber, and Ginsberg (1997) reported on attitudes and patterns of behavior they found when analyzing their interviews with 71 "successful adults with learning disabilities." This study population indicated that perseverance can compensate for a lack of natural potential in a number of academic areas. Other survival strategies these educators mentioned were self-advocacy, creative problem-solving, humor, maintaining a positive outlook on life, and reframing negative experiences in terms of what could be learned from them. Considering the significance of perseverance, the following ten suggestions are for students with dyslexia who are faced with a foreign language requirement:

1. Avoid "linguistic bears" such as taking a foreign language until the educational system says: "You *must* do this!" Then, carefully orchestrate each semester of learning, recognizing that sometimes a solo is needed. Enroll in one course—the foreign language.

2. Balance hard work and good health. If you have dyslexia and are in the process of learning a foreign language, recognize that feeling overwhelmed is normal. However, prepare to work three times harder than your intellectual peers, and allow time to repeat the course. Get plenty of rest, eat well, and never study for longer than 30 minutes without taking a short break.

3. Work with an instructor who uses the board to visually display structural concepts and who is willing to use English for teaching or clarification of grammatical principles.

4. Use books that explain grammar rules in English. If the assigned textbook presents all content in the foreign language, acquire an arsenal of books that clearly presents the linguistic structure of the foreign language in English (e.g., *The Essentials of French Grammar*, Ellis 1995; *500 French Verbs*, Kendris 1990). After you understand the grammatical rules and metalinguistic vocabulary in English, return to the assigned text. Learn all metalinguistic terms in the foreign language so you will comprehend these terms when they are used in instruction. Auxillary books that teach grammar principles in English serve the same function that *Cliff's Notes* serve for passing other courses.

5. Prepare. Read and reread a chapter before it is covered in class. Prepare for that moment of comprehension to occur in class when you have the instructor available to clarify anything that is still slightly "fuzzy."

6. Make course content meaningful to you. During class, write notes clarifying grammar in the text, so that all instructional information is in one place. When the instructor reviews homework, write the answers in the book so you have examples of structural concepts that make sense to you. Make a pronunciation key for all vowels, unusual consonants, or reoccurring verb endings where the written language does not parallel the pronunciation.

7. Accept without debate the logic of the foreign language. To spend time and energy on questioning the logic of a foreign language is futile; the foreign language will not change. Do what you need to do to understand the linguistic system rather than cluttering your mind with a resistant attitude. For example, assigning gender to nouns might not seem logical, but find a way to learn it (e.g., coding each noun with a pink or blue marker). Summarize key grammar rules on one page. Visualize the page during exams.

8. "Apply! Apply! Apply!" one of my instructors once told the class. Most college libraries have foreign language drills on computer, and drills are available on the internet. Computer drills provide immediate feedback so you can quickly learn a grammatical rule by applying it and you have the opportunity to analyze your error patterns.

9. Review regularly and prepare for exams. Earlier chapters set the stage for the current chapter being studied; review the key principles regularly. Outline each chapter at least three days before an exam. Prepare this outline in a place where you can say (at least at a whisper) everything you are writing. During this multisensory experience, linguistic rules that were once "fuzzy" suddenly become clear. Each day before the test, review the outline. Do not even *think* about beginning your review the night before an exam!

10. Discover ways to make foreign language learning motivating. For example, choose a language and culture that fascinate you. Find "parallel texts" that have English on one side of the page and the language you are learning on the other side, or books that are audiotaped.

The following is a list of six suggestions for foreign language instructors who teach students with dyslexia:

1. Teach *how* to learn what is being taught. Regularly ask students to share study strategies that have helped them master difficult foreign language principles and provide additional strategies of your own.

2. Provide multisensory support for learning linguistic concepts. For example:

    (a) Let students "play" with blocks that represent structural elements so they can see the deletions, additions and permutations that occur with replacements (e.g., a pronoun for a noun or noun phrase), negation, and construction of interrogatives;

    (b) Encourage students to develop charts that summarize linguistic principles and show predictable relationships among linguistic elements;

    (c) Provide opportunities to engage in memorized dialogues and sing songs that emphasize the grammatical principles you are teaching;

    (d) Help students establish an understanding of word boundaries by regularly giving dictation;

    (e) Provide immediate feedback by displaying the content in large print on an overhead transparency; and

(f) Ask students to correct their own work, using a pen with a different color of ink, and to analyze the types of errors they made. Have them submit the corrected dictation and give credit for the accuracy of the correction.

3. Provide early and continued support for learning sound/symbol relationships as well as opportunities to apply the knowledge. Regularly provide opportunities for students to develop fluency and intelligibility. Most listeners prefer clear (intelligible) sentences over poorly articulated complex sentences. In the absence of a solid grounding in the phonology of a foreign language, one's communication skills are stunted.

4. Provide incentives to speak the foreign language during each class period. For example:

(a) Ask pairs of students to engage in one-minute foreign language interactions, where they speak only in the foreign language. Give students points for maintaining a foreign language conversation for one-minute, but do not give penalties for lapsing into their native language;

(b) Ask students in advanced classes to create short plays of three to five minutes in length that have no more than three or four characters. Each week, distribute these mini-scripts to beginning and intermediate students. Assign roles and ask them to be fluent "radio performers" on the day they are scheduled to perform. It is important for students to hear themselves sounding fluent in a foreign language.

5. Develop compensatory grading procedures that encourage students with dyslexia to stay in a difficult course like that of a foreign language. For example:

(a) Give extra credit for time spent with a tutor. Ask students to summarize what they learned during the tutoring session. Have the tutor sign the paper and submit it to you;

(b) Give extra credit for grammar drills that are completed on the computer. Ask students to analyze their error patterns and formulate a grammar rule that will help them to stabilize their understanding of problematic structures;

(c)   Encourage students to watch films in the foreign language. Give extra credit for plot summaries of the films written in the foreign language. In addition, ask them to comment on cultural characteristics and interactional styles they observed.

6.   Make learning a foreign language an attainable goal. If students ask for visual support (i.e., seeing structures written on the board)—provide it. In an immersion class, if students ask for clarification in their native language, provide it. If students who are struggling ask you to call on them only when they volunteer, respect that request.

CONCLUSION

The purpose of this article has been to describe the challenges that a person with dyslexia faces when learning a foreign language. Through perseverance and modification of one's academic schedule to accommodate the need for focus on one type of linguistic input (i.e., the foreign language being learned), it is possible to pass foreign language courses that are required for graduation. La récompense (the reward) is a linguistic passport to another culture.

Address correspondence to: Charlann S. Simon, 5630 S. Rocky Point Road, Tempe, Arizona 85283. Telephone and Fax: (480) 839-5507.

References

Adams, M. J. 1997. The great debate: Then and now. *Annals of Dyslexia* 47:265–76.
Brown-Azarowicz, M., Stannard, C., and Goldin, M. 1992. *Yes! You Can Learn a Foreign Language*. Lincolnwood, IL: Passport Books.
Carroll, J. 1973. Implications of aptitude test research and psycholinguistic theory for foreign language teaching. *International Journal of Psycholinguistics* 2:5–14.
Carroll, J. 1962. The prediction of success in intensive foreign language training. In *Training and Research in Education*, ed. R. Glaser. Pittsburgh: Univeristy of Pittsburgh Press.

Catts, H. W. 1989. Defining dyslexia as a developmental language disorder. *Annals of Dyslexia* 39:50–64.

Chall, J. S. 1997. Are reading methods changing again? *Annals of Dyslexia* 47:257–64.

Chaney, C. 1990. Evaluating the whole language approach to language arts: The pros and cons. *Language, Speech, and Hearing Services in Schools* 21:244–49.

Chen, T. Y. 1995. In search of an effective grammar teaching model. *English Teaching Forum* 33:58–61.

Chomsky, N. 1959. A review of "Verbal Behavior" by B. F. Skinner. *Language* 35:1–22.

Cohen, J. 1983. Learning disabilities and the college student: Identification and diagnosis. In *Adolescent Psychiatry: Developmental and Clinical Studies, Vol. 11*, ed. M. Sugar. Chicago: University of Chicago Press.

Commeyras, M. 1995. What can we learn from students' questions? *Theory into Practice* 34:101–6.

Crawford, J. 1991. *Bilingual Education: History, Politics, Theory, and Practice*. Los Angeles: Bilingual Educational Services, Inc.

Dahl, K. L. 1995. Challenges in understanding the learner's perspective. *Theory into Practice* 34:124–30.

Damico, J. S., and Simon, C. S. 1993. Assessing language abilities in school-age children. In *Language-Related Learning Disabilities: Their Nature and Treatment*, ed. A. Gerber. Baltimore: Paul H. Brookes Publishing Co.

Das, J. P., Mishra, R. K., and Kirby, J. R. 1994. Cognitive patterns of children with dyslexia: A comparison between groups with high and average nonverbal intelligence. *Journal of Learning Disabilities* 24(4):235–42.

Dinklage, K. T. 1987. The learning disabled college student. Unpublished paper.

Dinklage, K. T. 1971. Inability to learn a foreign language. In *Emotional Problems of the Student*, eds. G. Blaine and C. McArthur. New York: Appleton-Century-Crofts.

Ehri, L. 1992. Reconceptualizing the development of sight word reading and its relationship to recoding. In *Reading Acquisition*, eds. P. Gough, L. Ehri, and R. Treiman (pp.107–143). Hillsdale, NJ: Lawrence Erlbaum.

Ehrman, M. 1990. The role of personality type in adult language learning: An ongoing investigation. In *Language Aptitude Reconsidered*, eds.T. Parry and C. Stansfield. Englewood Cliffs, NJ: Prentice-Hall.

Ellis, M. 1995. *The Essentials of French Grammar*. Piscatoway, NJ: Research and Education Association.

Ellis, R. 1985. *Understanding Second Language Acquisition*. Oxford: Oxford University Press.

Fink, R. 1998. Literacy development in successful men and women with dyslexia. *Annals of Dyslexia* 48:311–46.

Ganschow, L., and Sparks, R. 1993. Foreign language learning disabilities: Issues, research and teaching implications. In *Success for College Students with Learning Disabilities*, eds. S. Vogel and P. Adelman. New York: Springer-Verlag.

Ganschow, L., Sparks, R. L., and Javorsky, J. 1998. Foreign language learning difficulties: An historical perspective. *Journal of Learning Disability* 31:248–58.

Ganschow, L., Sparks, R., and Schneider, E. 1995. Learning a foreign language: Challenges for students with language learning difficulties. *Dyslexia* 1:75–95.

Gardner, R. 1985. *Social Psychology and Second Language Learning: The Role of Attitudes and Motivation*. London: Arnold.

Gass, S., and Selinker, L. 1994. *Second Language Acquisition: An Introductory Course*. Hillsdale, NJ: Lawrence Erlbaum Associates.

Gathercole, S. E., and Baddeley, A. D. 1993. *Working Memory and Language*. Hillsdale, NJ: Lawrence Erlbaum Associates, Publishers.

Gerber, P. J. 1994. Researching adults with learning disabilities from an adult-development perspective. *Journal of Learning Disabilities* 27:6–10.

Gerber, P. J., and Reiff, H. 1991. *Speaking for Themselves*. Ann Arbor, MI: University of Michigan Press.

Goodman, K. 1986. *What's Whole in Whole Language?* Portsmouth, NH: Heinemann.

Kendris, C. 1990. *500 French Verbs*. New York: Barron's Educational Series, Inc.

Koda, K. 1992. The effects of lower-level processing skills on foreign language reading performance: Implications for instruction. *Modern Language Journal* 76:502–12.

Krashen, S. 1982. *Second Language Acquisition and Second Language Learning*. New York: Pergamon Press.

Lescano, A. A. 1995. The remedial English project. *English Teaching Forum* 33:40–41.

Levin, M. D. 1987. *Developmental Variation and Learning Disorders*. Cambridge, MA: Educators Publishing Service.

Long, M. H. 1983. Does second language instruction make a difference? A review of the research, *TESOL Quarterly* 17:359–82.

Mann, V., Cowin, E., and Schoenheimer, J. 1989. Phonological processing, language comprehension and reading ability. *Journal of Learning Disabilities* 22:76–89.

Michaelides, N. N. 1990. Error analysis: An aid to teaching. *English Teaching Forum* 28:28–30.

Murphy, S. T. 1992. *On Being L.D.: Perspectives and Strategies of Young Adults*. New York: Teachers College, Columbia University Press.

Ossipov, H. 1999. Informal interview. Tempe, AZ: Arizona State University.

Oxford, R. 1990. Styles, strategies, and aptitude: Connections for language learning. In *Language Aptitude Reconsidered*, eds. T. Parry and C. Stansfield. Englewood Cliffs, NJ: Prentice Hall.

Pompian, N., and Thum, C. 1988. Dyslexic/learning disabled students at Dartmouth. *Annals of Dyslexia* 38:276–84.

Post, Y. V., Foorman, B. R., and Hiscock, M. 1997. Speech perception and speech production as indicators of reading disability. *Annals of Dyslexia* 47:1–28.

Reiff, H. B., Gerber, P. J., and Ginsberg, R. 1997. *Exceeding Expectations: Successful Adults with Learning Disabilities*. Austin, TX: PRO-ED.

Savignon, S. J. 1987. What's what in communicative language teaching. *English Teaching Forum* 25:16–21.

Scott, M. V. 1989. An empirical study of explicit and implicit teaching strategies in French. *The Modern Language Journal* 73:14–21.

Service, E. 1992. Phonology, working memory, and foreign language learning. *Quarterly Journal of Experimental Psychology* 45A:21–50.

Simon, C. S. 1999. On being dyslexic: An inside view. *Asha* 41:18–23.

Simon, C. S. 1998a. When big kids don't learn: Negotiating meaning in academic contexts for age 8–18 at-risk students. *Clinical Linguistics and Phonetics* 12:249–80.

Simon, C. S. 1998b. *Assessment of Classroom Communication and Study Skills*. Tempe, AZ: Communi-Cog Publications.

Simon, C. S. 1995. School-based SLP services in 2001: A career odyssey. In *Language Intervention Beyond the Primary Grades*, ed. D. F. Tibbits. Austin, TX: PRO-ED.

Simon, C. S. 1994. School language specialist: Defining an SLP niche within a culturally diverse setting. *Seminars in Speech and Language* 15:125–36.

Simon, C. S. 1991. (Ed.). *Communication Skills and Classroom Success: Assessment and Therapy Methodologies for Language and Learning Disabled Students* (Rev.). Eau Claire, WI: Thinking Publications.

Simon, C. S. 1989. Group screening of academic language skills: Finding at-risk students in classrooms. A paper read at the American Speech-Language, Hearing Association Conference, November 1989, St. Louis, MO.

Simon, C. S. 1987. Out of the broom closet and into the classroom: The emerging SLP. *Journal of Childhood Communication Disorders* 11:1–16.

Simon, C. S. 1986. *Evaluating Communicative Competence: A Functional-Pragmatic Procedure.* Tucson, AZ: Communication Skill Builders, Inc.

Simon, C. S. 1984. Functional-pragmatic evaluation of communication skills in school-age children. *Language, Speech, and Hearing Services in Schools* 15:83–97.

Sparks, R. L. 1995. Examining the linguistic coding differences hypothesis to explain individual differences in foreign language learning. *Annals of Dyslexia* 45:187–214.

Sparks, R. L., Artzer, M., Ganschow, L., Patton, J., Siebenhar, D., and Plageman, M. 1997. Prediction of foreign language proficiency. *Journal of Educational Psychology* 89:549–61.

Sparks, R., and Ganschow, L. 1991. Foreign language learning difficulties: Affective or native language aptitude differences? *Modern Language Journal* 75:3–16.

Sparks, R. L., Ganschow, L., Kenneweg, S., and Miller, K. 1991. Use of an Orton-Gillingham approach to teach a foreign language to dyslexic/learning disabled students: Explicit teaching of phonology in a second language. *Annals of Dyslexia* 41:96–118.

Sparks, R., Ganschow, L., and Pohlman, J. 1989. Linguistic coding deficits in foreign language learners. *Annals of Dyslexia* 39:179–97.

Sparks, R., Philips, L., and Ganschow, L. 1996. Students classified as learning disabled and the college foreign language requirement: A case study of one university. In *Patterns and Policies: The Changing Demographics of Foreign Language Instruction,* ed. J. Liskin-Gasparro. New York: Heinle & Heinle.

Sparks, R. L., Philips, L., and Javorsky, J. 1998. Students classified as learning disabled and the college foreign language requirement: A quantitative analysis. *Journal of Learning Disabilities* 31:248–58.

Vallar, G., and Baddeley, A. D. 1984. Fractionation of working memory: Neuropsychological evidence for a short-term store. *Journal of Verbal Learning and Verbal Behavior* 23:151–61.

Vellutino, F., and Scanlon, D. 1986. Linguistic coding and metalinguistic awareness: Their relationship to verbal and code acquisition in poor and normal readers. In *Metalinguistic Awareness and Beginning Literacy,* eds. D. Yaden and S. Templeton. Portsmouth, NH: Heinemann.

Zhenhui, R. 1999. Modern vs. traditional. *English Teaching Forum* 37(3):27–29.

Foreign Language Learning, Hyperlexia, and Early Word Recognition

Richard L. Sparks

College of Mount St. Joseph
Cincinnati, Ohio

Marjorie Artzer

Northern Kentucky University
Highland Heights, Kentucky

Children with hyperlexia read words spontaneously before the age of five, have impaired comprehension on both listening and reading tasks, and have word recognition skill above expectations based on cognitive and linguistic abilities. One student with hyperlexia and another student with higher word recognition than comprehension skills who started to read words at a very early age were followed over several years from the primary grades through high school when both were completing a second-year Spanish course. The purpose of the present study was to examine the foreign language (FL) word recognition, spelling, reading comprehension, writing, speaking, and listening skills of the two students and another high school student without hyperlexia. Results showed that the student without hyperlexia achieved higher scores than the hyperlexic student and the student with above average word recognition skills on most FL proficiency measures. The student with hyperlexia and the student with above average word recognition skills achieved higher scores on the Spanish proficiency tasks that required the exclusive use of phonological (pronunciation) and phonological/orthographic (word recognition, spelling) skills than on Spanish proficiency tasks that required the use of listening compre-

Annals of Dyslexia, Vol. 50, 2000
ISSN 0736-9387

hension and speaking and writing skills. The findings provide support for the notion that word recognition and spelling in a FL may be modular processes and exist independently of general cognitive and linguistic skills. Results also suggest that students may have stronger FL learning skills in one language component than in other components of language, and that there may be a weak relationship between FL word recognition and oral proficiency in the FL.

Generally, children learn to read by being taught to do so when they enter school. However, children with hyperlexia learn to read words well before entry into school and often before, or in conjunction with, the onset of oral language (Aram 1997). Children with hyperlexia exhibit three primary characteristics: (1) spontaneous reading of words before the age of five; (2) impaired comprehension on both listening and reading tasks; and (3) word recognition (decoding) skill above expectations based on measured cognitive and linguistic abilities (Healy 1982). Studies with hyperlexic children have shown that the majority exhibit some degree of intellectual limitation and that many are classified as having borderline intelligence or as mildly retarded (Aram and Healy 1987). Nonetheless, researchers have found that children with hyperlexia read words very well although they have limited language comprehension and production (Glosser, Grugan, and Friedman 1997). In many of the studies, the outstanding reading ability of children with hyperlexia is accompanied by compulsive and ritualistic reading behavior (Rispens and Van Berckelaer 1991). However, Sparks (in press) has found that hyperlexic children may not remain voracious readers over time.

Researchers have questioned how children with hyperlexia learn to read words so well and at such a young age prior to formal reading instruction without understanding what they read. Although there is no consensus, some studies have shown that children with hyperlexia have a strong ability to utilize regular phoneme-grapheme correspondence rules and read pseudo (nonsense) words that follow phonological rules as well as or better than normal readers (see e.g., Frith and Snowling 1983; Glosser, Grugan, and Friedman 1997; Goldberg and Rothermel 1984; Siegel 1984). Some researchers have speculated that the efficient use of phoneme-grapheme conversion rules by hyperlexic children for reading and spelling words may be modular processes that exist independently of general linguistic and cognitive skills (O'Connor and Hermelin 1994; Siegel 1994). Some researchers have hypothesized that children with hyperlexia might have well-developed orthographic strategies for reading words (Aram, Rose, and Horwitz 1984; Temple 1990) or exceptional visual skills (Aram 1997). However, Healy et al. (1982) report research which shows that although children with hyperlexia are skilled in tasks requiring visual discrimination, they do poorly on visual-spatial tasks. Sparks (in press) has speculated that hyperlexic children may not exhibit orthographic strategies superior to those of normal readers. However, he did not rule out the possibility that the orthographic system of hyperlexic children was superior to normal readers when both groups were younger, but that the normal readers "caught up" in orthographic processing skill over time.

Given their poor language comprehension and production skills in their native language, learning to read, write, speak, and listen to a FL would be difficult for hyperlexic children. Sparks and his colleagues have posited that skill in native language learning serves as an indicator of FL learning ability, and also that a deficit in one native language component (e.g., semantics, or meaning) can lead to similar problems in the FL (i.e., the linguistic coding differences hypothesis) (Sparks 1995a; Sparks and Ganschow 1991, 1993a, 1995). One could speculate that a hyperlexic student could experience some success in learning to read and spell words in a FL if the language adhered to a fairly regular system of phoneme-grapheme correspondence and phonological rules. However, the student with hyperlexia likely would exhibit severe difficulties with language comprehension (listening, reading) and language production (speaking, writing) of the FL. Therefore, a hyperlexic student might do well in the phonological/orthographic aspects of the FL but poorly in the semantic, and perhaps syntactic, aspects of learning the FL.

To date, only one study has been published in the literature about hyperlexia and foreign languages. In that study entitled "Trilingual Hyperlexia," LeBrun, Van Endert, and Sziwowski (1988) describe a fourteen-year-old child who could read aloud words in three languages (French, Dutch, English) despite an IQ in the mild to moderate range of mental retardation. The child did not show precocious reading skills and it was not discovered that she could read words until age five. Her native language was Dutch but she also knew some French. At the age of nine, the mother began to teach her to read English words and short sentences. The child's English pronunciation skills were good but contrasted with her difficulty in pronouncing words in Dutch during spontaneous speech. Generally, her pronunciation of words was much better reading words aloud than in conversation. The child could not write words from memory but had some limited writing skills. She displayed great difficulty with language comprehension and production, and seemed unable to derive meaning from what she had read.

It seems counterintuitive to suggest that a student with hyperlexia would be enrolled in formal FL classes in high school. Nonetheless, the first author of the present study had been following the progress of a student with hyperlexia and a student with above average word recognition skills, both of whom read words at a very early age, over a period of nine years from the primary grades through high school (Sparks 1995b, in press). In the course of his recent follow up study, he found that two of the three students were enrolled in regular sections of high school Spanish. Both had completed first year Spanish and were currently enrolled in a second-year Spanish course. Given the dearth of research about hyperlexia and word recognition in FL learning, the authors were interested in determining the two students' level of proficiency in oral and written Spanish after two years of FL study. A student without hyperlexia was chosen at random from a regular high school Spanish class for comparison purposes.[1]

PURPOSE OF THE STUDY

The purpose of the present study was to examine the FL word recognition, spelling, reading comprehension, writing, speaking, and listening skills of a high school student with hyperlexia, a high school student with above average word recognition but lower reading comprehension skills who read words at a very early age, and a high school student without hyperlexia, each of whom had competed two years of high school Spanish.[2] All three students had been enrolled in regular Spanish courses, completed all course requirements, and obtained passing course grades. The first author evaluated the stu-

---

[1] The author conducted a search over several months for a student without hyperlexia who was currently enrolled in second-year Spanish and whose IQ was similar to the two children with hyperlexia in this study. However, he was unsuccessful in locating such a student.

[2] The distinction between the student with hyperlexia and the student with above average word recognition but low reading comprehension skills is maintained in this paper to be consistent with the first author's previous papers on the two students (Sparks 1995b; in press).

dent with hyperlexia and the student with above average word recognition skills in 1990–1991 and 1998 using a test battery that assessed cognitive, reading, spelling, writing, arithmetic, oral language, verbal memory, general knowledge, and phonemic awareness skills. The student without hyperlexia was administered the same test battery.

In the present study, the authors predicted that the student without hyperlexia would achieve higher scores than the student with hyperlexia and the student with above average word recognition skills on all measures of FL proficiency. However, they expected the student with hyperlexia and the student with above average word recognition skills to perform better on those Spanish proficiency tasks requiring the exclusive use of phonological (pronunciation) and phonological/orthographic skills (i.e., word recognition, spelling) than they performed on Spanish proficiency tasks that required the use of syntactic and semantic skills (i.e., reading comprehension, written language, speaking, listening comprehension, syntax). If the hypotheses were confirmed, results would provide additional support for the idea that word reading and spelling are modular processes and exist independently of general cognitive and linguistic skills (Siegel 1994).

The authors present some brief background information about each of the three participants first, followed by a description of the procedure and testing instruments. Then, they present results and discuss them in the context of current research about the nature of native and FL learning.

METHOD

PARTICIPANTS

The first author reported extensive histories of the participant with hyperlexia (DZ) and the participant with above average word recognition skills (GM) in two earlier studies in which they participated (Sparks 1995b, in press).

DZ was evaluated first in 1990. He had learned to read words at two years of age and was reading books by the age of three. He read frequently each day throughout his primary school years. DZ exhibited oral language difficulties, especially prosodic and intonation irregularities, and an abnormal rate of speech. Test results showed that DZ had an IQ in the borderline range of intelligence. He displayed excellent word reading skills but poor reading and listening comprehension. DZ attended regular classes in parochial schools through his graduation from high school. He received some private tutoring and extensive academic support at home. When reevaluated in 1998, test results showed that although his word recognition skills remained strong, his score on word recognition measures had decreased significantly over time. However, DZ's word recognition skills were still above that predicted by his score on an intelligence test. His reading comprehension, listening comprehension, and oral language skills were still impaired. His parents reported that he had read much less over the years and that reading was no longer a "compulsive" activity. At the time of the present study, DZ was 17 years old, in the twelfth grade, and enrolled in college preparatory courses including second-year Spanish.

The first author initially evaluated GM in 1991 when she was ten years old. She had been enrolled in a public school classroom for children with severe behavior handicaps (SBH) since the second grade. GM had learned to read words at 18 months of age and was reading the newspaper when she was two years old. By the time she was ten years old, GM visited the library five to six times a week to obtain books. She displayed variable and fleeting eye contact, spoke in a loud voice, exhibited noticeable prosodic and intonation difficulties, and demonstrated little awareness of the listener. Test results showed that GM had an overall IQ in the borderline range of intelligence although verbal intelligence was in the average range. She displayed strong word reading skills but lower reading and listening comprehension. GM had remained in the SBH program through high school although she was now mainstreamed for several classes. Although the mainstream classes were at a college preparatory level, teachers modified the work for her. GM continued to exhibit behavior problems at school. When reevaluated in 1998, test results showed that her word recognition skills remained strong but had decreased somewhat over time. However, her word recognition skills were still above her overall intellectual functioning although they were now more consistent with her Verbal IQ. Her reading comprehension, listening comprehension, and oral language skills were still lower generally than her word recognition skills. GM had remained a "voracious" reader for whom reading was still a "compulsive activity." At the time of the present study, GM was 17 years old, in the eleventh grade, and enrolled in a second-year Spanish class.

BR was a tenth grade student who was enrolled in a college preparatory level of courses at a single sex, parochial high school. She was chosen at random from all students enrolled in second-year Spanish at this school and agreed to participate. BR had an overall high school GPA of 3.5, had achieved an A in Spanish I, and received As in the first three-quarters of Spanish II. She had no history of learning difficulties, had never been enrolled in special education, and had not received speech and language therapy. BR described herself as a good reader who enjoyed reading. At the time of the present study, BR was 15 years old.

PROCEDURE

DZ and GM had been assessed in 1990–91 and 1998 with a comprehensive battery of cognitive, academic achievement, oral language, and phonemic awareness measures (Sparks 1995b; in press). For the present study, BR was administered the same battery of tests by the author at the end of the 1999 school year.

The oral and written proficiency measures were administered by the second author during the last four weeks of the students' second-year Spanish course. The author had been trained in developing, administering, and evaluating FL proficiency measures. The American Council for the Teaching of Foreign Languages (ACTFL) Guidelines (1989) were used as the basis for the evaluations. The FL reading comprehension, writing, word recognition, and spelling measures lasted 50 minutes. The FL syntax and working memory measures took approximately 20 to 25 minutes to complete. The FL listening/speaking test, an oral interview, lasted approximately 15 to 20 minutes. All measures requiring an oral response were taped for later scoring.

The FL writing and FL listening/speaking measures were scored by two different raters, both of whom had been trained to evaluate FL proficiency measures using ACTFL Guidelines.[3] Neither of the raters had met nor directly evaluated the participants.

INSTRUMENTS

The complete battery of testing instruments administered to the three participants has been described in detail elsewhere (Sparks 1995b; in press). For the present study, the type of test and the names of the instruments are listed.

---

[3] The authors thank Dr. Maria Garriga and Dr. Nancy Humbach for their assistance in evaluating the FL writing and FL listening/speaking measures.

Achievement. Woodcock Reading Mastery Test-Revised (WRMT-R) (Woodcock 1987); Gray Oral Reading Test-Revised (GORT-R) (Wiederholt and Bryant 1986); Test of Written Spelling-3 (TWS-3) (Hammill and Larsen 1994); Woodcock-Johnson-Revised (WJ-R) (Woodcock and Johnson 1989): Broad Mathematics, Broad Written Language, and Broad Knowledge Cluster; and listening comprehension to text assessed by converting the alternate form of the WRMT-R into a listening comprehension measure (Aaron 1991).

Oral language. Peabody Picture Vocabulary Test-Revised (PPVT-R) (Dunn and Dunn 1981); and the Test of Language Competence-Expanded Edition (TLC-E) (Wiig and Secord 1989).

Memory. Woodcock-Johnson Psychoeducational Battery (WJPB): Memory Cluster (Woodcock and Johnson 1978).

Phonemic awareness. Lindamood Auditory Conceptualization Test (LAC) (Lindamood and Lindamood 1979); Rosner Auditory Analysis Test (Rosner and Simon 1971); and a Pig Latin test developed by Pennington et al. (1990).

Intelligence test. Kaufman Brief Intelligence Test (K-BIT) (Kaufman and Kaufman 1990). DZ had been administered the Wechsler Intelligence Scale for Children-Revised (WISC-R) (Wechsler 1974) in 1990 and the WISC-III (Wechsler 1991) in 1998. GM had been administered the WISC-R in 1991.

FL Proficiency measures. The oral and written FL proficiency measures with the exception of the syntax tests were developed by the second author, a professor of Spanish, who has extensive experience working with high school students and beginning and intermediate university students. The FL proficiency tests were designed to measure the four skills of listening, speaking, reading, and writing in a FL, and were based on tasks at the novice and intermediate levels of the ACTFL Proficiency Guidelines (1989). The FL proficiency tests and the scoring system have been described in detail in previous studies (Sparks et al. 1998; Sparks et al. 1998). The FL proficiency tests are described briefly here.

To assess FL reading comprehension, each student was asked to read two different passages silently (a letter and an article from *Seleccionis* [*Readers' Digest* in Spanish]) and answer ten, multiple-choice comprehension questions written in English about each passage. The students were given 15 minutes for each passage. A student could achieve a maximum score of 20 on the two passages.

To assess FL writing, each student was given 15 minutes to write a response in Spanish to the fictitious letter he or she had

read for the reading comprehension task. The students' performance on the writing task was evaluated by assigning a global
score of 0 to 5 for each of the following writing skills: vocabulary, cultural appropriateness, structure, comprehensibility, and
spelling.[4] A student could achieve a maximum score of 25 on
the writing measure.

To assess FL listening/speaking, a 10 to 15 minute oral interview was conducted with each student. The interview pro-
ceeded according to ACTFL Guidelines and was audiotaped for
later scoring. The students' performance was evaluated by assigning a global score of 0 to 5 on each of the following skills:
pronunciation, vocabulary, grammar, comprehensibility, and listening comprehension.[5] A student could achieve a maximum
score of 25 on the listening/speaking measure.

To assess word recognition in Spanish, students read a list of
20 words, some of which they had never seen before. This task
assessed directly phonological/orthographic skills in Spanish,
and indirectly, pronunciation ability. The vowel sounds in
Spanish, diphthongs, words with diacritical marks, and multi-
syllabic words were included. The list of Spanish words is presented in Appendix A.

To assess spelling in Spanish, students were asked to spell
20 words, many of which they may not have encountered either
in first- or second-year Spanish.[6] This task directly assessed
phonological/orthographic skills in Spanish. Words for spelling
were chosen according to the same criteria used to select the
Spanish words for reading. The spelling words also are presented in Appendix A.

To assess syntax in Spanish, students were administered an
informal oral cloze (incomplete sentences) measure. This task
directly assessed syntax in Spanish. Ten sentences with one
word omitted were read aloud to the student and he or she was
asked to fill in the blank. The words that were omitted included
prepositions, conjunctions, verbs with different tenses, and adverbs (e.g., Marta metío el pavo _____ el horno).

---

[4] Using the ACTFL Guidelines, global scores were assigned according to the
following criteria: 0 = no production, 1 = Intermediate/Low, 2 = Novice/Mid,
3 = Novice/High, 4 = Intermediate/Low, 5 = Intermediate/High. A score of 0
was included if a student was unable to produce any response in Spanish.

[5] Global scores in each of the five areas on the oral interview were assigned
according to ACTFL Guidelines using the same criteria as the FL writing test
(0 = no production, 1 = novice/low, and so forth).

[6] Three pseudowords were included unintentionally in the spelling list.

To assess working memory (memoria de trabajo) in Spanish, students were administered sixteen sentences with the last word in the sentence omitted.[7] The students were asked to complete the sentence by saying a word orally (e.g., Mis manos tienen diez _____.) This task assessed working memory such as the short-term memory system involved in the temporary processing and storage of information (Gathercole and Baddeley 1993) in Spanish.

RESULTS

Tables I, II, III, and IV show the test results of the three students. Table I presents their standardized intelligence test results. Table II presents their performance on the phonemic awareness measures. Table III shows their performance on the native language achievement tests. Table IV presents their performance on the FL proficiency measures. The students' ages at the time of testing are included in all tables.

INTELLIGENCE TESTS

DZ's Composite IQ on the K-BIT was in the borderline range of intelligence (78). His scores on the Verbal scales of the WISC-R (74) and WISC-III (84) were somewhat lower than his score on the Vocabulary scale of the K-BIT (93).

Table I.   Performance of the Three Participants on the Intelligence Tests.

Test	Participants				
	DZ		GM		BR
	1990	1998	1991	1998	1999
	(9-8)	(18-3)	(8-5)	(17-0)	(15-7)
WISC-R/WISC-III					
Verbal IQ	74	84	102	—	—
Performance IQ	72	75	55	—	—
Full Scale IQ	71	79	77	—	—
K-BIT					
Vocabulary	—	93	—	93	118
Matrices	—	68	—	56	105
Composite IQ	—	78	—	72	113

[7] Margaret Lesperance developed the oral cloze and memoria de trabajo tasks. The authors thank Dr. Linda Siegel for permitting us to use these tasks in our study.

Table II.   Performance of the Three Participants on the Phonemic Awareness Measures.

Test	Participants		
	DZ	GM	BR
	(18-3)	(19-0)	(15-7)
Lindamood Auditory Conceptualization Test[a]	68/100	81/100	100/100
Rosner Auditory Analysis Test[b]	12/40	24/40	38/40
Pig Latin Test[b]	0/30	11/30	29/30

[a] The Lindamood is a criterion-referenced test. Its results are expressed in raw scores. Each participant's raw score is reported and followed by the criterion established by the test's authors at the participant's grade level.

[b] Each participant's raw score is reported and followed by the number of items on the task.

GM's Composite IQ on the K-BIT was in the borderline range of intelligence (72). Her score on the Verbal scales of the WISC-R (102) was somewhat higher than her score on the Vocabulary scale of the K-BIT (93).

BR's Composite IQ on the K-BIT was in the above average range of intelligence (113). She scored somewhat higher on the Vocabulary scale than on the Matrices scale.

PHONEMIC AWARENESS

DZ had substantial difficulty on all three phonemic awareness measures. He scored well below the expected criterion when compared to his grade-level peers on the Lindamood. (His performance on the Lindamood was also well below the expected criterion in 1990.) On the Rosner, DZ reached a ceiling level quickly when he encountered items on which he had to delete single consonants in the medial position. DZ could not perform the Pig Latin task and did not appear to understand the directions.

GM also achieved below her expected criterion on the Lindamood. (Her performance on the Lindamood was also extremely poor in 1991.) On the Rosner, GM missed several items on which she had to delete an initial, final, or medial consonant from a word. GM's performance on the Pig Latin task was erratic and she missed some of the easiest items.

BR achieved a perfect score on the Lindamood. She exhibited little or no difficulty on either the Rosner or Pig Latin tasks.

Table III. Performance of the Three Participants on the Cognitive, Academic Achievement, and Oral Language Measures[a]

Area	Test	Participant				
		DZ		GM		BR
		1990	1998	1991	1998	1999
		(9-8)	(18-3)	(9-8)	(16-3)	(15-7)
Reading	Woodcock Reading Mastery Test-Revised					
	Word Identification	116	96	115	106	104
	Word Attack	110	92	94	103	117
	Word Comprehension	90	81	106	99	114
	Passage Comprehension	83	79	95	97	108
	Total Reading	101	87	107	103	116
	Gray Oral Reading Test-Revised	55	75	87	80	111
	Passage Comprehension (Listening)	81	67	87	86	108
Spelling	Test of Written Spelling-3					
	Predictable Words	103	104	94	110	117
	Unpredictable Words	105	109	84	111	116
	Total Test	106	106	91	112	117
Written Language	Woodcock-Johnson-Revised					
	Broad Written Language	74	84	83	91	109
Arithmetic	Woodcock-Johnson-Revised					
	Broad Mathematics	76	86	55	62	126
Oral Language	Test of Language Competence-Expanded Edition					
	Expressing Intents	70[b]	<65	81[b]	79	109
	Interpreting Intents	72[b]	73	89[b]	97	108
	Total Test	69[b]	<65	84[b]	86	108
	Peabody Picture Vocabulary Test-Revised	88	89	112	113	115
Verbal Memory	Woodcock-Johnson Psychoeducational Battery					
	Memory Cluster	79	81	79	74	115
General Information	Woodcock-Johnson-Revised					
	Broad Knowledge	99	86	118	98	104

[a] All scores expressed in standard scores (Mean = 100, SD = 15)
[b] Test of Language Development - Intermediate

Table IV.   Performance of the Three Participants on the Foreign Language
Proficiency Meausres.

FL Measure	Participants					
	DZ		GM		BR	
	(19-1)		(17-2)		(15-7)	
	Raw Score	%	Raw Score	%	Raw Score	%
Reading Comprehension[a]	6	30	13	65	15	75
Word Recogition[a]	13	65	13	65	16	80
Spelling[a]	11	55	14	70	15	75
Syntax[b]	2	20	4	40	6	60
Working Memory[c]	2	12	8	50	6	38
	Rater 1 Raw Score	Rater 2 Raw Score	Rater 1 Raw Score	Rater 2 Raw Score	Rater 1 Raw Score	Rater 2 Raw Score
Writing[d]	3	3	7.5	9	13	19
Listening/Speaking[d] (Oral Proficiency	2.5	10	5.5	13	13	21

[a] Maximum raw score = 20

[b] Maximum raw score = 10

[c] Maximum raw score = 16

[d] Maximum raw score = 25

NATIVE LANGUAGE ACHIEVEMENT

DZ and GM's scores on the achievement measures have been described in detail elsewhere (Sparks 1995b; in press). Here, the authors provide a brief summary of each individual's scores.

DZ's word recognition score was above that predicted by his intellectual ability. However, his listening and reading comprehension scores were low and generally consistent with his intellectual ability. DZ's spelling skills were in the average range but his oral language skills were significantly impaired. DZ's word recognition skills had declined by more than one standard deviation over eight years. However, his spelling skills had not changed in that same time period.

GM's word recognition score was above that predicted by her overall intellectual ability (Full Scale IQ) but consistent with that predicted by her Verbal IQ on the WISC-R and her Vocabulary IQ score on the K-BIT. Her listening comprehension and reading comprehension skills on the GORT-R were somewhat lower than her Verbal IQ on the WISC-R. GM's word recognition skills had declined somewhat over a seven-year period. Her spelling skills were in the above average range and had increased by more than one standard deviation over seven years. Her oral language skills, particularly verbal expression, were poor.

BR's scores on all testing measures were in the average to above average range. Her scores on all achievement measures were consistent with her intellectual ability.

FOREIGN LANGUAGE PROFICIENCY

DZ exhibited great difficulty on the reading comprehension measures on which he answered only 6 of the 20 questions correctly. He performed better on the word recognition measure on which he read 13 of the 20 words correctly. DZ spelled 11 of the 20 spelling words correctly. He exhibited substantial difficulty on both the syntax (2 out of 10) and working memory (2 out of 16) measures. DZ received low ratings on the writing measure (3 and 3). He also received very low ratings on the listening/speaking (oral interview) measure (2.5 and 10).

GM answered 13 of the 20 reading comprehension questions correctly. On the word recognition measure, she achieved a level similar to DZ, reading 13 of the 20 words correctly. GM spelled 14 of the 20 spelling words correctly. She exhibited difficulty with the syntax (4 out of 10) measure but achieved the highest score of the three participants on the working memory (8 out of 16) measure. GM received low ratings on the writing measure (7.5 and 9). She also received low ratings on the listening/speaking (oral interview) measure (5.5 and 13).

BR achieved the highest score of the three participants on the reading comprehension measure, answering 15 of the 20 questions correctly. She achieved the highest scores of the three participants on both the word recognition (16 out of 20) and spelling (15 out of 20) measures. BR also achieved the highest score on the syntax measure (6 out of 10) but did poorer than GM on the working memory measure (6 out of 16). She received strong ratings on both the writing measure (13 and 19) and the listening/speaking (oral interview) measure (13 and 21).

DISCUSSION

The purpose of the present study was to examine the FL word recognition, spelling, reading comprehension, writing, speaking, and listening skills of a high school student with hyperlexia, a high school student with above average word recognition but below average comprehension skills who read words at a very early age, and a high school student good in both word recognition and reading comprehension, each of whom had completed two years of high school Spanish. The authors predicted that BR, the student without hyperlexia, would achieve higher scores than DZ, the student with hyperlexia, and GM, the student with above average word recognition skills, on all measures of FL proficiency; and that DZ, the student with hyperlexia, and GM, the student with above average word recognition but below average reading comprehension skills, would perform better on those Spanish proficiency tasks that required the exclusive use of phonological (pronunciation) and phonological/orthographic (word recognition, spelling) skills than on Spanish proficiency tasks that required the use of language comprehension (i.e., reading comprehension, written language, speaking, listening comprehension, syntax).

In this study, the first hypothesis was supported in part; that is, BR, the student without hyperlexia, achieved higher scores than the student with hyperlexia, DZ, and the student with above average word recognition skills, GM, on most measures of oral and written Spanish proficiency. BR's scores also were higher than DZ and GM on all measures of native language skill. This finding is supportive of Sparks and Ganschow's linguistic coding differences hypothesis that suggests students with stronger native language skills have stronger FL aptitude and achieve higher levels of FL proficiency than students with weaker native language skills (Sparks 1995a; Sparks and Ganschow 1991, 1993a, 1995).

A related finding is that GM, the student with the stronger native language skills, scored higher than DZ, the student with hyperlexia, on most measures of FL proficiency. DZ performed as well as GM on only one FL proficiency measure, word recognition. This finding is also supportive of the linguistic coding differences hypothesis that suggests FL aptitude and FL learning exist on a continuum from very good to very poor FL learners, and that one's position on the continuum is determined largely by one's level of native language skill (Sparks 1995a; Sparks and Ganschow 1995).

However, the first hypothesis was not fully supported. On two measures of FL proficiency—working memory and reading comprehension—GM performed almost as well as or better than BR. Perhaps GM did well on the FL reading comprehension measure because she exhibited strong word recognition skills in Spanish, displayed adequate working memory skills in

Spanish, possessed a strong native language vocabulary, and exhibited average to low average native language reading comprehension skills.

Findings also showed that the second hypothesis was supported in part; that is, the student with hyperlexia and the student with above average word recognition skills performed better on most Spanish proficiency tasks requiring the exclusive use of phonological and phonological/orthographic skills than on Spanish tasks requiring the use of language comprehension skills. DZ achieved a higher percentage of correct answers on the word recognition (65 percent) and spelling (55 percent) measures than on any of the remaining FL proficiency measures, all of which required the use of syntactic (grammar), semantic (meaning), and comprehension skills. GM achieved a higher percentage of correct answers on the spelling (70 percent) and word recognition (65 percent) measures than on all the remaining FL proficiency measures except reading comprehension. DZ and GM's scores on the FL word recognition and FL spelling measures were similar to BR, the student without hyperlexia. Furthermore, the two FL proficiency evaluators rated both DZ and GM higher on the phonological criterion of FL listening/speaking (i.e., pronunciation) and the phonological/orthographic criterion of FL writing (i.e., spelling) than on all other criteria on the FL writing (vocabulary, cultural appropriateness, structures, comprehensibility) and FL listening/speaking (vocabulary, grammar, comprehensibility, listening comprehension) measures. These findings are supportive of Siegel (1994) who hypothesizes that word reading and spelling are modular processes that exist independently of general cognitive and linguistic skills.

The present findings also show that an individual with strong FL word recognition skill can have weaker skill in FL listening comprehension and FL reading comprehension (i.e., the hyperlexic pattern). In this study, DZ achieved very low scores on the FL listening/speaking measure and the FL reading comprehension measure. In a review of the second language (L2) literature, Geva (2000) found that FL reading comprehension relates to FL oral proficiency; however, research did not support the idea that word-based reading skills in a FL relates to FL oral proficiency (i.e., listening/speaking). Geva and her colleagues have conducted research that showed weak relationships between students' performance on word recognition tasks and measures of oral proficiency in the FL (Geva and Clifton 1994; Geva, Wade-Woolley, and Shany 1997; Gholamain and Geva

1999). Other researchers report that FL word recognition skills are best predicted by students' native language phonemic awareness and native language word recognition skills (see, e.g., Durgunoglu, Nagy, and Hancin-Bhatt 1993; Dufva and Voeten 1999). The findings of the present study and the research cited here support Sparks and Ganschow's previous finding that secondary and postsecondary level students learning a FL can exhibit stronger skills in some aspects of FL learning (e.g., word recognition and pronouncing words) than in other aspects of FL learning (e.g., speaking and listening) (see, e.g., Sparks and Ganschow 1993b).

In previous studies with the student with hyperlexia and the student with above average word recognition skills (Sparks 1995b, in press), the first author found that despite their strong word recognition skills, both students' phonemic awareness skills were poor (see table II). He speculated whether hyperlexic children and children with above average word recognition skills who read words at a very early age might fail to demonstrate phonemic awareness skill because of difficulties with language comprehension, information processing, and/or abstract and conceptual thinking. In this study, both students also achieved relatively strong scores on FL word recognition and spelling measures despite their difficulties completing phonemic awareness tasks successfully. This finding provides additional evidence that suggests students with hyperlexia and children with above average word recognition skills who read words at a very early age possess adequate phonemic awareness skill but cannot demonstrate it on typical measures of phonemic awareness (i.e., Lindamood, Rosner, Pig Latin).

One finding of the author's previous studies was that despite their low levels of phonemic awareness, the student with hyperlexia and the student with above average word recognition skills appeared to rely on grapheme-phoneme conversion rules for word analysis. Thus, the author questioned whether they would use grapheme-phoneme conversion rules to read (decode) Spanish words. Analysis of the students' errors showed that both students relied predominantly on grapheme-phoneme conversion rules to read Spanish words. For example, DZ made the following errors: *inventado*—/in//ven//tä//do/; *la amada*—/lä//ä//mä//dä/; *agencia*—/ä//gen///sē//ä/; *entrenamiento*—/e//trē//rē//mē//en//tō/; and *filólogo*—/fē//lō//lē//jē//gō/. On two words, *salon* and *antena*, DZ read their English pronunciation. GM made the following errors: *orilla*—/ō//rē//lu/; *entrenamiento*—/en//tru//mē//en//tō/;

filólogo—/feel//lō//gō/; and *antena*—/an//ten//yä/. GM read the word *mural* with its English pronunciation. Both GM and DZ failed to pronounce the Spanish *d* as *th* in the words *inventado* and *la amada*. Most of DZ and GM's spelling mistakes were also related to grapheme-phoneme conversion errors. For example, DZ spelled *letro* as *litro* and GM spelled *arpa* as *arapa*. Table V provides a list of the two students' misspelled words. It seems likely that Spanish was an appropriate choice of FL for these students because it has a more transparent orthography than English. Nonetheless, findings suggest that students with hyperlexia and students with above average word recognition skills who read words at a very early age also rely on phoneme-grapheme conversion rules for word recognition and spelling Spanish words, despite their inability to demonstrate adequate levels of phonemic awareness.

IMPLICATIONS

There are several important theoretical implications of this study. First, reading and spelling words in a FL may be modu-

Table V. Spelling Errors of DZ and GM on the Spanish Spelling Task	
Spelling Errors of DZ on the Spanish Spelling Task	
litro	letro
maiz	mayes
paisaje	picahe
tranquilo	tranquillo
mirande	miande
zebajo	sebajo
horarios	oraejos
felicidad	falicidad
zanahoria	sanaonea
abecedario	avecetario
Spelling Errors of GM on the Spanish Spelling Task	
arpa	arapa
maiz	maize
transuilo	transuillo
periodico	perodicol
zanahoria	fanahoria
abecedario	abesadio

lar processes that exist independently of general cognitive and linguistic skills. One's ability to read and spell words in a FL is likely to depend on phonological skills. Moreover, one's phonological skills can be superior to one's syntactic and semantic skills, making it easier to read words in the FL than to comprehend the meaning of the words.

Second, children with hyperlexia are also good in spelling. This finding suggests that superior word reading skills are not only a product of mere recognition phenomenon but also a product of good recall skills. Moreover, both DZ and GM were good in spelling "regular" as well as "exception" words. This finding may have some implications for the role of nonphonetic skills in spelling.

Third, the processes supporting reading development in one's native language and a second (foreign) language are likely to be similar. Geva (2000) suggests that one's ability to develop good reading comprehension skill in a FL depends on a combination of both good FL word recognition and some measure of proficiency in the FL. A student is unlikely to comprehend text in a FL very well if he or she cannot read (decode) words in the FL with ease and automaticity. FL researchers should consider investing more time in research devoted to the development of FL word recognition skill and its relationship to FL reading comprehension (e.g., see Koda 1992, 1996, 1999).

Fourth, one's ability to read words in a FL is not necessarily related to one's oral proficiency in the FL. That is, some students enrolled in FL courses may be able to learn to read, spell, and pronounce words in a FL quite well because they have at least average phonological and phonological/orthographic skills in their native language. They may do less well in their FL courses as the demands for the use of syntactic and semantic (i.e., writing, listening, speaking) skills increase.[8] The findings of the present study suggest that adequate phonological processing is a necessary but not sufficient condition for efficient FL learning; by the same token, adequate syntactic and semantic skills (i.e., language comprehension) are necessary but not sufficient conditions for efficient FL learning. A student must possess adequate phonological, syntactic, and semantic skills (i.e., similar to BR) to be a good FL learner.

---

[8] However, Sparks and Ganschow have also found that secondary (i.e., Grades 9 to 12) and postsecondary (college and university) level students who have problems with the phonological and phonological/orthographic aspects of their native language do less well not only in reading, writing, and spelling the FL but also in speaking and listening to the FL (e.g., see Sparks et al. 1998).

Fifth, FL educators should consider the idea that knowledge of one's first (native) language can transfer to a second (foreign) language (i.e., cross-language transfer). For several years, the author and his colleagues have conducted research on the impact of one's native language skills on one's FL learning ability. (For a review of these studies, see Ganschow, Sparks, and Javorsky 1998; Sparks 1995a; Sparks et al. 1998.) Through the study of cross-language transfer of phonological and linguistic awareness, FL researchers might uncover improved pedagogical techniques for teaching bilingual students to read English, and for teaching a FL to secondary and postsecondary level students in United States schools.

And sixth, it seems possible that a very few, select children could be classified as "hyperlexic" in two languages. That is, they are able to read (and spell) words in two languages with a high level of skill but do poorly in listening and reading comprehension in both languages. The possibility of studying children with hyperlexia who are attempting to learn a FL is not likely to occur often because most of these students do not learn a second language nor do they enroll in FL courses in high school or college. If the opportunity presents itself, however, other researchers studying this phenomenon should consider adding additional measures to a test battery, such as reading pseudowords in the FL, phonemic awareness and orthographic awareness tasks in English and the FL, and extended reading comprehension and listening comprehension tasks in the FL.

APPENDIX A

Word Lists in Spanish for Reading and Spelling

Word Recognition	Spelling Words
anoche	bien
enero	arpa
isla	dulce
orilla	gafas
usted	litro
mesa	maiz
señora	tago
jefa	después
entrenamiento	secroto
salón	paisaje
inventado	placeta
mural	tranquilo

la amada	mirande
agencia	zebajo
filólogo	horarios
alto	pegamento
corriente	periódico
antena	felicidad
repentinamente	zanahoria
extensión	abecedario

Address correspondence to: Richard L. Sparks, College of Mount St. Joseph, 5701 Delhi Road, Cincinnati, Ohio 45233. Telephone: 513-244-4208. Fax: 513-244-4867. Email: richard_sparks@mail.msj.edu.

References

Aaron, P. G. 1991. Can reading disabilities be diagnosed without using intelligence tests? *Journal of Learning Disabilities* 24:178–91.

American Council for the Teaching of Foreign Languages (ACTFL) Guidelines. 1989. Hastings-on-Hudson, NY: American Council on the Teaching of Foreign Languages.

Aram, D. 1997. Hyperlexia: Reading without meaning in young children. *Topics in Language Disorders* 17:1–13.

Aram, D., and Healy, J. 1987. Hyperlexia: A review of extraordinary word recognition. In *The Exceptional Brain*, eds. L. K. Obler and D. Fein. New York: Guilford Press.

Aram, D., Rose, D., and Horwitz, S. 1984. Hyperlexia: Developmental reading without meaning. In *Dyslexia: A Global Issue*, eds. R. Joshi and H. Whitaker. Netherlands: Martinus Nijhoff.

Dufva, M., and Voeten, M. 1999. Native language literacy and phonological memory as prerequisites for learning English as a foreign language. *Applied Psycholinguistics* 20:329–48.

Dunn, L., and Dunn, L. 1981. *Peabody Picture Vocabulary Test-Revised*. Circle Pines, MN: American Guidance.

Durgunoglu, A., Nagy, W., and Hancin-Bhatt, B. 1993. Cross language transfer of phonological awareness. *Journal of Educational Psychology* 85:453–65.

Frith, U., and Snowling, M. 1983. Reading for meaning and reading for sound in autistic and dyslexic children. *British Journal of Developmental Psychology* 1:329–42.

Ganschow, L., Sparks, R., and Javorsky, J. 1998. Foreign language learning problems: An historical perspective. *Journal of Learning Disabilities* 31:248–58.

Gathercole, S., and Baddeley, A. 1993. *Working Memory and Language*. Hillsdale, NJ: Lawrence Erlbaum Associates.

Geva, E. 2000. Issues in the assessment of reading disabilities in L2 children: Beliefs and research evidence. *Dyslexia* 6:13–28.

Geva, E., and Clifton, S. 1994. The development of first and second language reading skills in early French immersion. *Canadian Modern Language Review* 50:646–67.

Geva, E., Wade-Woolley, L., and Shany, M. 1997. The development of reading efficiency in first and second language. *Scientific Studies of Reading* 1:119–44.

Gholamain, M., and Geva, E. 1999. The concurrent development of word recognition skills in English and Farsi. *Language Learning* 49:183–218.

Glosser, G., Grugan, P., and Friedman, R. 1997. Semantic memory impairment does not impact on phonological and orthographic processing in a case of developmental hyperlexia. *Brain and Language* 56:234–47.

Goldberg, T., and Rothermel, R. 1984. Hyperlexic children reading. *Brain* 107:759–85.

Hammill, D., and Larsen, S. 1994. *Test of Written Spelling-3*. Austin, TX: PRO-ED.

Healy, J. 1982. The enigma of hyperlexia. *Reading Research Quarterly* 17:319–38.

Healy, J., Aram, D., Horwitz, S., and Kessler, J. 1982. A study of hyperlexia. *Brain and Language* 17:1–23.

Kaufman, A., and Kaufman, N. 1990. *Kaufman Brief Intelligence Test*. Circle Pines, MN: American Guidance.

Koda, K. 1992. The effects of lower level processing skills on foreign language reading performance: Implications for instruction. *Modern Language Journal* 76:502–12.

Koda, K. 1996. L2 word recognition research: A critical review. *Modern Language Journal* 80:450–60.

Koda, K. 1999. Development of intraword orthographic sensitivity and decoding skills. *Modern Language Journal* 83:51–61.

LeBrun, Y., Van Endert, C., and Sziwowski, H. 1988. Trilingual hyperlexia. In *The Exceptional Brain*, eds. L. K. Obler and D. Fein. New York: Guilford Press.

Lindamood, C., and Lindamood, P. 1979. *Lindamood Auditory Conceptualization Test*. Austin, TX: PRO-ED.

O'Connor, N., and Hermelin, B. 1994. Two autistic savant readers. *Journal of Autism and Developmental Disorders* 24:501–15.

Pennington, B., Van Orden, G., Smith, S., Green, P., and Haith, M. 1990. Phonological processing skills and deficits in adult dyslexics. *Child Development* 61:1753–78.

Rispens, J., and Van Berckelaer, I. 1991. Hyperlexia: Definition and criterion. In *Written Language Disorders*, ed. R. Joshi. Netherlands: Kluwer.

Rosner, J., and Simon, D. 1971. The auditory analysis test: An initial report. *Journal of Learning Disabilities* 4:40–48.

Siegel, L. 1984. A longitudinal study of a hyperlexic child: Hyperlexia as a language disorder. *Neuropsychologia* 22:577–85.

Siegel, L. 1994. The modularity of reading and spelling: Evidence from hyperlexia. In *Handbook of Spelling: Theory, Process, and Intervention*, eds. G. Brown and N. Ellis. United Kingdom: Wiley and Sons.

Sparks, R. in press. Phonemic awareness and reading skill in hyperlexic children: A longitudinal study. *Reading and Writing: An Interdisciplinary Journal*.

Sparks, R. 1995a. Examining the linguistic coding deficit hypothesis to explain individual differences in foreign language learning. *Annals of Dyslexia* 45:187–219.

Sparks, R. 1995b. Phonemic awareness in hyperlexic children. *Reading and Writing: An Interdisciplinary Journal* 7:217–35.

Sparks, R., Artzer, M., Patton, J., Ganschow, L., Miller, K., Hordubay, D., and Walsh, G. 1998. Benefits of multisensory language instruction for at-risk learners: A comparison study of high school Spanish students. *Annals of Dyslexia* 48:239–70.

Sparks, R., and Ganschow, L. 1991. Foreign language learning difficulties: Affective or native language aptitude differences? *Modern Language Journal* 75:3–16.

Sparks, R., and Ganschow, L. 1993a. Searching for the cognitive locus of foreign language learning difficulties: Linking native and foreign language learning. *Modern Language Journal* 77:289–302.

Sparks, R., and Ganschow, L. 1993b. The impact of native language learning problems on foreign language learning: Case study illustrations of the linguistic coding deficit hypothesis. *Modern Language Journal* 77:58–74.

Sparks, R., and Ganschow, L. 1995. A strong inference approach to causal factors in foreign language learning: A response to MacIntyre. *Modern Language Journal* 79:235–44.

Sparks, R., Ganschow, L., Artzer, M., Siebenhar, D., and Plageman, M. 1998. Differences in native language skills, foreign language aptitude, and foreign language grades among high, average, and low proficiency foreign language learners: Two studies. *Language Testing* 15:181–216.

Temple, C. 1990. Auditory and reading comprehension in hyperlexia: Semantic and syntactic skills. *Reading and Writing: An Interdisciplinary Journal* 2:297–306.

Wechsler, D. 1974. *Wechsler Intelligence Scale for Children-Revised*. San Antonio, TX: Psychological Corporation.

Wechsler, D. 1991. *Wechsler Intelligence Scale for Children-III*. San Antonio, TX: Psychological Corporation.

Wiederholt, L., and Bryant, B. 1986. *Gray Oral Reading Test-Revised*. Austin, TX: PRO-ED.

Wiig, E., and Secord, W. 1989. *Test of Language Competence-Expanded Edition*. San Antonio, TX: Psychological Corporation.

Woodcock, R. 1987. *Woodcock Reading Mastery Test-Revised*. Circle Pines, MN: American Guidance.

Woodcock, R., and Johnson, M.B. 1978. *Woodcock-Johnson Psychoeducational Battery: Tests of Cognitive Ability*. Chicago, IL: Riverside.

Woodcock, R., and Johnson, M.B. 1989. *Woodcock-Johnson Revised: Tests of Achievement*. Chicago, IL: Riverside.

PART V
Reading Disabilities
in Other Languages

In 1997, when The Orton Dyslexia Society took on its new name, the organization made a commitment to promote and facilitate crosscultural understanding of the nature, diagnosis, and remediation of dyslexia. The two articles presented here reflect current research and thinking about reading disabilities in other parts of the world.

The first article by Haynes and his colleagues represents a collaborative effort between American and Japanese educators on teacher perceptions of learning disabilities in the United States and Japan. The article is the first crosscultural research on teachers' perceptions of academic skills (reading, computation, listening, spelling, math) in children with learning disabilities. Among the results was the finding that American teachers identified 4 percent of children with LD, whereas Japanese teachers identified only 1.5 percent. The authors provide several plausible explanations for this finding, and discuss similarities and differences between teacher perceptions in light of distinctive features of the writing systems and cultural aspects in the two countries.

Most *Annals* readers are likely to be familiar with the research of C. K. Leong who is an authority on dyslexia research in both English and Chinese. Attention to similarities and differences across orthographies becomes important as researchers attempt to characterize dyslexia across alphabetic, syllabic, and morphosyllabic language systems. Professor Leong and his colleagues introduce readers to aspects of the linguistic structure of Chinese, a morphosyllabic language based on meaning-plus-speech sound. They describe the nature of the phonetic and semantic radicals involved in learning to read and spell Chinese, and explain how children in China acquire initial reading and spelling skills. The authors make a case for the reading-spelling connection as the main source of difficulties in Chinese. They suggest that spelling difficulties are particularly prominent among Chinese children with dyslexia, and their reading includes difficulties with automaticity and reading accuracy. The authors argue for systematic teaching of Chinese spelling patterns and their linkages to speech sounds and meaning. Their review of research on good and poor reader-spellers should be of particular interest to researchers who study dyslexia across different language systems.

As we continue to look toward what researchers are doing across the world, we will necessarily have to expand our view of what dyslexia is and what it means. Toward this end, we welcome articles from across the world that will increase our scientific understanding of reading disabilities.

Teachers' Skill Ratings of Children with Learning Disabilities: A Comparison of the United States and Japan

Charles Haynes, Ed.D.

MGH Institute of Health Professions,
Boston, Massachusetts

Pamela Hook, Ph.D.

MGH Institute of Health Professions,
Boston, Massachusetts

Paul Macaruso, Ph.D.

Community College of Rhode Island,
Providence, Rhode Island

Etsuko Muta, M.Ed.

Seikei University,
Musashino, Tokyo

Yoichi Hayashi, M.A.

Shirayuri University,
Chofu, Tokyo

Junko Kato, M.D.

Kanagawa Research Institute of Learning Disabilities
Yokohama, Kanagawa

Tokuko Sasaki, M.Ed.

Tsunashima Higashi School,
Yokohama, Kanagawa

Annals of Dyslexia, Vol. 50, 2000
ISSN 0736-9387

This study compared U.S. and Japanese grade school teachers' percep-tions of the strengths and weaknesses of children in their classrooms identified as fitting commonly used criteria for a learning disability. U.S. teachers identified 4.0 percent of their children as meeting the criteria and Japanese teachers identified 1.5 percent. The teachers then rated these children's abilities in the areas of listening, speaking, read-ing/writing, reasoning, mathematics, social, and study skills. Overall, U.S. and Japanese teachers' rating patterns were similar on 70 percent of the skills. In most areas where significant differences were found— listening, speaking, reading/writing and study skills—U.S. teachers rated higher percentages of their children as "weaker" than Japanese teachers. A noteworthy exception was the area of social skills where Japanese children received higher percentages of "weak" ratings. U.S. and Japanese teachers also differed in their perceptions of causative factors leading to their children's learning difficulties. We discuss the findings in terms of U.S.-Japanese differences in writing systems and cultural expectations.

Past studies comparing educational practices and outcomes in the United States (U.S.) and Japan have focused mainly on ethnographic data and, in some instances, direct measurement of children's academic and cognitive skills (White 1987, 1993; Shields 1993; Stevenson, Stigler, Lee, Lucker, Kitamura, and Hsu 1985; Yamada and Banks 1994). Relatively little attention has been paid to comparing *teachers' perceptions* of the specific aca-demic weaknesses of students in their classes. Teachers' percep-tions, informed by daily observations of children's behaviors and shaped by cultural values, are important because they in-fluence patterns of assessment, referral, and treatment (Hammill and Bryant 1998; Shaywitz, Shaywitz, Fletcher, and Escobar 1990).

In this study, we compare Japanese and U.S. teachers' iden-tification rates and evaluation of students who fit generic crite-ria for a learning disability. This comparison allows us to address cross-cultural differences in teachers' perceptions of specific skills in children with learning difficulties. These per-ceptions are likely to be influenced by expectations for class-room performance that may differ across the cultures. Previous studies have shown that cultural factors often influence teach-ers' perceptions and expectations for children's performance (Michaels 1981; Cazden 1988; Gallimore and Hu-Pei Au 1997). Below, we highlight social, educational, and linguistic factors in Japan and the U.S. that may affect teachers' perceptions of stu-dents' skills.

In the area of social interactions, Japan and the U.S. differ greatly in the importance they place on rules for social behavior (White 1987). Examples of Japan's highly evolved structures for social interaction include refined use of social distance, an elaborate system of honorific terms for precisely denoting social register, and firm rules for expected responses to authority figures. In the U.S., use of social distance is highly variable, and rules for denoting social register tend to be less elaborate and less strictly observed. Additionally, the countries differ with respect to the role of the individual in relationship to the group (Takahashi 1995). In Japan, a strong cultural value is placed on the group and the ability to collaborate harmoniously with others (Iwama 1993; LeVine 1995). Collective accomplishments are generally emphasized over those of the individual. On the other hand, in the U.S., individualistic behavior is generally tolerated, if not encouraged, and high esteem is often associated with positive accomplishments that distinguish the individual from the group.

With respect to educational environments, U.S. class sizes are relatively small and provide opportunities for individual attention. In Japan, class sizes are larger, and teachers employ positive peer pressure to promote group order and cohesion (Stevenson 1993). In addition, curricula for Japanese public schools are centrally controlled by the *mombusho*, Japan's Ministry of Education. Consistent with the value placed on conformity and group harmony, the content and sequence of curricula are highly regimented and generally consistent across school systems (Sheridan 1983, 1993; Iwama 1993). In contrast, curricula and teaching approaches in the U.S. tend to be locally controlled, varying from district to district, from school to school, and even from class to class within schools.

Curricular differences between the U.S. and Japan are particularly evident in the area of reading and are complicated by differences in orthography. English employs an alphabetic orthography, premised on grapheme-phoneme relationships. Numerous researchers have documented the unique demands that reading of alphabetic text places on phonemic awareness and efficiency of grapheme-phoneme conversion (Liberman and Shankweiler 1979; Brady and Shankweiler 1991; Treiman and Baron 1981). In the face of these demands, U.S. schools vary greatly in their approaches to teaching children how to read. Some districts embrace meaning-based approaches to reading, others employ phonics-based methods, and still others promote "balanced" approaches that incorporate varying degrees of both methods. In contrast to the variable approaches seen in the U.S., reading instruction in Japan involves highly uniform, incremental teaching of kana and kanji. Kana, a syllabary system with a relatively small and consistent set of syllable-sound relationships, is introduced in kindergarten and usually mastered by the end of first grade. Specific groups of kanji, abstract ideographs representing whole word-symbol relationships, are taught at each grade level. Reading instruction is generally uniform across grade schools in Japan (Sheridan 1993; Takeda 2000).

Based on these contrasting orthographies and instructional approaches, Makita (1968) asked Japanese teachers to estimate the number of children with reading disabilities in their classes and reported a 1 percent incidence in Japan compared with 10 to 20 percent incidence levels in the U.S. and western European countries. This finding led Makita to maintain that alphabetic texts are inherently more difficult to process than kana and kanji orthographies (see also Rozin, Poritzsky, and Stotsky 1971). This theoretically attractive hypothesis has been challenged by Hirose and Hatta (1988), Stevenson, Stigler, Lucker, and Lee (1982), and Yamada (1994; 2000), who measured children's reading skills directly and found similar percentages of reading disabilities—6 to 7 percent—in Japan and the U.S.. The present study reconsiders U.S. and Japanese teachers' perceptions of reading difficulties, in this case, addressing teachers' perceptions of specific reading-related skills in children they have identified as meeting commonly used criteria for a learning disability.

Within the context of these cross-cultural differences, it is not surprising that the U.S. and Japan diverge with respect to educators' awareness of learning difficulties and individualized education for children with disabilities. In the U.S., momentum toward recognizing learning disabilities arose in the 1960s with the pioneering work of Kirk (1962), Johnson and Myklebust (1967), and Kephart (1971). In contrast, public awareness of learning disabilities in Japan did not start until the late 1980s (Takeda 2000). In fact, it was not until 1999 that the *mombusho* formally recognized the concept of "learning disabilities." Furthermore, while the U.S. has a long history in the implementation of Individualized Education Plans (IEPs), they have begun to be implemented only in the last decade in Japan (Muta 1997).

In the present study, we compare Japanese and U.S. grade school teachers' perceptions of children with learning difficulties in their classrooms. We consider whether there are differences between countries in teachers' identification rates for children meeting criteria for a learning disability. Given the greater attention to individual learning differences in the U.S. than in Japan, we ask whether this leads to cross-cultural discrepancies in teachers' awareness of weaknesses of children with learning disabilities in academic areas such as listening, speaking, reading/writing, and mathematics. The greater emphasis on social skills in Japan compared to the U.S. suggests cross-cultural differences also may be found in this domain.

METHODS

PARTICIPANTS

Participants in this study were teachers in Grades 1 through 6 employed by school systems in Yokohama (near Tokyo) and Worcester (near Boston). Students were assigned to regular education classrooms with inclusive enrollment. The students in the Yokohama schools were largely from middle-class socioeconomic (SES) backgrounds and virtually all native speakers of Japanese. The Worcester schools were selected because the students have similar SES backgrounds and are predominately monolingual (English-speaking). According to 1990 U.S. Census data, over 90 percent of the U.S. students were Caucasian, approximately 5 percent were African-American, and the remaining students were Asian, Latino or Native American. We approached 132 U.S. teachers (from 12 schools) for the study. Eighty-nine percent (118) responded by completing the Preliminary Questionnaire (see page 00). Of the 118 U.S. participants, 106 were female and 12 were male. These U.S. teachers were predominately monolingual, and their racial and ethnic distribution was approximately the same as for the students. In Japan, 357 teachers (from 23 schools) were approached and 292 responded (82 percent). Of the 292 participants, 219 were female and 73 were male. Virtually all the teachers in Japan were native speakers of Japanese.

PROCEDURE/ INSTRUMENTS

We asked teachers to identify students in their classrooms who met generic criteria for a learning disability (Teacher Survey, Appendix A). For each student identified, the teacher completed a Main Survey (Skill Areas, Appendix B) in which he or she rated the student's skills across a range of areas. Teachers filled out the questionnaires about six months after the school year started in each country.

Preliminary Questionnaire. We designed the Preliminary Questionnaire to gather background information on the teachers and to guide them in identifying students who fit the criteria for a learning disability. In an effort not to bias teacher judgments, we omitted the term "learning disability" from the Preliminary Questionnaire. The first set of items queried the teachers about their class size, teaching experience, and availability of educational and personnel resources. The teachers were then asked to identify students in their classes who lagged at least two years in acquisition or use of listening, speaking, reading, writing, reasoning, and/or mathematical skills. We selected skill areas in accordance with the U.S. National Joint Committee on Learning Disability's definition of a learning disability (NJCLD 1990/1994). Although the issue of whether to use a two-year lag criterion is controversial in the U.S., we elected to include it because it reflects accepted practice in Japan for diagnosing a learning disability. The adoption of a shared definition provided an essential framework for comparing teachers' perceptions of learning disabilities in the two countries.

In accordance with standard exclusionary criteria found in most definitions of a learning disability, teachers were requested to eliminate any identified students who lagged behind because of mental retardation, sensory and/or motor impairment, primary emotional disturbance, cultural differences, or gross social or economic deprivation (Association for Children with Learning Disabilities 1984; Interagency Committee on Learning Disabilities 1987). The remaining students fit these commonly used criteria for a learning disability and are referred to, hereafter, as "the children" or "the students."

Main Survey. The Main Survey contains 47 items which list skills in the areas of listening, speaking, reading, writing, reasoning, mathematics, study, and social skills. Most of the skills overlap with published inventories used diagnostically to rate students with learning problems in the U.S. (Hammill and Bryant 1998; Levine 1996). However, we chose to create our own instrument in order to respond to the cross-cultural demands of the current study. Although not specifically targeted in published inventories, we added study and social skills to the Main Survey because of their cultural significance in Japan. The data reported in the recently published Learning Disabilities Diagnostic Inventory (LDDI) suggest that the reliability and validity levels for our Main Survey would be high (Hammill and Bryant 1998). Content of the two questionnaires is similar, in terms of general categories of assessment as well as specific skill items.

Teachers rated the students on specific skills using a 3-point scale (1 = "weak", 2 = "average", 3 = "strong"). A fourth option was labeled d.k. ("don't know"). We adopted a 3-point scale because teachers in Japan indicated during pilot testing that a 7-point scale was too cumbersome and likely to give rise to artificial degrees of precision. In the last section, Teacher's Opinions, we queried teachers about possible causes of the student's learning difficulties. For this section, we used a 5-point Likert scale with responses ranging from 1 ("disagree") to 5 ("agree").

We conducted a series of Chi-square tests using raw totals to compare results from the U.S. and Japan on the Preliminary Questionnaire and the Main Survey. Significance levels were set at <.01 to control for elevated family-wise error rates due to multiple tests.

RESULTS

PRELIMINARY QUESTIONNAIRE

In this section, we compare U.S. and Japanese teachers' responses to the Preliminary Questionnaire. Teachers reported an average of 18.3 years teaching experience in Japan compared to 20.1 years in the U.S.. The mean class size of 33 (n = 9,564 children) in Japan is significantly higher than the mean class size of 23 (n = 2,676) in the U.S. [$t(403)$ = 18.5, $p<.01$]. Teachers in both countries reported about 27 hours a week direct instructional time. Ten percent of Japanese teachers indicated they had taught one or more years in a special education setting compared with 21 percent of U.S. teachers [$X^2(1)$ = 7.7, $p<.01$]. There was a significantly higher proportion of male teachers in Japan (25 percent) than in the U.S. (10 percent) [$X^2(1)$ = 10.6, $p<.01$].

When asked to assess educational resources, 79 percent of Japanese teachers categorized them as "sparse" compared to 23 percent of U.S. teachers [$X^2(1)$ = 95.0, $p<.01$]. Similarly, 54 percent of Japanese teachers rated personnel resources as sparse, compared to 30 percent of U.S. teachers [$X^2(1)$ = 18.1, $p<.01$].

Teachers in the U.S. identified a significantly higher percentage of children meeting the study's criteria for a learning disability than in Japan. The identification rate was 4.0 percent in the U.S. compared to 1.5 percent in Japan [$X^2(1) = 67.2$, $p<.01$]. Overall, teachers identified fewer children in the early grades compared to the later grades. In the U.S., identification rates rose from 2.8 percent in first and second grade to 5.7 percent in sixth grade. A similar pattern is apparent in the Japanese data, with a peak of 2.4 percent in fifth grade compared to an average of 1 percent in first and second grades; however, the percentage of children identified by sixth grade teachers dropped to 1.3 percent. Teachers in both countries identified higher percentages of boys than girls; the ratios of boys to girls were approximately 3:1 in Japan and 2:1 in the U.S.

MAIN SURVEY

In this section, we compare U.S. and Japanese teachers' skills ratings for the identified children. First we provide an overview of rating patterns, then discuss salient findings within each skill area. Our analyses are based on U.S.-Japanese comparisons of frequencies of "weak" versus "average"/ "strong" ratings for each item. There were relatively few "strong" ratings given in the two countries (less than 5 percent for 51 of the 58 items); as a result, "average" and "strong" ratings were combined into one category. "Don't know" responses were also infrequent (less than 5 percent for 48 of the 58 items) and were excluded from the analyses. We note items on which teachers in one or both countries gave a relatively high percentage of "strong" or "don't know" responses. The number of children rated was 105 in the U.S. and 140 in Japan.

OVERVIEW

There were no significant differences found between Japanese and U.S. teachers 'ratings on 70 percent of the items. On 19 percent of the items, U.S. teachers rated a significantly higher percentage of students as "weak," and on the remaining 11 percent of the items, Japanese teachers rated a significantly higher percentage of students as "weak." Across four of the skill areas—listening, speaking, reading/writing, and study skills—U.S. teachers rated a significantly higher percentage of children as "weak" on eight of 20 items (figure 1). No differences between countries were found in either reasoning or mathematics skills. In the area of social skills, Japanese teachers rated a significantly higher percentage of children as "weak" on five of nine items. Results for individual skill areas are examined in more depth below.

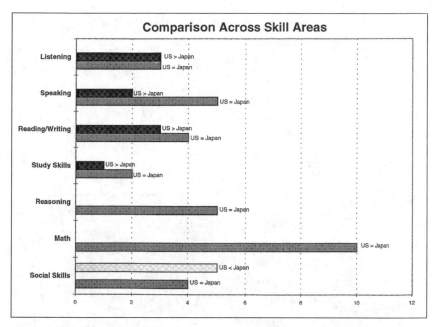

Figure 1:   *For each skill area, number of skills in which significant (or nonsignificant) differences in "weak" ratings were found across countries.*

SKILL AREAS

Listening skills.   As reported in table I, teachers in the U.S. and Japan displayed similar ratings on three of the six listening skills (attention to teacher, listening vocabulary, story comprehension). Teachers in both countries rated over 70 percent of the children as "weak" in ability to attend when the teacher is speaking. The three listening skills on which the U.S. teachers rated a significantly higher percentage of children as "weak" were auditory discrimination (hearing differences between sounds in words), responding to differences in vocal intonation, and following directions. In the latter skill, the U.S. teachers rated a noteworthy 83 percent of the children as "weak."

Speaking skills.   The majority of ratings in speaking skills did not differ between the countries (table II). Teachers in both countries rated a relatively large percentage of children as "weak" in prompt and accurate recall of people, places, and things, and in telling the events of a story in proper sequence. On the other hand, relatively few ratings of "weak" were given in the area of articulation in both countries. Differences between the U.S. and Japan were found in two areas: U.S. teachers identified

Table I. Percentage of Children Rated as "Weak" in Listening Skills.				
Item	Description	U.S.		Japan
A1	attention to teacher	71		72
A2	vocal intonation	38	*	16
A3	auditory discrimination	45	*	14
A4	listening vocabulary	39		46
A5	following directions	83	*	59
A6	story comprehension	52		58

* p<.01 for chi square

Table II. Percentage of Children Rated as "Weak" in Speaking Skills.				
Item	Description	U.S.		Japan
B1	pronouncing sounds	27		20
B2	intonation and stress	37	*	18
B3	repeating information	57		44
B4	recall of names	56		56
B5	playing sound games	60	*	25
B6	gram. correct speech	51		40
B7	story sequencing	59		69

* p<.01 for chi square

more students as "weak" in use of appropriate intonation and stress in speaking and playing sound games. In the latter case, teachers in both countries responded with a relatively high percentages of "don't know" responses (U.S. 34.6 percent, Japan 13.6 percent).

Reading/writing skills. Table III (Part A) presents results from reading/writing skills which are relatively comparable across countries (skills only moderately affected by characteristics of the writing systems). Comparisons of less comparable skills are presented in Part B. Examination of the combined results indicates high percentages of children rated as "weak" in reading/writing skills in both countries. U.S. teachers rated 70 percent or more of their children as "weak" on nine of twelve items, and Japanese teachers rated 70 percent or more of their children as "weak" on six of twelve items. Similarities are quite apparent in the higher level functions of reading and writing; percentages in reading comprehension, composing sentences, and sequencing ideas are nearly identical for the two countries.

In the case of comparable skills (Part A), U.S. teachers rated higher percentages of children as "weak" in using precise vocab-

Table III. Percentage of Children Rated as "Weak" in Reading/Writing Skills.

Part A: Comparable Skills

Item	Description	U.S.		Japan
C5	reading connected text	80	*	65
C6	reading comprehension	75		72
D8	copying words/sentences	50		54
D9	writing from dictation	90	*	73
D10	precise vocabulary	86	*	53
D11	composing sentences	87		86
D12	sequencing ideas	85		86

Part B: Less Comparable Skills

Item	Description	U.S.		Japan
C1,C3	applying phonics/reading kana	72	*	51
C2,C4	reading sight words/reading kanji	66		72
D5,D2	motor formation of print/ motor formation of kanji	56		68
D6,D3	spelling regular words/ producing kana for words	74	*	54
D7,D4	spelling irregular words/ producing kanji for words	90		78

* p<.01 for chi square

ulary in writing, reading connected text, and writing from dictation. Contrasts based on less comparable skills (Part B) are necessarily speculative because of important differences between the two countries' writing systems. Comparisons were made separately for word recognition and spelling/character formation skills that are mainly phonological and for those that rely more heavily on visual processing. When phonic reading and regular word spelling are compared respectively with kana (syllabary) reading and kana spelling, U.S. teachers gave significantly higher percentages of "weak" ratings than Japanese teachers did. It should be noted that prompt and accurate reading of kana was the *only* skill on the Main Survey on which teachers in either country rated more than 10 percent of children as "strong." Eleven percent of the students in Japan were rated as "strong" in reading kana. When sight (irregular) word spelling was compared with kanji character formation, teachers in both countries gave high percentages of "weak" ratings (>70 percent).

Reasoning and math skills. There were no significant differences between countries in the areas of reasoning and mathematics skills. Teachers in both countries rated more than 70 percent of children as "weak" in nearly all areas of reasoning except differentiating real events from imaginary ones. Teachers in both countries also rated over 80 percent of the children as "weak" in mathematical word problems. "Don't know" responses were relatively high in the U.S. (but not in Japan) in "understanding geometry concepts" (16 percent) and "understanding unit concepts" (18 percent).

Study skills. There was only one significant difference in the area of study skills. U.S. teachers rated a higher percentage of students as "weak" in completing tasks. Close to 70 percent or more of children in both countries were rated "weak" in concentrating on assignments and organization skills.

Social skills. Japanese teachers gave significantly higher percentages of "weak" ratings on five of the nine items in the area of social skills (table IV). This is a complete reversal of our typical findings; in all other areas where significant differences exist, U.S. teachers rated a greater percentage of students as "weak" than did their Japanese counterparts. The Japanese teachers identified difficulties in cooperating with others, maintaining peer relationships, maintaining social distance, recognizing social authority, and taking turns.

Table IV.   Percentage of Children Rated as "Weak" in Study Skills and Social Skills.

Item	Description	U.S.		Japan
Study Skills				
G1	concentrating on assign.	78		73
G2	organization skills	74		69
G4	completing tasks	68	*	49
Social Skills				
G3	cooperating with others	42	*	60
G5	joining class discussion	60		65
G6	peer relationships	41	*	58
G7	social distance	25	*	56
G8	gestures/facial express.	32		42
G9	social authority	19	*	52
G10	taking turns	35	*	55
G11	initiating conversation	48		36
G12	maintaining topic	48		53

* $p < .01$ for chi square

Etiological/causative factors.   Table V provides results regarding U.S. and Japanese teachers' responses to five different statements about the etiology or cause of each child's learning problems. For each statement, teachers indicated whether they disagreed, were neutral, or agreed. U.S. and Japanese teachers did not differ in their opinions about the possible contributory roles of lack of motivation or borderline intellectual abilities. Cross-cultural differences were found in responses to items concerning teacher training, family support, and the presence of a specific learning disability. Unlike their Japanese counterparts, U.S. teachers most often disagreed with the statement that insufficient teacher training played an important role in the child's learning problems. Differences between countries on the remaining items were due mainly to larger percentages of neutral responses by the Japanese teachers. A large percentage of teachers' responses in both countries either disagreed or were neutral with regard to the statement that the identified child has a "specific learning disability." This is somewhat surprising, given that the children were initially selected on the basis of meeting criteria for a specific learning disability.

DISCUSSION

This study compared U.S. and Japanese grade school teachers' identification rates and skills ratings of children who met commonly used criteria for a learning disability. We employed a

Table V.   Comparison of Agreement with Causative Factors.

Item	Description	% Disagree		% Neutral		% Agree		Significance
		U.S.	Japan	U.S.	Japan	U.S.	Japan	
H1	lacks motivation	35	34	18	30	48	36	ns
H2	inadequate family support	38	26	12	32	51	42	*
H3	insufficient teacher training	81	17	10	51	9	32	*
H4	specific learning disability	28	22	15	47	57	32	*
H5	borderline intellect. abilities	31	22	27	22	42	56	ns

* p<.01 for chi square

Preliminary Questionnaire to gather background data on the teachers and provide them with criteria for selecting these children. On a Main Survey, U.S. and Japanese teachers rated the skills of the identified children.

Several background factors differentiated the U.S. and Japanese teachers. Larger class sizes were reported by Japanese teachers, a distinction noted previously in the cross-cultural literature (Stevenson et al. 1985; White 1987). Despite larger class sizes, Japanese teachers indicated that they have less special education experience and fewer educational and personnel resources than U.S. teachers. Consistent with their perceived lack of resources, Japanese teachers were more likely than their U.S. counterparts to report insufficient teacher training as a cause of their children's learning difficulties. This may reflect the fact that "learning disabilities" have only been recognized recently by the Japanese educational establishment. Teacher education programs in Japan have not included systematic training to address learning difficulties. Further evidence of Japanese teachers' lack of familiarity with learning disabilities is that they "agreed" with the statement that their identified children have a "specific learning disability" for only 32 percent of the children. Japanese teachers' lower awareness of learning disabilities may also reflect a reluctance to detract from group harmony by singling out students whose learning deviates from the norm.

Given these background factors, it is not surprising that Japanese teachers identified a significantly lower percentage of children as fitting criteria for a learning disability than U.S. teachers. The Japanese figure of 1.5 percent is approximately 5 percent lower than test-based identification rates for reading disabilities in Japan (Stevenson et al. 1982; Yamada and Banks 1994).

With respect to U.S. teachers, the identification rate of 4 percent is similar to the 5 percent incidence of learning disabilities noted by the National Institute of Health (Lyon, 1996, 1997). U.S. teachers, however, "agreed" with the statement that their identified children have a "specific learning disability" for only 57 percent of the children. The percentage is higher than in Japan but suggests continued uncertainty among U.S. teachers as to what constitutes a learning disability. This is again not surprising given that U.S. researchers and policy-makers continue to debate existing definitions (Francis, Fletcher, Shaywitz, and Rourke 1996; Lyon 1996).

Teachers in both countries tended to identify a greater percentage of children in the upper grades. This may be related in part to the study's use of a two-year lag criterion. Applied to first- and second-grade children, this standard is likely to identify a more severely impaired child and, therefore, a smaller number of children. Also, first- and second-grade teachers may have trouble recognizing academic difficulties because the criterion requires them to make comparisons with preschool level performance.

With regard to identification rates by gender, this study's ratios of boys to girls (U.S. 2:1; Japan 3:1) are consistent with school-identified ratios reported in Shaywitz et al. (1990). Higher ratios have been reported in studies using clinical criteria (Miles, Haslum, and Wheeler 1998; Pennington 1991); in contrast, exclusively test-based ratios are closer to 1:1 (DeFries 1989; Shaywitz et al. 1990; Wadsworth, DeFries, Stevenson, Gilger, and Pennington 1992). As Miles et al. (1998) point out, differences in gender ratios stem largely from a "definition" issue. The definition of a learning disability based solely on an IQ-discrepancy gives rise to ratios close to 1:1, whereas the utilization of a constellation of difficulties which may be recognized clinically leads to higher identification rates for boys. It appears that teachers in both countries may have considered broader, clinical signs such as behavioral concerns to identify more boys than girls with learning problems.

There were 13 skill areas (out of 58) in which teachers in *both* countries rated 70 percent or more of their students as "weak." These skill areas fall into three broad categories:

1. attention (paying attention to the teacher, concentrating on assignments);

2. rote memory and working memory (spelling of irregular words/formation of kanji, single/multi-digit computation); and

3. high level language and thinking skills (reading comprehension, drawing conclusions and inferences, differentiating details from main ideas, sequencing ideas in writing and composing sentences, mathematical word problems, and geometric and unit concepts).

These areas of agreement are consistent with U.S. research findings indicating that large percentages of children with learning disabilities show deficits in attention (Hallowell and Ratey 1994), memory functions, and high-level language processing (Torgeson and Wong 1986). For language processing, both Japanese and U.S. teachers identified higher percentages of deficiencies in complex learned skills involving written language than in listening and speaking. Teachers' perceptions in both countries are consistent with data from the U.S. National Institute of Health indicating that 60 to 80 percent of children with learning disabilities have difficulties with written language (Lyon 1997).

We observed a number of cross-cultural differences in rating patterns in the areas of listening and speaking. U.S. teachers gave higher percentages of "weak" ratings in skills related to phoneme-level processing (auditory discrimination and sound manipulation) and in recognizing and producing correct intonation and prosody. The higher percentages for phoneme-level skills may reflect U.S. teachers' greater attention to speech sounds due to their salience for alphabetic orthography. In the case of sound manipulation skills, however, differences may be due in part to a discrepancy in the complexity of games provided as examples. The Japanese children's sound manipulation game, Shiritori, requires movement of syllables and is typically mastered by age six (Hara 1998). Pig Latin, the U.S. example, requires complex manipulation of speech sounds at the phoneme level and is usually not mastered until age nine (Rath 1994). With regard to vocal intonation, the cross-cultural differences may be related to the observation that spoken English places greater demands on recognition and use of stress and intonation to convey meaning than Japanese, which is comparatively neutral in prosody (Seward 1994).

We also observed cross-cultural differences in a number of reading/writing skills. We found differences between phonic reading and kana reading, and between regular word spelling and kana spelling. In both cases, U.S. teachers rated higher percentages of children as "weak." This likely reflects the less complex phonological demands of kana, in which written symbols map consistently onto a relatively small set of spoken syllables, compared to the much larger number of context dependent, grapheme-phoneme correspondence rules needed to master the alphabetic system of English.

We also found significant differences between countries in using precise vocabulary in writing, with higher percentages of U.S. children rated "weak." This finding may again reflect differences in the orthographic systems. In the case of Japanese kanji, only a limited number of characters are taught each year. Japanese children rely on a restricted set of kanji characters and/or highly predictable kana to express their ideas in writing. Therefore, Japanese teachers may not perceive a weakness in vocabulary use in children with deficits in written expression. In the U.S., however, once the alphabetic system has been mastered—usually by the end of third grade--children are expected to use a wide range of words in writing (more comparable to their spoken vocabularies). Children with difficulties acquiring the alphabetic system may often rely on words they can spell, thus reducing the richness of their written vocabulary. We also obtained cross-cultural differences in reading-connected text and writing to dictation. However, percentages of children rated "weak" in these skills were high for both countries (65 percent or higher).

A striking difference in rating patterns was observed in the area of social skills. Japanese teachers consistently rated higher percentages of children as "weak" than U.S. teachers. This robust finding appears to reflect different cultural perspectives, with Japanese teachers highly sensitive to children's abilities to engage in social activities such as cooperating with others, developing peer relationships, maintaining appropriate social distance, and recognizing authority. This is consistent with the strong emphasis in Japanese culture on well-defined rules for social interaction (White 1987; 1993). While social activities are important for children in both countries, the interactive skills developed by grade-schoolers appear more salient to Japanese than U.S. teachers (LeVine 1995; Takahashi 1995).

As with most survey-based research, there are obvious concerns regarding the degree to which our data can be considered valid indicators of children's abilities. As mentioned earlier, teachers' perceptions sometimes differ from behavioral information gathered by researchers. In our subsequent work, we intend to validate teacher impressions with follow-up studies examining actual performance patterns. Also in this study, we sampled teachers from multiple schools in two representative urban-suburban school districts matched by socioeconomic levels. Nevertheless, in order to control for potential regional differences in teachers' perceptions, future researchers may want to sample from disparate geographical regions within each country.

Independent of these validity or sampling considerations, our data provide valuable insights regarding the skills teachers consider critical for children's success in school. As we have observed, there are important similarities and differences in teachers' perceptions across U.S. and Japanese cultures. An increased understanding of teachers' perceptions is essential in both countries, given potential effects of these perceptions on the identification, referral, and instruction of children with learning disabilities.

APPENDIX A

Teacher Survey, Japan–United States Learning Study

PRELIMINARY INFORMATION

1. School's name: _____
2. Location of school (town, city): _____
3. Study code: ____-____-____-____
4. Sex of teacher (circle):   female male
5. Grade level currently teaching: ____   Years of teaching experience (any type): ____
6. How many children are in your class? ____
7. Number of hours teaching per week:_____   Subject(s) you teach:_____
8. Years of teaching experience, if any, with special education: ____
9. Kind(s) of teaching experience with special education (if applicable): _____
10. [U.S. only] Method for meeting special education needs of children in your class (circle primary approach): inclusion pull-out   combination   inclusion-pullout
11. Educational resources (materials and equipment) available to you in your school (please circle): sparse adequate plentiful
12. Personnel resources (support and consultative staff) available to you in your school (please circle): sparse adequate plentiful
13. How many children in your class lag by at least two years (behind their age level peers) in their acquisition or use of listening, speaking, reading, writing, reasoning, and/or mathematical abilities? _____
14. Of the children you noted in 13 above, how many lag behind in their learning because of one or more of the following conditions: mental retardation, sensory and/or motor impairment (e.g., visual or hearing impairment, cerebral palsy), primary emotional disturbance, cultural differences, gross social or economic deprivation?_____
15. Subtract 14 above from 13 above. What number of children remain? _____

If the number of children listed in 15 is zero, please STOP. If the number you listed in 15 is one or more, please fill out *one* of the attached "Main Survey" forms for *each* of these remaining students; that is, children who lag at least two years behind their age level peers in a major aspect of their learning, yet do not exhibit any of the conditions listed in 14.

APPENDIX B

Skill Areas Ranked by Teachers on the Main Survey

PART A. LISTENING SKILLS

A1. Paying attention to the teacher when he/she is speaking
A2. Responding to meaningful changes in the speaker's vocal intonation
A3. Hearing differences between sounds in words (auditory discrimination)
A4. Understanding the meanings of spoken words (listening vocabulary)
A5. Following multi-step oral directions
A6. Comprehending orally presented stories

PART B. SPEAKING SKILLS

B1. Pronouncing sounds in words accurately (e.g., not saying "thith" for "this", or "evelator" for "elevator")
B2. Employing appropriate intonation and stress when speaking
B3. Repeating information that has just been presented orally (e.g., repeating a phone number or lines of poetry)
B4. Prompt and accurate recall of names for people, places, and things
B5. Playing games with sounds in words (as with "Pig Latin" for American children, or "Shiritori" for Japanese)
B6. Speaking in grammatically correct sentences
B7. Telling in proper sequence the events of a story

PART C. READING SKILLS

C1. [U.S. only] Applying phonics to read unfamiliar words
C2. [U.S. only] Prompt and accurate reading of familiar words

C3. [Japan only] Prompt and accurate reading of hiragana and katakana
C4. [Japan only] Prompt and accurate reading of kanji
C5. Reading connected text promptly and accurately
C6. Comprehending what has been read

PART D. WRITING SKILLS

D1. [Japan only] Fine motor formation of hiragana and katakana characters
D2. [Japan only] Fine motor formation of kanji characters
D3. [Japan only] Hiragana and katakana spelling of orally dictated words
D4. [Japan only] Kanji production of orally dictated words
D5. [U.S.] Fine motor formation of print or script
D6. [U.S. only] Spelling of phonetically consistent words (e.g., get, cabin, sand)
D7. [U.S. only] Spelling of phonetically irregular words (e.g., yacht, sword)
D8. Copying words and/or sentences from the board
D9. Writing down orally dictated words or sentences
D10. Using precise vocabulary in writing
D11. Composing written sentences of age-appropriate complexity
D12. Sequencing ideas in writing

PART E. REASONING SKILLS

E1. Discriminating real events from imaginary ones
E2. Distinguishing details from main ideas
E3. Recognizing cause and effect relationships
E4. Drawing inferences from facts
E5. Forming conclusions from facts

PART F. MATHEMATICAL SKILLS

F1. Counting and stating the number of objects in a set
F2. Understanding place value
F3. Reading and writing multi-digit numbers
F4. Comprehending the functions of arithmetic operations (e.g., addition, division, etc.)
F5. Performing single or multi-digit computations promptly and accurately

F6. Solving arithmetic word problems
F7. Estimating quantities of objects in environment (e.g., How many apples are in this basket?)
F8. Understanding concepts of time
F9. Understanding geometry concepts (if applicable)
F10. Understanding unit concepts (length, height, area etc.)

PART G. STUDY SKILLS/SOCIAL SKILLS

G1. Concentrating while doing assignments in class
G2. Organizing and keeping track of homework assignments
G3. Cooperating with others during group activities
G4. Completing tasks assigned in class
G5. Joining in class discussion
G6. Developing peer relationships
G7. Employing appropriate social distances between self and others
G8. Using appropriate gestures and facial expressions when communicating
G9. Responding appropriately to persons of different social authority levels
G10. Taking turns during discussions and other group activities
G11. Initiating conversation
G12. Staying with and maintaining the topic of conversation

PART H. TEACHER'S OPINIONS

What do you think are the main causes of this child's learning difficulties?

H1. This child lacks motivation
H2. This child has not received adequate family support
H3. My training did not prepare me to teach this child
H4. This child has Specific Learning Disabilities
H5. This child has borderline intellectual abilities (low end of normal range)

ACKNOWLEDGMENTS

The authors wish to thank the Japan Foundation for Global Partnership and Seikei University for their generous support. A preliminary analysis of data from this study was reported in the *Journal of the Japanese Academy of Learning Disabilities* (see Muta, Hayashi, Kato, Nakagawa, Sasaki, Morinaga, Haynes, Hook, Macaruso, and Johnson 1998).

Please address correspondence to: Charles W. Haynes, Ed.D., CCC-SLP, MGH Institute of Health Professions, 101 Merrimac Street, Boston, MA 02114. Telephone: 617-724-6311. Fax: 617-726-8022. Email: chaynes@partners.org.

References

Association for Children with Learning Disabilities (ACLD). 1984. Definition adopted by the ACLD Board of Directors, September 22.

Brady, S., and Shankweiler, D. Eds. 1991. *Phonological Processes in Literacy: A Tribute to Isabelle Y. Liberman*. Hillsdale, NJ: Lawrence Erlbaum Associates.

Cazden, C. 1988. *Classroom Discourse*. Portsmouth: Heineman.

DeFries, J.C. 1989. Gender ratios in reading disabled children and their affected relatives: A commentary. *Journal of Learning Disabilities* 22:544–55.

Francis, F., Fletcher, J., Shaywitz, B., and Rourke, B. 1996. Defining learning and language disabilities: Conceptual and psychometric issues with the use of IQ tests. *Language, Speech and Hearing in the Schools* 27:132–43

Gallimore, R., and Hu-Pei Au, K. 1997. The competence/incompetence paradox in the education of minority culture children. In *Mind, Culture and Activity*, eds. M. Cole, Y. Engestrom, and O. Vasquez. Cambridge, UK: Cambridge University Press.

Hallowell, E., and Ratey, J. 1994. *Driven to Distraction: Recognizing and Coping with Attention Deficit Disorder from Childhood Through Adulthood*. New York: Random House.

Hammill, D., and Bryant, B. 1998. *Learning Disabilities Diagnostic Inventory: A Method to Help Identify Intrinsic Processing Disorders in Children and Adolescents*. Austin, TX: PRO-ED.

Hara, K. 1998. Development of phonological awareness in normally developing children. In *Report of Comparative Study in Japan and the U.S.: Children with Learning Disabilities*, ed. J. Kato. Yokohama: Kanagawa Research Institute of Learning Disability.

Hirose, T., and Hatta, T. 1988. Reading disabilities in modern Japanese and Chinese. *Journal of Research in Reading* 11:152–60.

Interagency Committee on Learning Disabilities (ICLD). 1987. Organization's 1987 definition.

Iwama, H. 1993. Japan's group orientation in secondary schools. In *Japanese Schooling: Patterns of Socialization, Equality and Political Control*, ed. J. Shields. University Park: Penn State Press.

Johnson, D., and Myklebust, H. 1967. *Learning Disabilities: Education Principles and Practices*. Austin, TX: PRO-ED.

Kephart, N. 1971. *The Slow Learner in the Classroom*. Columbus, OH: Merrill

Kirk, S. 1962. *Educating Exceptional Children*. Boston: Houghton Mifflin.

Levine, M. 1996. *The ANSWER System: School Questionnaire for Developmental, Behavioral and Health Assessment of the Elementary School Child*. Cambridge, MA: Educators Publishing Service.

LeVine, R. 1995. Public harmony, private doubts. *Harvard Graduate School of Education Bulletin*, June, 14–15.

Liberman, I., and Shankweiler, D. 1979. Speech, the alphabet, and teaching to read. In *Theory and Practice of Early Reading*, vol. II, eds. L. Resnick and P. Weaver. Hillsdale, NJ: Lawrence Erlbaum Associates.

Lyon, R. 1996. Learning disabilities. *The Future of Children: Special Education for Students with Disabilities* 6(1):54–76.

Lyon, R. 1997. Personal correspondence with the National Institute of Child Health and Human Development at the National Institutes of Health, Bethesda, MD.

Makita, K. 1968. The rarity of reading disability in Japanese children. *American Journal of Orthopsychiatry* 38(4):599–614.

Michaels, S. 1981. "Sharing time": Children's narrative styles and differential access to literacy. *Language in Society* 10:423–42.

Miles, T., Haslum, M., and Wheeler, T. 1998. Gender ratio in dyslexia. *Annals of Dyslexia* 48:27–55.

Muta, E., Hayashi, Y., Kato, J., Nakagawa, K., Sasaki, T., Morinaga, Y., Haynes, C., Hook, P., Macaruso, P., and Johnson, D. 1998. Regular education teachers' assessment of academic and social skills in children with LD : A comparative study in the U.S. and Japan. *Journal of the Japanese Academy of Learning Disabilities* 6(2):80–89.

Muta, E. 1997. Personal correspondence with Education Department, Seikei University, June 15.

Muta, E. 2000. Personal correspondence with Education Department, Seikei University, March 30.

National Joint Committee on Learning Disabilities. 1990. In NJCLD 1994, *Collective Perspectives on Issues Affecting Learning Disabilities: Position Papers and Statements*. Austin, TX: PRO ED.

Pennington, B.F. 1991. *Diagnosing Learning Disorders: A Neuropsychological Framework*. New York: Guilford.

Rath, L. 1994. Phonemic awareness: Segmenting and blending the sounds of language. In *Teaching Reading: Language, Letters, and Thought*, ed. S. Brody. Milford, NH: LARC Publishing.

Rozin, P., Poritzsky, S., and Stotsky, S. 1971. American children with reading problems can easily learn to read English represented in Chinese characters. *Science* 171:1264–67.

Seward, J. 1994. *Easy Japanese: A Guide to Spoken and Written Japanese*. Lincolnwood, IL: Passport Books.

Shaywitz, S., Shaywitz, B., Fletcher, J., and Escobar, M. 1990. Prevalence of reading disability in boys and girls: Results of the Connecticut Longitudinal Study. *Journal of the American Medical Association* 264:998–1002.

Sheridan, E. 1983. Reading disabilities: Can we blame the written language? *Journal of Learning Disabilities* 16(2):81–86.

Sheridan, M. 1993. Reading disabilities: Are there fewer in Japan? *Reading-Horizons* 33(3):245–57.

Shields, J. Ed. 1993. *Japanese Schooling: Patterns of Socialization, Equality and Political Control*. University Park: Penn State Press.

Stevenson, H. 1993. The Asian advantage: The case of mathematics. In *Japanese Schooling: Patterns of Socialization, Equality and Political Control*, ed. J. Shields. University Park: Penn State Press.

Stevenson, H., Stigler, J., Lucker, G., and Lee, S. 1982. Reading disabilities: The case of Chinese, Japanese, and English. *Child Development* 53:1164–81.

Stevenson, H., Stigler, J., Lee, S., Lucker, W., Kitamura, S., and Hsu, C. 1985. Cognitive performance and academic achievement of Japanese, Chinese, and American children. *Child Development* 56:718–34.

Takahashi, M. 1995. "I" or "We"? *Harvard Graduate School of Education Bulletin*, June, 8–9.

Takeda, K. 2000. Personal communication with Japanese Academy of Learning Disabilities, March 15.

Torgeson, J., and Wong, B. 1986. *Psychological and Educational Perspectives on Reading Disabilities*. New York: Academic Press.

Treiman, R., and Baron, J. 1981. Segmental analysis ability: Development and relationship to reading ability. In *Reading Research: Advances in Theory and Practice*, vol. 3, eds. G. MacKinnon and T. Waller. New York: Academic Press.

Wadsworth, S., DeFries, J., Stevenson, J., Gilger, J., and Pennington, B. 1992. Gender ratios among reading-disabled children and their siblings as a function of parental impairment. *Journal of Child Psychology and Psychiatry* 33:1229–39.

White, M. 1987. *The Japanese Educational Challenge: A Commitment to Children*. New York: The Free Press.

White, M. 1993. *The Material Child: Coming of Age in Japan and America*. Berkeley: University of California Press.

Yamada, J., and Banks, A. 1994. Evidence for and characteristics of dyslexia among Japanese children. *Annals of Dyslexia* 44:105–19.

Yamada, J. 2000. The myth of absence of dyslexia in Japan. *Perspectives* 26(1):22–23.

Exploring Reading-Spelling Connection as Locus of Dyslexia in Chinese

Che Kan Leong

University of Saskatchewan,
Saskatoon, Canada

Pui-Wan Cheng

The Chinese University of Hong Kong,
Hong Kong

Catherine C. C. Lam

Hong Kong Department of Health,
Hong Kong

This paper advances the argument that in learning to read/spell Chinese characters and words, it is important for learners to understand the role of the component parts. These constituents consist of phonetic and semantic radicals, or bujians, made up of clusters of strokes in their proper sequence. Beginning readers/spellers need to be sensitive to the positional hierarchy and internal structure of these constituent parts. Those Chinese children diagnosed with developmental dyslexia tend to have more difficulties in spelling Chinese characters and in writing to dictation than in reading. A lexical decision study with two groups of tertiary students differing in their Chinese language ability was carried out to test their efficiency in processing real and pseudo characters as a function of printed frequency of the

Annals of Dyslexia, Vol. 50, 2000

characters, and the consistency of their component semantic radicals.
There is some evidence that even for adult readers differing in their
Chinese language ability, lexicality, frequency of characters and the
consistency of the semantic radicals affect accurate and rapid character
identification. Suggestions for research and teaching approaches are
made to enhance the analysis and synthesis of the phonetic and seman-
tic radicals to promote efficient reading and spelling in Chinese.

It was some twenty years ago that the topic of dyslexia in the
context of different orthographies was discussed systematically
(Kavanagh and Venezky 1980). The research and clinical questions emerging were whether or not there are common and specific processing factors to explain developmental dyslexia
across different language systems. In the intervening years,
these questions have been pursued with both vigor and rigor.
The advances owe much to our greater understanding of processes of reading and spelling, and their difficulties across
alphabetic (e.g., English), syllabic (e.g., Japanese), and morphosyllabic (e.g., Chinese) language systems (for details, see Leong
1999a, 1999b; Leong and Joshi 1997; Leong and Tamaoka 1998;
Lundberg, Tønnessen, and Austad 1999).

   In keeping with this quest and to advance our understanding, the International Dyslexia Association also has affirmed the
need to study the clinical manifestations and the scientific basis
of dyslexia across languages through seminars in IDA's annual
conferences and its official publications. Within this context, the
present paper explores the locus of developmental dyslexia in
the Chinese language which is *morphosyllabic*, and is based on
meaning-plus-speech sound relation, as compared with English
which is *phonemically* based. This paper posits the reading-
spelling connection as the main source of difficulties for
students with developmental dyslexia and as the focus of instruction and remediation. In learning Chinese, analyzing
spelling patterns and linking these orthographic patterns and
their constituent parts to speech-sounds and to meaning are an
integrative activity and must be taught systematically.

   More than thirty years ago, the doyen of dyslexia,
Macdonald Critchley, pointed out the need to examine the writing and spelling of those with dyslexia even though they may
be able to transcribe from print to script. He noted that ". . . re-
markable errors occur as soon as he [the dyslexic individual]
writes spontaneously or to dictation. . . . In the case of the
'cured' dyslexic, defective writing and spelling may continue to

appear long into adult life. Where some degree of writing lies within the capacity of a dyslexic, the mistakes are of such a nature as often to make it possible to diagnose the reading defect from a mere perusal of the script" (Critchley 1970, pp. 36–37). In his books, Critchley provided many examples of spelling errors of his patients such as fusion of consecutive letters; omission and addition of letters, syllables and words; and inconsistent spelling of words or "neographisms." Critchley's portrayal of his patients reminds us of Orton's (1925, 1937) classic symptoms of strephosymbolia and the latter's call for reeducation in auditorization of these individuals.

Given these classic studies spanning some thirty to sixty years, it should be noted that the current working definition of dyslexia seems to place considerable emphasis on reading disorders. It does, however, acknowledge that this condition is "manifest by variable difficulty with different forms of language, often including, in addition to problems with reading, a conspicuous problem with acquiring proficiency in writing and spelling" (Lyon 1995, p. 9). Similarly, in a volume on theory-to-practice in dyslexia, Høien and Lundberg 2000 also acknowledge that poor writing skills most often remain with those with dyslexia even though their reading difficulties may be "cured." Nevertheless, both research and clinical studies of spelling in children with and without dyslexia are underemphasized as compared with studies of reading. While the spelling of dyslexics is more primitive than that of their nondyslexic counterparts, they have difficulties in carrying out fine-grained analysis of spoken words and tend to produce in a persistent manner the kinds of errors as noted by Critchley, Orton, and others (Treiman 1997).

PERSISTENT SPELLING DIFFICULTIES IN CHINESE CHILDREN WITH DYSLEXIA

This persistent difficulty with spelling, particularly writing to dictation, seems to apply even more so to Chinese children with dyslexia, as compared with children using alphabetic language systems (Leong 1999b). It is only during the last seven years or so that real progress has been made in greater public awareness and understanding of developmental dyslexia in Hong Kong. These advances are due to the efforts of parents, developmental pediatricians, and child neurologists working through the Hong Kong Society of Child Neurology and Developmental

Paediatrics (HKCNDP), the Department of Health, and members of the Education Department. In the several professional meetings and symposia held under the auspices of HKCNDP in mid and late 1999, it was estimated that there could be as many Chinese children with specific learning disabilities as estimated in western countries. Of the 1998 cohort of children assessed in one of the centers of the Hong Kong Health Department Child Assessment Service, over 80 percent were diagnosed with dyslexia as the main presenting disability, and there were between 15 to 28 percent overlapping disabilities in speech/language, mathematics, and developmental coordination (Lam 1999). Clearly, these children need appropriate provisions with systematic and sustained teaching and adaptive curriculum materials. The need is all the more urgent in face of the comprehensive Education Reform now taking place in Hong Kong to provide for more humane and equitable education for all (Hong Kong Education Commission 2000).

In working with Chinese children with suspected or diagnosed dyslexia, teachers and clinicians observe signs and symptoms analogous to those in children with dyslexia in English. The reading of the Chinese dyslexics is labored (lack of automaticity) and with lots of errors and repetitions although the meaning of the text is generally grasped. One main feature, however, is in the area of copying characters and words and writing to dictation. This is shown in the spelling of a bright seven-year-old in figure 1. The wrongly spelled characters are circled and the missing characters are shown with crosses. To native Chinese speakers and readers, it is immediately apparent that this individual child has considerable problems in spelling. These include poor character formation, lack of proportionality in writing the component parts (the radicals or *bujians* containing clusters of strokes), and the general lack of awareness of the positional hierarchy (morphographical aspects) and internal structure of the characters (morphological aspects). This portrayal is quite typical of many of the children with dyslexia in Chinese. The difficulties of these children in their spelling and handwriting should be seen in the total context of disorders in written expression analogous to Axis I of Learning Disorders in the multi-axial DSM-IV (American Psychiatric Association 1994). The same written language disorder is coded as Specific Developmental Disorders of Scholastic Skills in the multi-axial system of ICD-10 (World Health Organization 1992).

If the pervasive writing and spelling disorders are characteristic of dyslexia in Chinese, just as we are reminded by Orton

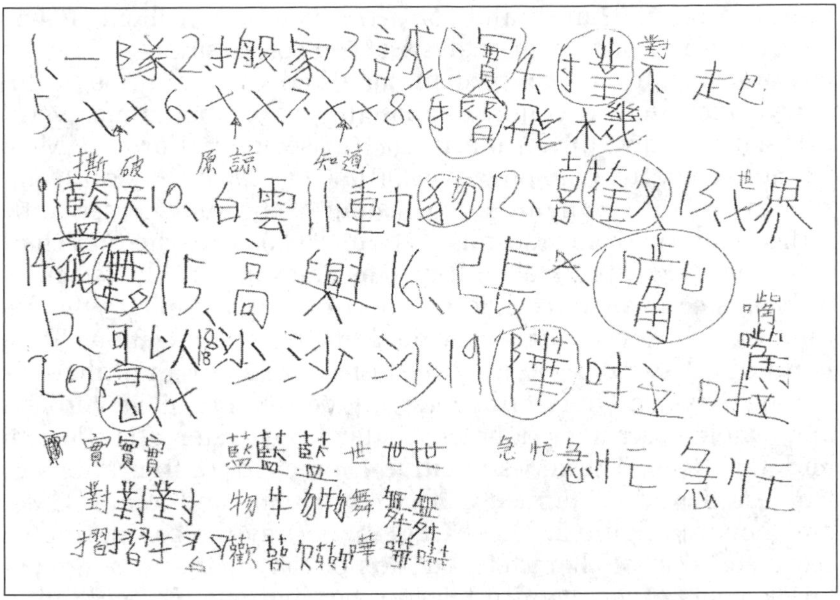

Figure 1. Sample Chinese writing to dictation and spelling errors.

(1925, 1937) and Critchley (1970) of their English speaking children, adolescents, and adults, there are pertinent research and clinical questions. We would like to know how Chinese learners come to acquire and develop knowledge of Chinese characters and symbol-sound correspondence. Do they segment characters first by an analysis-by-synthesis iterative process? If so, what are the subcomponents of the characters most conducive to learning to read and spell, and by inference, as impediments to reading and spelling? Are these subcomponents the individual strokes of the characters together with their ordered stroke sequences in both reading and writing? Are they the phonetic radicals or the semantic radicals (bujians) in terms of their *functions* and not so much their left-right and vertical positional effects? In short, what are the integrative activities in learning the characters and words as building blocks in reading and spelling and in preventing reading/spelling difficulties?

READING/SPELLING CHINESE CHARACTERS AS AN INTEGRATIVE ACTIVITY

A brief discussion of the nature of Chinese characters is in order as a necessary preliminary. The character, or *zi*, is the basic graphic unit in Chinese and corresponds to a morpheme (Chao 1968). Figure 2 shows an analysis of the composition of Chinese characters with their constituent parts known as radicals or bujians, which, in turn, consist of different strokes (horizontal, vertical, slanting, and the like) arranged in sequential orders. Most Chinese characters are of the *compound*, or *composite*, kind (sample Rows 2 to 8 in figure 2) consisting of meaning or semantic radicals and phonetic radicals (Leong 1999a). Take the first character meaning "sprinkle" in Row 5 as an example. The left most radical is equivalent to "hydro" and provides meaning whereas the two right constituents provide a clue to pronunciation. There is no direct symbol-sound correspondence as in an alphabetic language system. In fact, the mapping between phonetic radicals and whole character phonology is far from systematic (Perfetti and Tan 1998). The representative geometric configurations of Chinese characters, termed GEONS by Huang and Wang (1992), are shown in figure 2. These GEONS portray the compositional nature of Chinese characters, but do not convey the autosegmental elements of *tones* which refer to the rhythmic rise and fall of the pitch contour of the voiced part of characters and which carry changes in meaning (see Leong 1999a).

` GEONS ´ (Geometrical Ions) of Chinese Characters	
A	日 (sun) 月 (moon) 兩 (two)
AB	休 (rest) 好 (good) 暗 (dim)
A, B in A	國 or 国 (country) 園 or 园 (park)
A B	早 (early) 否 (no) 音 (sound)
ABC	淋 (sprinkle) 謝 (thank) 假 (false)
A AB BC or C	森 (forest) 箱 (box) 染 (dye) 雙 (double)
A BC or A C (B A)	新 (new) 船 (boat)
A C B D	慢 (slow)
ABC D	變 (change)

After Huang and Wang (1992)

Figure 2.   *"Geometric ions" or GEONS of Chinese characters (after Leong 1999a).*

The compositionality of Chinese characters as summarized in figure 2 raises some pertinent research questions in terms of reading aloud real and pseudo Chinese characters in some recent studies of Chinese word reading development (Ho and Bryant 1997a, 1997b; Hu and Catts 1993; So and Siegel 1997). These emergent and important studies are typically modeled after the influential dual-route paradigm of single-word reading of Coltheart (1978) to explain developmental and acquired dyslexia. The 1978 Coltheart two-route model postulates the lexical route for direct word-specific access to phonology for reading English exception words (e.g., PINT, VAGUE), and the nonlexical route to assemble phonology from graphemes for reading regular words and pseudowords. While this model is updated in the Coltheart, Curtis, Atkins, and Haller (1993) cascaded two-route, parallel-distributed processing model, the logic of the Chinese studies cited above relies mainly on the reading of regular, exception, and pseudo Chinese characters via the dual-route.

The research literature explains regular, exception, and pseudo Chinese characters in this way. Regular Chinese (compound) characters are those pronounced the same way as their constituent phonetic radicals with the same tone (regular consistent) or variant tone (regular inconsistent); exception characters are those pronounced with sounds and tones different from those of the constituent radicals; and pseudo characters are those with radicals in legal positions but are not strictly pronounceable (Leong 1999a, 1999b; Liu, Wu, and Chou 1996). Given this generally accepted definition, we may ask if the classical Coltheart (1978) dual-route model for converting print to sound can strictly be applied to the reading aloud of pseudo Chinese characters, as in a number of studies referred to earlier. Coltheart himself (Coltheart and Perry 1998) has recently cautioned against the direct application of his dual-route, or DRC, model to reading Chinese characters mainly because the Chinese morphosyllabic system does not have a nonlexical procedure. Specifically, the phonological information carried by components of Chinese characters differs from the phonological information of phonemes, and there are no comparable grapheme-to-phoneme correspondence (GPC) rules that permit the assembly of phonology as in the Coltheart (1978) dual-route model. The phonological information obtained from the phonetic radicals is not segmental as in the case of English but paradigmatic and is more akin to that of English sublexical units of onsets and rimes rather than the segmental phonemes (Leong 1997).

This cautionary note does not mean that phonological processing is not involved in reading Chinese characters and words (see Leong 1997); but it does serve to remind us that the reading aloud of pseudo Chinese characters as information processing for symbol-sound correspondence needs reappraisal. Coltheart and Perry (1998) further elucidate their position by invoking access to the orthographic lexical entry for the phonetic radical. In fact, Ho and Bryant (1997b) also noted that sensitivity to subsyllable structure and making orthographic analogies are important for reading Chinese characters. More recently, Ho, Wong, and Chan (1999) have shown in two studies that Chinese children in first and third grades can be trained in phonological and semantic analogies, and have suggested the explicit teaching of the functional roles of these constituents in young Chinese readers.

Two of us (Cheng and Lam, in progress) have been conducting a modest training study using similar logic with a small number of clinic-referred children between the ages of five and eight, using a sample of characters from a carefully selected corpus of 409 compound characters. This ongoing study follows from the Ho et al. (1999) study. Specially prepared teaching materials help teachers in teaching explicitly Chinese word knowledge. Children are taught systematically the compositionality of the characters with their constituent phonetic and semantic radicals through games, songs, rhymes, alliterations, and other enjoyable linguistic activities designed to enhance their word identification skills. The preliminary results are encouraging. Data of the sort obtained by Ho et al. (1999) and Cheng and Lam (in progress) help toward a better understanding of the psycholinguistic nature of reading and spelling in Chinese, and reading and spelling errors of Chinese students with dyslexia.

To summarize the argument thus far, clinical evidence suggests that Chinese children with developmental dyslexia experience many more difficulties in spelling than in reading. This clinical observation parallels that made by clinicians working with clients using the alphabetic English language system. To understand the reading/spelling connection, there have been studies on phonological involvement in reading Chinese characters. Notwithstanding some interesting findings, the weight of evidence points to the importance of the integrative nature of the phonetic radical and semantic radical as necessary preliminaries to learning to read and spell Chinese.

FINE-GRAINED ORTHOGRAPHIC ANALYSIS

It is logical, therefore, to study functional orthographic units that are important in reading and spelling in Chinese. If recognition of Chinese characters were mainly a holistic process, we would expect the visual complexity of the configuration of characters in terms of number of strokes to be important in lexical decision and naming tasks of Chinese characters. There is some evidence for this as shown by Huang and Wang (1992) and Leong, Cheng, and Mulcahy (1987). Huang and Wang suggested that the number of strokes, their order, and interaction all serve a cueing function in activating the constituent parts of characters. Leong et al. (1987) found in two experiments that character complexity in terms of number of strokes affected both lexical decision and naming latency of these characters. However, Huang and Wang and Leong et al. took care to emphasize that the concept of complexity goes beyond stroke number and the configuration of characters, and needs some more fine-grained analyses. Some answers in this direction are provided in recent studies by Chen, Allport, and Marshall (1996), Feldman and Siok (1999), Li and Chen (1999), and an exploratory study by the present authors.

Chen, Allport, and Marshall (1996) examined the number of strokes, orthographic units in simultaneous same-different judgment of pairs of real Chinese characters, pseudo characters, and noncharacters by skilled native Chinese readers. They found that these readers showed a bias in terms of speed and accuracy toward the phonetic radical in phonological tasks and a bias toward the semantic radical in semantic tasks. They suggested that stroke patterns rather than stroke numbers are the salient and functional higher-order orthographic units for the recognition of Chinese characters.

In four experiments, Feldman and Siok (1999) demonstrated that a function-specific characteristic influences character decision and that the semantic attributes of semantic radicals are particularly potent in activating character recognition. This function-specific aspect, in some contrast to the left-right positional effect, is important for further research and instruction. Li and Chen (1999) demonstrated that lexical decision performance was affected by the semantic relatedness between radicals and characters in addition to type frequency of the radicals and their lexical status.

A STUDY OF CHARACTER IDENTIFICATION

There thus seems to be some convergent evidence that the quest for reading and writing Chinese characters should be on the functions of the constituent radicals or bujians in addition to printed frequency and stroke numbers. To test this, we conducted a study on lexical decision of real and pseudo Chinese characters with two groups of skilled native Chinese readers differing in their Chinese language ability. We controlled for lexicality (real or pseudo characters), printed frequency of each character, and the constituent semantic radical frequency or consistency (semantic radicals with many "neighbors" forming many characters or those with few "neighbors" forming few characters). We hypothesized that the processing efficiency (latency) of the lexical items would differ according to the Chinese language ability of the two groups, even though both groups were proficient Chinese readers. There would also be main effects of lexicality (real or pseudo characters), printed frequency of the token characters, and the consistency of the semantic radicals or bujians in the accurate and rapid lexical decision of characters. The details are summarized below.

PARTICIPANTS

There were eleven beginning Bachelor of Education students (seven females and four males) from one tertiary institution (Group 1 or Gp1), and their mean age was 252.10 months with a standard deviation of 20.25 months. There were thirty-two Post-Graduate in Education students after their first degrees (twenty-four females and eight males) from another tertiary institution (Group 2 or Gp2), and their mean age was 301.13 months with a standard deviation of 35.52 months. These participants were paid for the experiment. The Chinese language results of the publicly administered Hong Kong Advanced Level Examination taken just prior to admission to the bachelor's programs were used as a yardstick in differentiating the Chinese language ability of these two groups. The Advanced Level Examination scaled scores ranged from the "pass" grade of E (treated as 1 for the data analysis) to the maximum grade of A (as 5). According to this criterion, the group 1 students had a mean of 1.47 with a standard deviation of .48 and the Group 2 students had a mean of 3.36 with a standard deviation of 1.09. It was reasoned that even though both groups were skilled readers of Chinese, Group 1 would be less efficient in processing simple lexical items as compared to Group 2. This processing difference would be a function of linguistic factors.

MATERIALS

The materials consisted of twenty high-frequency real Chinese characters (mean printed frequency of 2262.95 and mean stroke number of 7.4) and twenty low-frequency real Chinese characters (mean printed frequency of 14.55 and mean stroke number of 7.5) from Cheng's frequency corpus (1982). These single characters were all of the AB left-right symmetrical combinatorial GEONS type (figure 2, Row 2) and were at about the primary six reading level. The character as a whole frequency has an effect on the efficiency of processing because a character represents a morpheme. Moreover, the semantic radical is central to the meaning of the character and may have an impact on the identification of the character. Hence, the forty real characters were also checked for the "consistency" of the semantic radicals. This was done in terms of the number of occurrence of "friendly neighbors" in the tokens and the resultant percentage frequency occurrence in the types from a corpus of 21.7 million Chinese character tokens subsumed under 7,785 character types in the Chinese Language Data Processing Dictionary (Shanghai Chiao Tung Ta Hsueh 1988). For the twenty high-frequency characters, the mean percentage occurrence of the semantic radicals was 32.23 with a standard deviation of 1.61. For the twenty low-frequency characters the corresponding values were 31.14 and 1.56. What appeared to be the very close means for the high- and low-frequency characters was accounted for by the four characters (items 12, 16, 26, and 30 in Appendix A) with the semantic radical meaning "mouth". This semantic radical has the highest percentage occurrence of 5.637 in the corpus of nearly twenty-two million character tokens subsumed under 7,785 character types (Shanghai Chiao Tung Ta Hsueh 1988). The correlation between the frequency of the character as a whole and that of the semantic radical for the twenty high-frequency characters was .363 and for the twenty low-frequency characters .052. The correlation for the two kinds of frequencies for all forty characters was .166.

Forty corresponding pseudo characters were formed by retaining in each pseudo character either the same semantic or the same phonetic radical as that of the corresponding real character and by adding another radical. The resultant pseudo characters must conform to the psycholinguistic principle of maintaining all radicals in their "legal" left-right symmetrical positions (see Leong 1999a for details). The forty real characters with their printed frequency and percentage frequency of the semantic radicals and the corresponding pseudo characters are shown in Appendix A.

PROCEDURE

The underlying notion of this study was to examine if skilled native readers of Chinese differing in their Chinese language ability would also differ in the efficiency with which they process simple, single Chinese characters accurately and rapidly. Further, it was hypothesized that this differential processing would relate to the frequency of the characters considered as wholes and according to their constituent semantic radicals. The computerized work was conducted with individual students in a quiet room in the two tertiary institutions by the first author or his assistant. All items were centered on the computer screen and presented at random.. The participants were asked to press YES or NO keys which were color-coded for the experiment. Feedback took the form on the computer screen in Chinese characters of either: "Your answer is good" or "This is a good try" for correct or incorrect lexical decisions, and this message was shown together with the YES or NO response time. Both accuracy and latency scores were recorded on the hard disk for data analyses.

RESULTS

Before the main data analyses, all the reaction time scores for the correct answers were scrutinized for outliers according to the principles of the Winsorizing technique (Barnett and Lewis 1984). The general idea was to replace those reaction times (RTs) two standard deviations above (or below) the mean RT for each individual item with the value(s) just below (or just above) the M+ 2 (or M- 2) s.d. times an adjustment factor. The iterative process was repeated so that all outliers at the first pass would fall within the M+ 2 (or M- 2) s.d. bounds. This was a refinement of the approach used by the first author in previous studies using RT measures. There was little speed-accuracy trade-off as shown in the scattergram in figure 3. It should be noted that there was much greater variability in both accuracy and latency among the eleven Group 1 members as reflected in the correlation between the two measures of .143. There was closer correspondence between the accuracy and latency measures for the

thirty-two Group 2 members as shown by the correlation coefficient of .281. The wrong responses for one member (subject No.
21) lying farther in the accuracy continuum were all in the
pseudo characters corresponding to the high-frequency real
characters

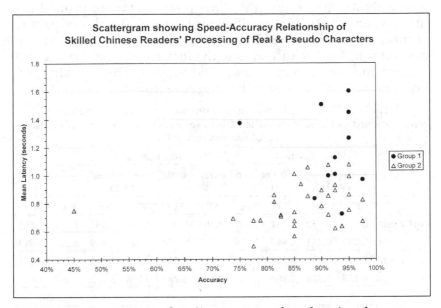

Figure 3.   Scattergram showing accuracy plotted against latency
scores.

Taking the adjusted RT measures of the correct answers as
indices of processing efficiency, a 2 (group) by 2 (lexicality) by
2 (frequency/consistency) ANOVA with the last two factors repeated was carried out. There were highly significant effects in
favor of the higher language ability group ($F[1, 41] = 30.45, p =
.000$). On the surface, it would appear that the eleven Group 1
participants tended to be more accurate than the thirty-two
Group 2 participants, but the difference was not significant
($F[1, 41] = 2.54, p = .12$). There were lexicality effects in favor
of real characters ($F[1, 41] = 109.59, p = .000$) and
frequency/consistency effects in favor of higher frequency and
more consistent characters ($F[1, 41] = 31.57, p = .000$). However,
there was a significant lexicality x group interaction effect
($F[1, 41] = 6.90, p = .012$) and a significant lexicality x
frequency/consistency effect ($F[1, 41] = 43.64, p = .000$). These
significant interactions suggested that there were differential
effects of the real and pseudo characters on the two groups and

that the frequency and consistency of the real characters also affected the efficiency of processing differentially.

These results are summarized in table I and figure 4. Even though these results are based on sample sizes of eleven and thirty-two skilled readers of Chinese differing in Chinese language ability, they suggest that linguistic factors of printed frequency, and consistency of semantic radicals play a part in accurate and rapid identification of Chinese characters. What is needed is to further disentangle the involvement of printed frequency and consistency as they tend to go together and to carry out more refined studies with Chinese children.

Table I.   **Mean reaction time (in seconds) and accuracy scores and standard deviations of skilled Chinese readers' processing of Chinese real and pseudo characters.**

| | Real Characters | | | | Pseudo Characters | | | | | |
| | Higher Freq (R-H) | | Lower Freq (R-L) | | "Higher Freq" (P-H) | | "Lower Freq" (P-L) | | Total | |
	RT	Acc	RT	Acc	RT	Acc	RT	Acc	RT	Acc
Gp1 mean	0.982	19.182	1.134	18.727	1.305	18.091	1.269	17.182	1.169	73.182
s.d.	0.297	0.751	0.344	1.489	0.327	1.758	0.248	2.089	0.290	4.813
Gp2 mean	0.674	18.531	0.790	17.938	0.862	16.844	0.876	15.844	0.794	69.156
s.d.	0.133	1.814	0.168	2.063	0.169	3.244	0.158	3.102	0.151	7.858

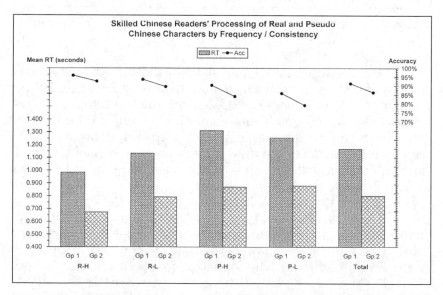

Figure 4.   *Skilled Chinese readers' processing of real (R) and pseudo (P) Chinese characters by high (H) and low (L) frequency of characters and "consistency" of constituent semantic radicals.*

RESEARCH AND TEACHING IMPLICATIONS

Taken together, the studies by Chen et al. (1996), Feldman and Siok (1999), Ho et al. (1999), Li and Chen (1999), and the authors' modest project provide evidence about the nature of the functional orthographic units important for reading and spelling the meaning-plus-sound morphosyllabic Chinese. The results also yield some clues for reading/spelling difficulties. The studies cited deal mainly with adult Chinese readers. There are some fairly recent data on Chinese children's sensitivity to the nature of the semantic and phonetic radicals and their role in reading/spelling acquisition (Chan and Nunes 1998; Shu and Anderson 1997, 1999; Tzeng, Lin, Hung, and Lee 1995). The consensus finding is that by about the third grade, Chinese children generally are aware of the roles of radicals in reading/spelling and they also use much broader orthographic knowledge to pronounce novel or new Chinese characters. By the third or fourth grade, children have developed clearer and deeper insight into the composition of Chinese characters and the functions of phonetic and semantic radicals as linguistic elements in providing clues to the phonology and semantics of the characters.

This is further shown in a recent developmental study in which 288 Primary 4 and 6, Secondary 2, and university students in Beijing were asked to judge if two characters, one familiar and one new, having the same phonetic radicals, were homophonous (Shu, Zhou, and Wu 2000). Shu et al. found that this judgment was influenced by the consistency of phonetic radicals in providing phonetic cues and that the participants needed to analyze the orthographic structure of the characters. The report by Shu et al. supports and adds to an earlier study with two experiments by Yang and Peng (1997). Yang and Peng found that the phonetic radicals play a fairly important part in children's naming of phonograms, the phonological information of which is represented more or less by the graphic form, but that naming relies more on the regularity and consistency effects as children develop. This kind of analysis-by-synthesis metalinguistic ability develops gradually and incrementally and needs to be taught systematically and explicitly to children.

Examination of teaching materials shows that systematic training should be done in the form of guided learning. The general steps are:

1.   Recognition through guided reading of the general shape or configuration of the characters in a well-

ordered sequence from global to specific, from top half to bottom half, and from left to right in the proper hierarchical order.

2. Understanding of the functional roles of phonetic and semantic radicals through the use of rhyming and alliterative characters in context and associative bujians with many "neighbors."

3. Practice in writing those characters appropriate to age and life experience in accordance with stroke sequence.

4. Use of orthographic patterns to derive phonology as a whole.

5. Development of handwriting ability, taking into account stroke sequence, well-formedness of the characters, and the overall habit of writing.

This instructional sequence follows the orthography-to-phonology correspondence in integrating orthographic patterns, phonology, and meaning in reading/spelling Chinese. Theory-based curriculum materials in primary grades all emphasize sensitivity to these interrelated linguistic aspects through the use of games, songs, and the like, moving to listening and speaking, then guided reading and writing of controlled characters. All these integrative activities are designed to promote both the precision and redundancy in learning Chinese characters, thereby reducing sources of errors (Leong 1999a).

The discussion above should not be taken to mean that phonological processing is not important in learning to read/spell Chinese. Analogous to the phonological awareness literature in reading/spelling English, the parallel process of explicit, conscious representation from the implicit, unconscious representation of the primary linguistic activities of listening and speaking to the secondary linguistic activities of reading and spelling still applies to learning to read/spell Chinese. But the difference is at the level and unit of phonological analysis. In learning to read and spell English, it is the analytic process at the segmental level, involving units of phonemes and sublexical units of onsets and rimes, that is of critical importance. In learning to read and spell Chinese, it is the paradigmatic analysis involving the hierarchical structure of initials (onsets) and finals (rimes) that is important (see Leong 1997 for explication).

There are some preliminary data involving adult Chinese students in the paradigmatic analysis of initials and finals in addressing phonology in reading Chinese words (Bertelson, Chen, and de Gelder 1997). There is also a preliminary report on Grades 3, 4, and 5 good and poor Chinese readers' (twenty students in each grade) development of phonological awareness, including onset-rime awareness (Tao and Peng 1999). It would appear that research in the metalinguistic awareness in reading and spelling Chinese should be at this paradigmatic level involving subsyllabic units and not so much at the segmental level involving phonemes. The first author and Dr. LiHai Tan have just carried out (May 2000) such a study with children in Primary 3, 4, and 5 in Beijing. Furthermore, the analysis-by-synthesis of the phonetic and semantic radicals, and the building up of the associative network of these components with many consistent characters, are necessary for proficient reading and spelling in Chinese.

ACKNOWLEDGMENTS

The writing of this paper was completed while the first author was Visiting Professor in the Department of Educational Psychology, Faculty of Education, the Chinese University of Hong Kong, in the spring of 2000. He thanks Dr. K. T. Hau, Head of the Department; Dr. Leslie N. K. Lo, Director of the Hong Kong Institute of Educational Research, CUHK; and Dr. Catherine C. C. Lam for the privilege of working with some teachers and children with developmental dyslexia. He is also grateful for the support of the Social Sciences and Humanities Research Council of Canada through SSHRC Research Grant 410-96-0186 for the studies summarized here. The second author also expresses her appreciation to CUHK for its assistance from its Research Committee. All three authors are grateful to the children, their parents, and the tertiary students for sharing their joys and tribulations in learning and developing Chinese. The authors thank W. K. Lai for assistance in running the experiment and in data analyses, the editor, and the anonymous reviewers for their insightful comments on the earlier draft. The authors alone are responsible for their shortcomings.

Appendix A

Frequency of Real Characters and of their Semantic Radicals together with Corresponding Pseudo Characters

Item No.	Real Character 正字	Frequency of Whole Character	Percentage Frequency of Semantic Radical	Pseudo Character 假字	Item No.	Real Character 正字	Frequency of Whole Character	Percentage Frequency of Semantic Radical	Pseudo Character 假字
1	那	4549	0.876		21	吻	30	5.637	
2	作	3315	2.131		22	注	29	1.333	
3	佢	2646	2.131		23	抒	25	1.232	
4	沒	2326	1.333		24	抄	20	1.232	
5	你	2067	2.131		25	伶	13	2.131	
6	佀	1802	2.131		26	呐	10	5.637	
7	每	1291	0.276		27	冊	10	0.956	
8	利	1196	0.956		28	妒	9	0.796	
9	形	1114	0.257		29	皂	4	0.923	
10	即	1078	0.264		30	吹	2	5.637	
11	到	5548	0.956		31	测	23	0.956	
12	和	5272	5.637		32	恬	22	0.619	
13	法	2312	1.333		33	帖	20	0.286	
14	物	2292	0.145		34	泣	19	1.333	
15	定	2204	0.910		35	玫	15	0.505	
16	知	2053	5.637		36	弧	10	0.123	
17	明	1327	2.277		37	怡	8	0.619	
18	空	996	0.910		38	帕	8	0.286	
19	近	946	1.330		39	荠	7	0.360	
20	放	925	0.608		40	昉	7	0.535	

Practice Examples

E1	加	1839	0.803		E2	伙	26	2.131	

Address correspondence to: Che Kan Leong, Department of Educational Psychology & Special Education, University of Saskatchewan, Saskatoon, Sask., Canada. S7N 0X1, Phone: (306) 966-5257, FAX: (306) 966-7719, Email: leong@sask.usask.ca; Pui-Wan Cheng, Department of Educational Psychology, Faculty of Education, The Chinese University of Hong Kong, Shatin, NT, Hong Kong, Phone: (852) 2609-6954, FAX: (852) 2603-6921, Email: pwcheng@cuhk.edu.hk; or Catherine C.C. Lam, Central Kowloon Child Assessment Centre, Hong Kong Department of Health, 147L Argyle St., Kowloon, Hong Kong, Phone: (852) 2246-6633, FAX: (852) 2463-5319, Email: clam@hk.gin.net.

References

American Psychiatric Association. 1994. *Diagnostic and Statistical Manual of Mental Disorders*, 4th ed. Washington, DC: Author.

Barnett, V., and Lewis, T. 1984. *Outliers in Statistical Data*, 2nd ed. New York: John Wiley.

Bertelson, P., Chen, H.-C., and de Gelder, B. 1997. Explicit speech analysis and orthographic experience in Chinese readers. In *Cognitive Processing of Chinese and Related Asian Languages*, ed. H.-C. Chen. Hong Kong: The Chinese University Press.

Chan, L., and Nunes, T. 1998. Children's understanding of the formal and functional characteristics of written Chinese. *Applied Psycholinguistics* 19:115–31.

Chao, Y. R. 1968. *A Grammar of Spoken Chinese*. Berkeley, CA: University of California Press.

Chen, Y. P., Allport, D. A., and Marshall, J. C. 1996. What are the functional orthographic units in Chinese word recognition: The stroke or the stroke pattern? *The Quarterly Journal of Experimental Psychology* 49A:1024–43.

Cheng, C. M. 1982. Analysis of present-day Mandarin. *Journal of Chinese Linguistics* 10:181–258.

Coltheart, M. 1978. Lexical access in simple reading tasks. In *Strategies of Information Processing*, ed. G. Underwood. New York: Academic Press.

Coltheart, M., Curtis, B., Atkins, P., and Haller, M. 1993. Models of reading aloud: Dual-route and parallel-distributed processing. *Psychological Review* 100:589–608.

Coltheart, M., and Perry, C. November 1998. *Reading Chinese: Dual-route theory and acquired dyslexia*. Paper read at the Advanced Study Institute on Advances on Theoretical Issues and Cognitive Neuroscience Research on the Chinese Language, University of Hong Kong, Hong Kong.

Critchley, M. 1970. *The Dyslexic Child*. (2nd and augmented ed. of *Developmental Dyslexia*). London: Heinemann Medical Books.

Feldman, L. B., and Siok, W. W. T. 1999. Semantic radicals in phonetic compounds: Implications for visual character recognition in Chinese. In *Reading Chinese Script: A Cognitive Analysis*, eds. J. Wang, A. W. Inhoff, and H.-C.. Chen. Mahwah, NJ: Lawrence Erlbaum Associates.

Ho, C. S-H., and Bryant, P. 1997a. Learning to read Chinese beyond the logographic phase. *Reading Research Quarterly* 32:276–89.

Ho, C. S.-H., and Bryant, P. 1997b. Phonological skills are important in learning to read Chinese. *Developmental Psychology* 33:946–51.

Ho, C. S.-H., Wong, W.-L., and Chan, W.-S. 1999. The use of orthographic analogies in learning to read Chinese. *Journal of Child Psychology and Psychiatry* 40:393–403.

Høien, T., and Lundberg, I. 2000. *Dyslexia: From Theory to Intervention*. Dordrecht: Kluwer Academic Publishers.

Hong Kong Education Commission. May 2000. *Review of Education System: Reform Proposals Consultation Document*. Hong Kong-SAR: Author.

Hu, C. F., and Catts, H. W. 1993. Phonological recoding as a universal process? Evidence from beginning readers of Chinese. *Reading and Writing: An Interdisciplinary Journal* 5:325–37.

Huang, J.-T., and Wang, M.-Y. 1992. From unit to Gestalt: Perceptual dynamics in recognizing Chinese characters. In *Language Processing in Chinese*, eds. H.-C. Chen and O.J.L. Tzeng. Amsterdam: North-Holland.

Kavanagh, J. F., and Venezky, R. L. Eds. 1980. *Orthography, Reading, and Dyslexia*. Baltimore: University Park Press.

Lam, C. C. C. 1999. Developmental dyslexia and other specific learning disabilities. The state of practice: International and Hong Kong perspectives. *Hong Kong Journal of Paediatrics* (New Series) 4:145–50.

Leong, C. K. 1997. Paradigmatic analysis of Chinese word reading: Research findings and classroom practices. In *Cross-language Studies of Learning to Read and Spell: Phonologic and Orthographic Processing*, eds. C.K. Leong and R.M. Joshi. Dordrecht: Kluwer Academic Publishers.

Leong, C. K. 1999a. What can we learn from dyslexia in Chinese? In *Dyslexia: Advances in Theory and Practice*, eds. I. Lundberg, F. I. Tønnessen, and I. Austad. Dordrecht: Kluwer Academic Publishers.

Leong, C. K. 1999b. Psychological and educational aspects of specific learning disabilities. *Hong Kong Journal of Paediatrics* (New Series) 4:151–59.

Leong, C. K., Cheng, P.-W., and Mulcahy, R. 1987. Automatic processing of morphemic orthography by mature readers. *Language and Speech* 30:181–97.

Leong, C. K., and Joshi, R. M. Eds. 1997. *Cross-language Studies of Learning to Read and Spell: Phonologic and Orthographic Processing*. Dordrecht: Kluwer Academic Publishers.

Leong, C. K., and Tamaoka, K. Eds. 1998. *Cognitive Processing of the Chinese and the Japanese Languages*. Dordrecht: Kluwer Academic Publishers.

Li, H., and Chen, H.-C. 1999. Radical processing in Chinese character recognition: Evidence from lexical decision. *Psychologia* 42:199–208.

Liu, I.-M., Wu, J.-T., and Chou, T.-L. 1996. Encoding operation and transcoding as the major loci of the frequency effect. *Cognition* 59:149–68.

Lundberg, I., Tønnessen, F. E., and Austad, I. Eds. 1999. *Dyslexia: Advances in Theory and Practice*. Dordrecht: Kluwer Academic Publishers.

Lyon, G. R. 1995. Toward a definition of dyslexia. *Annals of Dyslexia* 45:3–27.

Orton, S. T. 1925. "Word blindness" in school children. *Archives of Neurology and Psychiatry* 14:581–615.

Orton, S. T. 1937. *Reading, Writing, and Speech Problems in Children*. New York: Norton.

Perfetti, C. A., and Tan, L. H. 1998. The time course of graphic, phonological, and semantic activation in Chinese character identification. *Journal of Experimental Psychology: Learning, Memory and Cognition* 24:101–18.

Shanghai Chiao Tung Ta Hsueh. 1988. *Hanzi xinxi zidian*. [A dictionary of Chinese character information]. Shanghai: Author. [in Chinese].

Shu, H., and Anderson, R. C. 1997. Role of radical awareness in the character and word acquisition of Chinese children. *Reading Research Quarterly* 32:78–89.

Shu, H., and Anderson, R. C. 1999. Learning to read Chinese: The development of metalinguistic awareness. In *Reading Chinese Script: A Cognitive Analysis*, eds. J. Wang, A. W. Inhoff, and C.-H. Chen. Mahwah, NJ: Lawrence Erlbaum Associates.

Shu, H., Zhou, X.-L., and Wu, N.-N. 2000. Utilizing phonological cues in Chinese characters: A developmental study. *Acta Psychologica Sinica* 32(2):44–49. [in Chinese.]

So, D., and Siegel, L. S. 1997. Learning to read Chinese: Semantic, syntactic, phonological and working memory skills in normally achieving and poor Chinese readers. *Reading and Writing: An Interdisciplinary Journal* 9:1–21.

Tao, J., and Peng, D.-L. 1999. Chinese phonological awareness of children and the difference between good and poor readers. *Acta Psychologica Sinica* 31:60–68. [in Chinese.]

Treiman, R. 1997. Spelling in normal children and dyslexics. In *Foundations of Reading Acquisition and Dyslexia*, ed. B. A. Blachman. Mahwah, NJ: Lawrence Erlbaum Associates.

Tzeng, O. J. L., Lin, Z. H., Hung, D. L., and Lee, W. L. 1995. Learning to be a conspirator: A tale of becoming a good Chinese reader. In *Speech and Reading: A Comparative Approach*, eds. B. de Gelder and J. Morais. Hove, Sussex: Lawrence Erlbaum.

World Health Organization. 1992. *The ICD-10 Classification of Mental and Behavioral Disorders: Clinical Descriptions and Diagnostic Guidelines*. Geneva: Author.

Yang, H., and Peng, D.-L. 1997. The learning and naming of Chinese characters of elementary school children. In *Cognitive Processing of Chinese and Related Asian Languages*, eds. B. de Gelder and J. Morais. Hong Kong: The Chinese University Press.

Annals of Dyslexia
Guidelines for Contributors

Annals of Dyslexia is an interdisciplinary peer-reviewed journal dedicated to the understanding and remediation of written language difficulties (reading, writing, spelling, handwriting) and related areas. Primary consideration is given to original research papers, significant reviews, and well-documented reports of effective practices. We evaluate a manuscript according to the following criteria: (1) its general significance for the *Annals* readership; (2) its specific contribution within the paradigm adopted; (3) the soundness of methodology and interpretation of results; and (4) clarity and organization. Only papers not previously published are considered for publication. Please do not submit your paper simultaneously to other journals. **Limit length of your manuscript to no more than 35 pages, double-spaced, and in 12 pt. font, including references, tables, and figures.**

Manuscripts should be received on or before January 10 in order to receive full consideration for publication that year. Manuscripts are reviewed by the Editor and at least two reviewers with expertise in the area to which the topic pertains; the initial review process seldom requires more than 3 months. It is our policy to provide authors such editorial assistance as is necessary to achieve conciseness and clarity in presenting their work; most accepted papers will require some revision. The editorial decision letter will communicate suggestions to the author that should facilitate the preparation of the revision. We require strict deadlines in order to meet the once-a-year publication schedule.

Beginning with the 2001 *Annals*, the most recent *Publication Manual of the American Psychological Association (APA)* will be the primary reference for journal style. We recommend that writers refer to it, scrutinizing language, usage, and mechanics in their manuscripts prior to submitting them. In these instructions are examples. Other examples are in journals such as *the Journal of Learning Disabilities, Exceptional Children,* and the *Journal of Educational Psychology.*

Submit the **original manuscript plus four copies** and retain a copy for your files. Do not staple manuscripts or copies. We also require **an abstract of the paper not to exceed 200 words**. Please enclose a self-addressed, stamped envelope so that we may notify you upon receipt of your manuscript. If we accept your paper, we will ask at a later point for a copy of the computer disk containing the word processing version of your manuscript.

List your name on the title page, followed by applicable affiliations, exactly as the publication should read, all double-spaced. Except for medical doctors, no degrees are used in *Annals*. Please include home and work addresses for correspondence with the author and co-authors (designating the primary address to use), phone numbers, fax numbers, and e-mail addresses for each author and co-author, as available.

Preparation of Manuscript

Spacing, Formatting, Headings
Manuscript should be double-spaced throughout using 12-point font. Microsoft Word is the preferred format. Please put an extra space between each reference. All margins, left, right, top, and bottom, should be at least one inch wide. Each page should have the author's name and abbreviated title at the left-hand top of the page. Make the title of the article concise and to the point. We suggest a three- or four-word running head to facilitate indexing and information retrieval.

A and B headings should be typed on separate lines with triple space in between each heading. Do not italicize or underscore the headings. "A" headings should be centered, and "B" headings should be placed at the left margin. "C" headings should begin at the appropriate paragraph, using capitals and lower case, followed by two spaces that run into the text; C heads should be underlined. No heads, A, B, or C, should be typed in all capital letters.

Page Numbering
Please number all pages of text, beginning with page one of the text. Do not number the title page or the Abstract page.

Number footnotes consecutively in the text, indicated by superscript numbers, and then typed on a separate page labeled Footnotes. Place this page after the text and before the references.

References in Text
References cited in the text should be followed, in parenthesis, by the author's surname (unless it is given in the text of the sentence, as in a and d below) and the date of the reference. Note that if

there are two or more references cited by the same author with the same year of publication, use lowercase letters after the date to distinguish them.

Examples:
a. The group is receiving the Auditory Discrimination in Depth Program as outlined by Lindamood and Lindamood (1984).
b. The brain of the rat has been altered as a result of hormone treatments (Diamond, Dowling, & Johnson, 1981).
c. In recent years, psychologists have referred extensively to metacognition (Brown, 1978).
d. Orton (1928c, 1928d) provided several case studies that support this position.
e. Kamhi and his colleagues indicated that extensive exposure might be necessary to retain accurate representation of a new lexical item if the phonological form of the word is imprecise or unstable (Kamhi, Catts, & Mauer, 1990).

Note: When a work has six or more authors, cite only the surname of the first author followed by "et al." and the year for the first and subsequent citations. In the reference list, however, provide the initials and surnames of **each** author.

Illustrations, Tables, and Figures
Illustrations should be original inked drawings in a form suitable for reduction without retouching or redrawing. Suggested size is 8-1/2 x 11 inches. Lettering, numerals, and symbols should be large enough so that they will be completely legible after reduction. Photographs should be the original and on glossy paper. Place overlays on all photographs to avoid damage. If only part of the photograph is to be used, indicate that part with penciled lines on the overlay. Permission must be obtained for any illustrative material previously published in a book or journal. Legends for illustrations should not be attached, but typed double-spaced on a separate page and clearly keyed to the illustrations. Electronic artwork should be submitted in EPS, TIFF, or PICT format only. Minimum resolution for all electronic artwork should be 300 pixels per inch. If you are unsure of how to provide electronic artwork, please submit original artwork (line art or photography suitable for scanning) with your paper. Hard copy must accompany all electronic files.

In the text, number the tables with Roman numerals in the order in which the tables are first mentioned. Citations in the text to the tables should also be in Roman numerals. Place the citation at the end of the paragraph in which you mention that table (for example, *Place table I about here*). Place the actual tables and figures at the end of the article after the references. Type a brief title directly above each table. Place explanatory material for the table in a footnote. Double-space the table, title, and explanatory material. Mark the authors' names on each table.

In the text, number the figures in sequence with Arabic numerals and in the order of their mention in the text. Their citations should be in Arabic numerals in the text. Place the citation at the end of the paragraph in which you mentioned that figure (for example, *Place figure 1 about here*). Place the actual figure at the end of the article after the references and before each table. Type the legend in double-space and in sequence on a separate page of the manuscript labeled figure 1, 2, 3, etc.; do not type the legend on the figure. Mark the authors' names on each figure.

Reference List
The reference list should include only those references cited in the text. *Entries in the reference list should be alphabetical by the author's surname. Do not number the references.* If there is more than one publication by a given author in the same year, add the letters a, b, etc. after the date. Double-space all entries (triple-space between references) and follow the style of the examples given below. (DO NOT, however, separate your references into these categories.) See *Publication Manual of the APA* or journals that use APA style for other examples.

Book
Adams, M. J. (1990). *Beginning to read: Thinking and learning about print*. Cambridge, MA: The MIT Press.

More Than One Publication by a Given Author in the Same Year
Stanovich, K. (1996a). Toward a more inclusive definition of dyslexia. *Dyslexia*, 2, 154–66.

Edited Book
Brady, S., & Shankweiler, D. (Eds.). *Phonological processes in literacy: A tribute to Isabelle Y. Liberman*. Hillsdale, NJ: Lawrence Erlbaum Associates.

Chapter in a Book
Fowler, A., & Liberman, I. (1995). Morphological awareness as related to reading and spelling ability. In L. Feldman (ed.), *Morphological aspects of language processing* (pp. 157–88). Hillsdale, NJ: Lawrence Erlbaum Associates.

Journal
Lyon, R. (1995). Toward a definition of dyslexia. *Annals of Dyslexia, 45*, 3–30.

Rack, J. P., Snowling, M. J., & Olson, R. K. (1992). The nonword reading deficit in developmental dyslexia: A review. *Reading Research Quarterly, 27*, 29–53.

Dissertation or Thesis
Jones, A. J. 1947. *Laterality and dominance in preschool deaf children.* Unpublished doctoral dissertation, Northeastern University, Boston.

Unpublished Paper Read at Meeting
Snow, C. 1999. *Preventing reading difficulties in young children.* Paper presented at 50th Annual Meeting of The International Dyslexia Association, November, 1999, Chicago.

Send manuscript to:
Editor, *Annals of Dyslexia*
c/o The International Dyslexia Association
8600 LaSalle Road, Chester Building, Suite 382
Baltimore, MD 21286-2044, USA

REMINDER: MANUSCRIPTS MAY BE SENT ANY TIME
BUT MUST BE RECEIVED NO LATER THAN JANUARY 10
IN ORDER TO BE CONSIDERED
FOR THAT YEAR'S PUBLICATION.

Index

(Page numbers in italics indicate material in figures or tables.)